Once A Carpenter

Once A Carpenter

Bill Counts

HARVEST HOUSE
PUBLISHERS
IRVINE, CALIFORNIA
92707

to my Father and Mother

ACKNOWLEDGMENTS

All Old Testament Scriptures quoted are from the New American Standard Bible © 1960, 1962, 1963, 1968, 1971, The Lockman Foundation. The New Testament passages are renderings by the author.

All rights reserved. No portion of this book may be used in any form without the written permission of the publishers, with the exception of brief excerpts in magazine articles, reviews, etc.

Printed in the United States of America

SPECIAL THANKS

I want to express special thanks to Juanita Sanders for many hours of typing and retyping manuscripts, to the faculty and students at the Light and Power House Biblical Training School for their encouragement and support, and to my wife Beverly for her patience, good judgment, and help in a long and difficult task.

CONTENTS

True Light . . . How to be Free . . . Fathers and Sons . . . A Theological Question . . . An Amazing Half-Mile Run . . . Looking for A Loophole . . . "Don't Confuse Us with the Facts!" . . . Love at First Sight . . .

ONE

◆ ◆

The Uncommon Common Man

◆ ◆

The wedding guests laughed uneasily. But their jokes could not relieve the tension. The normal trappings of a normal wedding were there—the songs, the ceremonies, the best wine, the joyous loving looks between the young bride and groom. But in the courtyard corners the old women were busily gossiping that *the bride was pregnant.*

Pregnant brides stir no scandal today. But this wasn't New York or Paris—or the twentieth century. This was Nazareth, Galilee, in 6 B.C., where piety reigned among the Jewish faithful, where women were supersecluded, where daughters rarely got beyond the front door unchaperoned.

The bride *was* pregnant. Her name was Mary, after her famed ancestor, Miriam, sister of Moses and prophetess of Israel. The story behind her pregnancy, as the New Testament tells it, was incredible—far too incredible to explain to town gossips. The Gospels of Matthew and Luke tell us with all sobriety that Mary was to be a *virgin* mother.

This raises the perplexing question: Can a virgin birth really happen? Some theologians and scholars have concluded the story is a myth added to Gospel accounts by

1

the early church, possibly borrowed from pagan lore. But virgin births were unknown in ancient mythology![1] Some skeptics argue that the rest of the New Testament doesn't mention the virgin birth, but Paul gives almost no other biographical information of Jesus either, and two Gospels don't discuss Jesus' birth at all, so that is only an argument from silence. When you think about it, the virgin birth is no harder to believe than Jesus' resurrection from the dead, his instantaneous healings, his walking on water, and his prophecies of future events. A supernatural virgin birth, or something similar, and other miracles would be expected of a divine being. If he was not a divine being, the New Testament is a colossal fraud at worst or a collection of folk tales at best, and its hero is the most tragic failure in literature. So the question is not whether we can believe in the virgin birth; the real question is: Can we believe in the New Testament record of Jesus and in him as a divine being?

THE INCREDIBLE REVELATION

The New Testament says that Mary, a teenager engaged to a pious Jewish carpenter named Joseph, received a vision from God. An angel told her she would soon give birth to a child and that she should name him after Joshua, the Old Testament hero who conquered Jericho and the land of the Canaanites. This name, transliterated from the Greek of the New Testament, is "Jesus." The angel revealed to Mary that her child would rescue his people from their sins, and that he would be Israel's long-awaited Messiah.

The astounded girl was probably no older than fourteen, the average age of marriage then. She asked, "How can this happen, since I'm a virgin?" The angel answered, "The Holy Spirit will come upon you, and the power of the Most High will overshadow you. Because of this the holy being you give birth to will be called God's Son" (Luke 1:34, 35). In plain terms, this revelation meant that Mary would conceive a child from God instead of a man, ("The Holy Spirit will come upon you and the power of the Most High will overshadow you"), her child would be holy instead of sinful by nature ("the holy being you give birth to"), and he would be divine instead of merely human ("will be called God's Son"). The women of Israel believed in angelic revelations—but they never dreamed of one like this!

THE INCREDIBLE RESPONSE

Mary's response was simple submission and faith: "Let it happen to me just as you have said" (v. 38).

This acceptance and trust were fantastic. Here is a girl probably no older than a high-school freshman who has to try to explain to parents, aunts, uncles, cousins—and most important, her fiance, Joseph—that she is pregnant from God himself! How she could ever explain it, how to keep Joseph's love, how such an unheard-of miracle could take place—all this she consigns to God as she submits to his plan! But before the angel departed he revealed that her relative, Elizabeth, had conceived a child in her old age and this was apparently related to the astounding revelation given to Mary. The girl soon left on a journey of nearly a hundred miles to see Elizabeth. She could talk it all over with Elizabeth and get mature counsel.

Mary hardly got past Elizabeth's door before Elizabeth broke into ecstatic praise over Mary's unborn child. Elizabeth could not have known! This was another miracle. Mary was so overwhelmed she broke into a spontaneous exultation of poetry and song, just as her namesake Miriam had done after Israel escaped from Egypt. Spontaneous, uninhibited emotions characterized the ancient Jewish people, so such expressiveness was natural to these women.

Mary stayed with Elizabeth for three months and they shared the wonder and possible meaning of the children in their wombs; they sensed they were all cast in a drama of cosmic proportions.

COULD SHE EXPECT ANYONE TO BELIEVE HER?

Mary returned home to the problem of explaining a virgin birth to Joseph and her family—and what a problem! On the way home she must have puzzled how it would all work out and whether she would lose Joseph. Could he—or any man—believe when he found his fiancee pregnant that she had been faithful to him?

Mary told Joseph, and we learn that he did not believe her, for the Gospel writer Matthew says, "Joseph wished to dissolve the marriage privately" (1:19). In ancient Israel, engagement was as binding as marriage, and could only be broken by divorce. A public dissolution of the marriage would expose Mary as an adulteress, which Joseph thought she was. A private dissolution, possible under Jewish law, didn't relieve his anguish, but it did spare Mary and her family humiliation.

As Joseph contemplated his shattered life, he received a vision just like Mary—only in a dream. An angel informed him that Mary's story was true and that he should not hesitate to marry her!

Whether anyone beyond the inner circle knew of this virgin birth, we cannot say. It seems that the young couple would not try to explain something so incomprehensible to outsiders. Years later the citizens of Nazareth would despise Jesus and even try to lynch him (Luke 4:16-30)—perhaps the story of his birth encouraged their scornful rejection. John's Gospel also records an unusual accusation his Jerusalem enemies once hurled at him: "*We* were not born from fornication" (John 8:41). In the course of investigating this revolutionary young rabbi, had they come across a rumor of a "shotgun wedding"?

A CHANCE TO GET OUT OF TOWN

A few months after the marriage, gossip in little Nazareth may have swirled uncomfortably around Mary and Joseph. Mary was obviously nearing delivery after only six months of marriage. When news came of a Roman census that required citizens to register in the town of their ancestral lineage, the young couple probably welcomed it as a good excuse to get out of town. Historical records reveal that the Roman government decreed such a census every fourteen years. Josephus, a Jewish historian, mentions one in A.D. 6, so we presume the preceding one was about 8 B.C. This apparently was not carried out in Palestine until about 6 B.C.[2]

Since Joseph and Mary traced their ancestral lineage back to King David and he was from Bethlehem, this meant a trip of more than eighty miles. Such a trip by ancient means of transportation—probably about ten days on a donkey—seems folly with Mary ready to deliver her child. But Joseph had no desire to leave Mary to the mercy of unsympathetic neighbors, and more important, they no doubt knew the words of the Old Testament prophet written seven centuries before which predicted Bethlehem as the Messiah's birthplace:

"But as for you, Bethlehem Ephrathah, too little to be among the clans of Judah, from you One will go forth for me to be ruler in Israel. His goings forth are from long ago, from the days of eternity" (Micah 5:2, *NASB*).

An eighty mile trip to fulfill the prophecy or escape unpleasant surroundings would be a contrived scheme. But the census required Joseph to go to Bethlehem. Yet if the edict had reached Palestine a few months earlier or later, they could not have fulfilled the prophecy naturally. But the New Testament even pictures pagan Roman government as an unwitting instrument of God, obeying his perfect timing.

The slow, arduous trip to Bethlehem over the Samaritan and Judean hills finally ended. Because of Mary's condition—perhaps labor pains had begun before they approached Bethlehem—they did not arrive in time to secure lodging. Many houses had small attached stables, however, and this provided a semi-comfortable, though not very sanitary setting for the wonder child to enter the world.

We can only guess the parents' thoughts that night. Perhaps they resented the taunts of friends in Nazareth, difficulties on the journey, and lack of a decent place for Mary to have her baby. But they believed in spite of it all that they were playing a pivotal role in the destiny of all men.

5

UNEXPECTED BIRTH NOTICES

This was confirmed a few hours after the baby's birth, when some excited shepherds ran into town claiming that they had received an angelic visitation that this baby, cradled in a manger (an animal feeding trough), was the promised Messiah! Shepherds were considered despicable and dishonest by many religious Jews, but they were the first to spread the news that Israel's Messiah had arrived!

Joseph and Mary evidently decided to remain in Bethlehem for a time. Matthew states that they secured a house, perhaps intending to remain close to Jersualem, the spiritual center of the nation, so Jesus could gain instruction from the great rabbis. A month after Jesus' birth, they went to the temple in Jerusalem to make animal sacrifices prescribed for the birth of a first-born son. Sacrifices were offered when each child was born, but the first-born son was dedicated to God in remembrance of the first-borns' protection from plague in Egypt. The poor sacrificed birds instead of the more costly lambs, and the impoverished Joseph and Mary offered birds (Luke 2:25).

TWO SENIOR CITIZENS

As the temple ceremony began, Simeon, an aged Jew, approached and gently took the baby in his arms. Then, in another of those beautiful paeans to God he exulted: "Now, Master, release your slave to death in peace, as you promised, because my eyes have seen your salvation which you prepared before all people, a light of revelation to the Gentiles and the glory of your people Israel" (vv. 29-32).

Joseph and Mary may have staggered at these words, though many memorable events had already accompanied Jesus' conception and birth. For Simeon announces that Jesus is God's salvation even to the Gentiles, a shocking possibility that the Jewish scribes (the rabbis of that time) did not teach. And Simeon adds that Jesus will be "the glory of Israel"—the fairest flower of spiritual genius ever grown by this nation which gave Abraham, Moses, and David to the world.

Then Simeon adds an ominous note: "This child is set for the fall and rising again of many in Israel, and for a sign spoken against—and a sword shall pierce your soul also—that the thoughts of many hearts may be revealed" (vv. 34, 35).

The prophetic words of the angels, of Elizabeth, and of the shepherds had all been positive—no hint of conflict—but now Simeon reveals that many in Israel would fall because of this Messiah, and others would conquer through him. He would be opposed and hated. Pain, like a sword, would slash his mother's soul. His life would expose the inner thoughts of people—their reaction to him would signal their relationship to God.

Simeon had barely finished when an old widow named Anna, a prophetess, entered the scene and, like Simeon, began to praise God and speak to the crowd about the baby though she had never seen him before. Joseph and Mary must have traveled the six miles back to Bethlehem with mixed feelings. What could Simeon have meant? The scribes taught that the Messiah would be a great victor and king, not a man burdened by grief and rejection. He was to vanquish the despised Gentiles, not bless them. What did all this mean?

It didn't take long to see some of the answers. Shortly after they returned from Jerusalem, some wealthy Gentiles, probably from Babylon or Persia, arrived and announced that they had come to worship the king of the Jews! Our familiarity with Christmastime versions of the wise men's visit has distorted its true significance. The Bible doesn't report that there were three men, or that they were kings, or that they worshiped Jesus in the manger stall. They were actually astrologers who studied the movements of the stars and looked for unusual developments as messages for humanity. Some astrologers were more scientific, similar to our modern astronomers, while others were superstitious charlatans whose advice often misled kings and whoever else could pay for their services.

MIXING THE BIBLE WITH SATURN, JUPITER, AND MARS

These astrologers may have studied the Old Testament, which had been available to the ancient world in Greek for some two hundred years. As they pursued their study of the heavens, they also noticed phenomena which passed unnoticed by most people.

In the year 7 B.C. they saw what astronomers call a triple conjunction of Saturn and Jupiter as their paths passed each other three times, an event which occurs only once in 125 years. Then in early 6 B.C., Jupiter and Saturn grouped close to the planet Mars, a configuration repeated only each 805 years. Later in the spring of 6 B.C. Venus, Jupiter, and Saturn also formed an unusual close grouping. Ancient astrologers believed that the area of the sky named Pisces, where all these phenomena occured, contained pertinent signs for the Hebrew nation. They also believed Saturn ruled the destiny of the Jews. It is possible that these astrologers, blending a knowledge of Old Testament prophecies about a Messiah with observation of the sky, were led to seek a new king in Palestine.

To cross the Mideast's Fertile Crescent to Bethlehem required weeks of travel, and the timing of the astral event with the census must have accentuated the importance of this baby to Joseph and Mary. The wealthy worshipers found Jesus in a Bethlehem house and gave gifts of gold, frankincense, and myrrh. Frankincense was a sweet-smelling gum used for incense; myrrh was also a gum used for perfume, medicine, and embalming. The gifts would provide income for Joseph and Mary when sold.

The only Gospel which records the visit of these astrologers is Matthew's. As a former tax collector for the Romans, Matthew, or Levi, had been abused by the highly religious Pharisees, and he repeatedly notes the hypocrisy and vanity of this group in his writing. Perhaps he felt the deep irony as he recorded the worship of the Jewish Messiah by Gentile astrologers while the Hebrew scribes and priests wandered on in spiritual darkness!

HEROD AT HIS PARANOID WORST

The wise men of the East were unaware of Palestinian politics and stopped to consult Herod the Great in their search for Jesus. History records much about this man which is not mentioned in the Bible. He was better equipped for ruling a concentration camp than God's chosen people. A cruel and paranoid genius, he married ten times, murdered his favorite wife, plus a mother-in-law, three brothers-in-law, and three of his sons, in addition to ordering mass slayings. A popular phrase among his contemporaries was: "It's better to be Herod's pig than Herod's son."

When Palestine's king discovered from the astrologers that a baby had been born in Bethlehem who would one day be king, he did what came naturally to him—he ordered all male children of the village two years old and under to be killed.

Before this massacre, God again spoke to Joseph in a dream and directed him to flee to Egypt until Herod was dead. Colonies of Jews there provided a place where Joseph and Mary could be in congenial surroundings. Providentially, the gifts from the wise men probably financed their journey.

THE AMAZING TWELVE-YEAR-OLD

The dramatic details surrounding Jesus' birth now fade, and the Bible gives little description of the next thirty years of his life. Matthew tells us that when Herod's son Archelaus succeeded to the throne in Judea, which encompassed Jerusalem and Bethlehem, Joseph and Mary were directed back to Nazareth. This hilltop town in Galilee provided a quiet and secluded locale for rearing Jesus.

The Bible notes only one incident during these years. At the age of twelve a Jewish boy was taken to the temple for Passover celebration, just before his *Bar Mitzvah* recognition. Mary and the smaller children may have started the journey homeward ahead of her husband, since they traveled slower, and Joseph apparently assumed Jesus was with her or other relatives. When they discovered he was not in the caravan Joseph and

Mary, probably near panic, rushed back to Jerusalem and searched until they found him in the temple area listening and talking to the rabbis. We're told that "all those who heard him were amazed at his intelligence and his answers" (Luke 2:46, 47).

The rabbis taught by responding to questions and questioning their audiences. Jesus' answers were so deep and thought-provoking that the teachers could hardly believe they came from a twelve-year-old boy. He also asked such profound questions that the rabbis strained for answers.

Into this scene burst the harried searchers. They were relieved to find Jesus, but Mary rebuked him in motherly concern: "Why did you do this to us? Your father and I were worried sick looking for you" (v. 48). Though Joseph and Mary knew Jesus was the Messiah, they still could not envision what this would mean.

DID HE WONDER WHO HE WAS?

"Why were you anxiously looking for me? Didn't you know that I must be involved in my Father's affairs?" Jesus asked his mother. He thought they would know he was profitably using his time and that God was watching over him. Most significant, he refers to his father as God, not Joseph. Jesus at this age was well aware of his identity. The nagging question in the rock opera, *Jesus Christ Superstar,* "Did you ever wonder who you are?" is clearly answered here. Still in his childhood, Jesus has consciously assumed the role of Man-God.

As an obedient son, Jesus submitted to his parents' desire and returned with them to Nazareth. All that happened to him and in him during the next eighteen years or so is summed up in Luke's single statement: "Jesus grew mentally and physically, and was well-regarded by God and man" (2:52).

These are often called Jesus' "silent years." The biblical writers evidently felt that knowledge of this period is not relevant to understanding Jesus' mission. Mark's Gospel refers to Jesus' four brothers and at least two sisters (6:3), so we assume that Mary and Joseph had at least six other children. Some Christians insist that Mary remained a virgin, but tradition rather than Scripture supports this view.

After Jesus began his public ministry, Joseph's name is not mentioned, so we assume he died during these unrecorded years. Jesus endured the pain of separation from this kind and good man and the grief of his mother's sorrow at losing her husband. Like other Jewish boys, Jesus learned his father's trade, in this case carpentry. He built houses, made furniture, and fashioned farm instruments. Evidently he called no attention to himself by supernatural deeds because later the Nazareth citizens were astounded at his miracle power (Luke 4:22, 23).

WHO TOLD THE BIBLICAL WRITERS THESE STORIES?

We might wonder where the Gospel writers Matthew and Luke obtained their knowledge of the events surrounding Jesus' birth. Luke's account contains such an intimate detail as: "Mary preserved all these things (the shepherd's report), pondering them in her heart" (2:19). Mary probably told Matthew much that he didn't include in his Gospel, and Luke, Paul's companion and assistant, diligently researched sources for his writing (Luke 1:1-3). Mary's children, including James, a leader in the Jerusalem church, were reliable first-hand sources.

Another question concerning the accounts of Jesus' early life concerns the lengthy genealogies in Matthew 1 and Luke 3.

Matthew's list traces Jesus' lineage through David and Judah to Abraham because the Old Testament repeatedly links the Messiah with these men. Curiously, Matthew includes the names of four women (1:3, 5, 6), highly unorthodox for a Jew. Two of them—Rahab and Ruth—were Gentiles, while the other two—Tamar and Bathsheba—were immoral. This genealogy emphasizes God's accessibility to Gentiles and the notorious as well as to the heritage-rich Hebrews. Matthew was again getting back at the Pharisees.

11

Since Jewish people carefully preserved their genealogies, and since Luke's genealogy is different from Matthew's, the probable explanation is that Luke traces Jesus' actual human lineage through Mary, though using the names of the husbands. While Matthew follows the royal line through Joseph, Solomon, and David, Luke continues back to Adam to accent the humanity of Jesus, the spiritual leader of mankind.

THE UNCOMMON COMMON MAN

What is the essence of Jesus' early years? The accounts emphasize Jesus' absolute uniqueness. Jesus is God's Son, the divine Messiah sent to rescue mankind from its predicament. We also see his genuine humanness, his humble and limiting circumstances.

Paul put this in theological perspective when he wrote that Jesus, though "existing in the form of God, did not consider equality with God something which must be held on to, but emptied himself, taking the form of a slave, coming to earth like a man" (Philippians 2:6, 7). Jesus was born a promised king, but in a stable instead of a palace. He narrowly escaped murder in infancy. He endured hardships and sorrows of poor people. His family did not really understand him; his relatives probably pitied him. Some disreputable shepherds, foreign astrologers, and two insignificant senior citizens recognized his eminence, but they didn't stay around long. Priests, kings, emperors, and philosophers paid little attention to him except when intent on killing him.

These things make Jesus appealing to the common people of this world. They sense that he is *one of them* despite his genius and profundity. His brilliance can always challenge the intellectuals, but unless he had lived as a common man he probably would not attract the great masses of ordinary men and women.

Today millions worship a man who never went to college but was wiser than any Ph.D., and a man who never earned more than a few pennies a day but walked in an abundance of life which the merely wealthy never dream of. He was the uncommon common man.

FOOTNOTES FOR CHAPTER ONE:

[1] Everett F. Harrison, *A Short Life of Christ,* (Eerdmans, 1968), pp. 44-46.
[2] The date generally used for Jesus' birth is now considered a miscalculation.

TWO

◆ ◆

Strange Happenings in the Desert

◆ ◆

Elijah was the cream of the crop among Israel's ancient prophets. He was a rugged, solitary figure who battled the infamous King Ahab and Queen Jezebel eight hundred years before Jesus came on the Israeli scene. He pronounced stern judgment on these evil leaders and called the wayward nation back to God. His rough and simple clothing matched his message: he disdained flowing robes with ornate "girdles" for a hair-skin garment with a rough leather belt.[1] Most incredible was the way he left this world: as he stood by the Jordan River near Jericho, God's fiery chariot swept him up to heaven (2 Kings 2:4-11).

Later prophets remembered Elijah. In fact, the last Old Testament prophet, Malachi, closed his book with this promise from God: "Behold, I am going to send you Elijah the prophet before the coming of the great and terrible day of the Lord. And he will restore the hearts of the fathers to their children and the hearts of the children to their fathers, lest I come and smite the land with a curse" (Malachi 4:5,6, *NASB*).

For the next four hundred years many Jews looked for Elijah's return. They weren't expecting a reincarnation—Elijah's spirit in another person's body—they looked for Elijah himself to appear and straighten out the nation.

Sometime between A.D. 26 and 30 another rugged figure appeared at the Jordan River near Jericho. He wore a hair garment with a rough leather belt, just like Elijah. He called the Jewish people back to God, just like Elijah. He denounced an evil royal couple—King Herod Antipas and Queen Herodias, just like Elijah. But his name was John the Baptist: he was the miracle child of Elizabeth, Mary's relative, conceived in her old age.

Though John was not Elijah—and the "terrible day of the Lord" was not yet at hand—John's ministry was enough like Elijah's so Jesus could say: "He is Elijah who was to come" (Matthew 11:14). This signified the importance of John's words to Jews who were sincerely seeking God.[2]

DID JOHN JOIN A COMMUNE?

The historian Josephus describes John's brief influence on Israel, but details of his early life are missing in both Josephus and the New Testament. Luke's Gospel tells us that he spent time in the Judean desert before he began his ministry (1:80). As his parents lived in the hill country, some scholars have suggested that John became part of a now famous commune.

In 1947, Bedouin shepherds probed the interiors of cliffside caves near the Dead Sea and found the remains of the Qumram community. This group was an ascetic Jewish sect which isolated itself to preserve its traditions. Their writings and documents have provided biblical scholars with a wealth of background material about Palestine in the times of Jesus, as well as preserving in earthen jars our most ancient manuscripts of Old Testament Scriptures. Their teachings are strikingly similar to John's in some respects, and as they followed a custom of adopting and training children, John may have been trained by them even as a boy.

But whatever their similarities with John, the differences are so significant that John must have broken away from any connection. The commune's strategy was to retreat into the desert, while John's was to confront the world and its sins. "Repent, for the kingdom of heaven is at hand!" John trumpeted (Matthew

3:2). The commune looked for several messianic personalities, but John announced one Messiah was coming and he was very near.

ASSAULT ON THE SELF-RIGHTEOUS

John began his ministry by the Jordan River because he used the water for baptizing his converts. This ritual was not new to the Jewish people. For many years they had demanded that Gentiles converting to the Jewish faith be baptized. But it was new for John to demand that Jews be baptized. And this was no casual ceremony, for John insisted that they first repent and confess their sins. Many balked at a public admission of sins when they had worked so hard to observe innumerable rituals.

John's message was so revolutionary that crowds from the cities flocked to hear him. The Jewish leaders decided to join the throngs and put this innovator in his place. When John spotted them approaching, he denounced their hypocrisy just as the fiery Elijah would have.

"You sons of snakes!" John shouted. "Who warned you to run away from the coming judgment? Show in your lives, then, that you have *really* repented!" (Luke 3:7, 8).

In one swing John had cut them down. And he added fuel to the fire by baptizing tax collectors, soldiers who assisted them, and disreputable Jews who were anathema to the religious elite.

The crowds grew and their excitement mounted. Here was a prophet who feared no man. Some began to say John was the Messiah, but he replied, "I baptize you with water, but someone else is coming far greater than I. I'm not even worthy to untie his shoes. He will baptize you with the Holy Spirit and fire" (v. 16). At these words the controversy and anticipation burned all the brighter.

JESUS' AMAZING ACT

Into the midst of this riverside turmoil came Jesus to perform his first public act. As tax collectors, soldiers, and Jewish rabble stood in line for the sinner's baptism, who joined them but Jesus! When he stood before John, the prophet objected: "I can't baptize you. You should baptize me instead."

Jesus replied firmly: "Let me be baptized, for this is the fulfillment of righteousness for me" (Matthew 3:14, 15). He was not saying he was a sinner, but that he wanted to identify himself publicly with those who are. The act foreshadowed his future ministry and reputation as the friend of sinners.

As John obediently baptized him, the Spirit of God descended on Jesus in visible form signifying to John that Jesus was the promised Messiah (John 1:33).

THE DEVIL AND THE DESERT

Jesus did not stay around long, but soon disappeared into the vast, frightening desert west of the Jordan River. Here he faced one of the most terrifying experiences imaginable—he met the devil himself in that eerie wasteland.

Sophisticated society has joked about the devil until recent years. That horned and bearded creation of artists has been relegated to superstitious fables of the Middle Ages, but the horrible evils of the twentieth century and the bizarre events of the last decade—UFO's, psychic phenomena, evil oppression—have brought the devil back into his own. Movies about demonic powers gross millions, TV shows on the occult are living room standbys, while occult book shops, witches, warlocks, and seances are popping up everywhere. More and more people are convinced that an evil being whom the Bible calls the devil or Satan is shaping the strange and evil events in our world.

TEST ONE: IT'S DESPERATION TIME

Jesus stayed in the desert forty days without food. Physically weak from hunger, he resisted unnamed temptations the whole forty days, then confronted Satan's most insidious traps at the last. Satan approached Jesus—in what form we don't know—and said: "Since you are God's Son, command these stone to become bread" (Matthew 4:3).

The desert was dotted with small round stones which resembled the pancake-shaped loaves of bread enjoyed in every family. By performing a miracle Jesus could avoid starvation even if he remained in the wilderness. The devil was suggesting it was desperation time and Jesus had better work fast because God has forgotten him.

But Jesus struck back with a statement from Deuteronomy: "Man shall not live on bread alone, but on every word which comes out of the mouth of God" (Deuteronomy 8:3; Matthew 4:4).

These words originally reassured Israel of God's care after they had spent forty years in wilderness living. Lacking productive land, the Israelis needed a God who could miraculously supply them with a food called "manna" for their survival. In the same way, children are not sustained by houses and food, but by parents who provide their necessities. God is the ultimate source of all provisions, and our relationship with him is more important than our supply of food.

Jesus was willing to wait until God signaled the end of the long fast. He believed that a God who sustained millions in a desert for forty years could sustain one man in a desert after forty days. Because he believed God was trustworthy, Jesus refused to perform a desperate and impulsive act. Such trust and patience in the face of adversity are hard to come by. Most of us doubt ourselves, others, and God, and leap to clutch any straw when things go wrong.

TEST TWO: PUT ON A SHOW

The devil next reversed his strategy. He escorted Jesus to the pinnacle of the Jerusalem temple, a high corner overlooking a deep valley, and suggested: "Throw yourself down, for it stands written in Scripture, 'He will command his angels concerning you, and they will hold you in their hands, lest you strike your foot on a stone'" (Matthew 4:6).

The devil smoothly quoted from the psalm where God promised to take care of the Messiah at all times and allow nothing to hurt him. Since Jesus had just displayed his faith concerning food, the devil challenged him to prove his faith unequivocally. Satan suggested that he leap from the top of the temple area, four hundred feet high, and let the angels catch him! God couldn't possible let him hit the ground, because Scripture says his foot won't even strike a stone. But Jesus' response was another admonition from Deuteronomy: "You shall not put to the test the Lord your God" (Deuteronomy 6:16; Matthew 4:7). Jesus believed God would protect him, but he refused to create an unnecessary emergency to force God to do so. Satan asked for a miracle tainted with a wrong motivation.

The first test appealed to the physical need of Jesus. This test appealed to his spiritual nature. It encouraged a spiritual pride, and reminds us of the tragic stories of sick people who refuse medical help because they demand that God work a healing miracle instead. To create our own emergencies and then to demand that God miraculously deliver us so our great faith can be on display is both tragic and self-centered. Such misguided belief has launched many dedicated persons on disillusioning ventures. These foolish undertakings starkly contrast with the triumphs of those who fully trust in genuine emergencies.

TEST THREE: AN OFFER YOU CAN'T REFUSE

The third test was the devil's offer of world power. He and Jesus returned to a high mountain in the wilderness and Satan showed him what must have been like a rapid slide presentation of Rome, Alexandria, Athens, Jerusalem and other great cities of the ancient world. "All these I will give you," Satan promised, "if you will prostrate yourself and worship me" (Matthew 4:9).

What an offer! To be king of the world boggles the mind. We wouldn't know what to do with such a proposition, but the Old Testament had promised all this to the Messiah (Psalms 2:8). Jesus can rule the world without waiting, suffering, or dying, if he accepts the devil's offer.

But Jesus rejected it by quoting from Deuteronomy again: "You shall worship the Lord your God, and him only shall you serve" (Deuteronomy 6:13; Matthew 4:10). Jesus' worship of God was not for sale at any price. The end of world dominion did not justify this evil means. Again he affirmed his trust in God—he was willing to suffer, die, and wait for the promised rule according to the divine plan.

In lesser ways the devil makes similar bargains with people today. The occult movement attracts increasing numbers because it offers supernatural power to its adherents. Since most of us feel powerless in our technological society, this has great appeal. But Jesus showed that replacing God with Satan, and selling out to evil to obtain supposed good is a poor bargain. No end ever justifies evil means.

As early believers later read about these temptations of Jesus, they could hardly avoid contrasting them with the biblical story of the fall of man. Adam was in a lush garden; Jesus, in a barren wilderness. Adam has a companion, Jesus was alone. Adam was rested and fed, Jesus was tired and hungry. Adam's test was simple but he failed without a struggle. Jesus' test was complex but he endured to success. What a difference between the two men!

Jesus defeated the devil here without resorting to miracles. His weapons were firm resistance combined with unwavering reliance on the character, commands, and promises of God. He defeated Satan in a way that any follower of Jesus can employ. As the ideal man,

Jesus set the example for all men in combatting the devil. "Resist the devil and he will run from you," James later wrote in the New Testament (James 4:7).

BACK TO WHERE THE ACTION IS

Jesus returned from the wilderness to the river valley where John was preaching and found the spiritual battle there blazing as hot as ever. The Jerusalem religious authorities increased their pressure through a delegation demanding to know what claims John makes for himself. Is he Elijah, or the Messiah, or the prophet who Moses foretold (actually also the Messiah), or who?

John replied that he was none of these—but rather a divine messenger pointing to the great person who was coming. The dissatisfied delegation left, and the very next day Jesus returned to the baptismal site. On seeing him this time, John began announcing that Jesus was the Son of God (John 1:34).

The usual crowds were evidently not present at the moment, but John's close followers were. A number of men had attached themselves to John, helping him baptize and vowing their allegiance to him. One of John's disciples was named Andrew, and another was probably John, the author of the fourth Gospel, for in his book he gives what appears to be an eyewitness account of this dramatic encounter—he even remembers the time of day (v. 39).

John and Andrew set out after Jesus when their first leader, John the Baptist, disclosed Jesus' real identity. Jesus invited the two men to stay with him the rest of that day. We don't know what Jesus said to them, but they headed out the door convinced that John's relevation was true. John says Andrew "first" got his brother Simon and brought him to Jesus, declaring: "We've found the Messiah" (vv. 40, 41). The word "first" implies that John next brought his own brother, James, another fisherman who also joined the group.

Jesus looked at Simon with a searching gaze (as the Greek original implies) and said, "You are Simon, the son of John; you will be called Peter" (v. 42). Ancient names often had particular meanings, and "Peter" meant "rock." One who went up and down like a yo-yo in his performance learned he would become solid as a rock. No doubt Peter never forgot that day and that hour, that look and that word as Jesus foretold the fisherman's spiritual future.

THE CASE OF THE HONEST ISRAELITE

The next day the group gained another follower, Philip. He was from Bethsaida, the same town on the Sea of Galilee as Peter and Andrew, and probably a friend of theirs. Philip in turn looked up Nathanael and told him they had found the Messiah—Jesus of Nazareth. Cana and Nazareth were obscure villages, located only nine miles apart. They probably looked down on one another, each insisting that the other was lower on the totem pole. Nathanael therefore replied with blunt skepticism, "Nazareth? Can anything good come from there?" (v. 46)

When Nathanael was introduced to him, Jesus said "Here is an Israelite who is without any deceit!" Nathanael was obviously a blunt, tell-it-like-it-is type of person.

"How do you know me?" he asked Jesus.

"Before Philip got you, I saw you under the fig tree," Jesus replied (v. 48).

This was the icing on the cake for Nathanael. Fig trees were favorite spots for devout Jews to meditate and pray, and Nathanael had been hidden from observers under such a tree, perhaps meditating about the future Messiah and the kingdom promises to Israel. Jesus' supernatural knowledge triggered Nathanael's praise: "Rabbi, you are the Son of God, you are the king of Israel!" (v. 50)

Jesus' associations with these six men demonstrated his sensitivity to individuals. He understood and accepted them as they were. His concern for the individual continued throughout his ministry, even when he was surrounded by crowds. From their first encounter these six believed Jesus was the Messiah and sensed his supernatural powers. But their concept of Israel's Messiah—like Joseph's and Mary's—was so inadequate that several years would pass before they discovered the majestic meaning of that name and destiny.

Realizing their unpreparedness, Jesus waited before calling them to leave their jobs and accompany him full time as committed disciples. Yet undoubtedly the vivid memories of those first days never left the minds of that little half dozen who were to have such effect on the world's history.

A HOMETOWN WEDDING

Jesus and his newfound friends kept traveling north and west into Galilee, and they arrived in Cana in time to attend a wedding in Nathanael's home town. Jesus' mother was present as a friend of the family, so Jesus and his friends were invited.

That Jesus attends is significant. While John the Baptist stayed in the desert areas and lived an ascetic life, Jesus moved from town to town and mixed with people. Some religious leaders have followed the ascetic road like John, but Jesus took a different path.

This wedding feast was not a simple three-hour reception with champagne and cake. Wedding feasts in Jesus' time went on for days with food and drink for all. And when the wine gave out at the Cana festivities it was super embarrassing. In fact, in those days when a host ran short, the guests could even sue and straddle him with an extra financial burden!

Jesus' mother implied that he should do something about the need as she informed him of it. Probably she expected no miracle, since she presumably had never seen him do one, but knowing his concern for the family and his dependability in all situations, she thought he could somehow take care of it.

Jesus replied, "Woman, what have I to do with you? My hour has not yet come" (John 2:4). He called her "woman," a courteous form of address in those times. Then he used an idiomatic expression which meant, "You and I aren't together on this." Then Jesus informed her his "hour" for Messianic action had not yet come. Mary probably thought he meant he would take care of the situation in a natural way, and she told the servants to follow his directions. Little did she know how spectacularly he would fulfill her request—in *his* timing.

This disagreement was probably painful for Mary. Joseph had been gone for some time, and Jesus had been the mainstay of the family. Now he was beginning to exchange his physical family relationships for attachments to the spiritual family of God, and Mary must learn to see him as the divine Messiah who took orders from God alone.

DEAD WATER AND LIVING WINE

At the right moment Jesus instructed the servants to fill six stone waterports to the brim—about 120 gallons of water. These waterports were used for the endless purification rites the Pharisees forced on the people. They frequently had to wash before, in the midst of, and at the end of meals. They had to wash certain ways and according to certain rules. This had no connection with sanitation—it was legalistic, traditional, and often useless ritual.

Jesus next commanded the servants to take water from the waterpots to the official in charge of the feast. The servants must have thought Jesus was crazy. But without their notice the water in the pots had miraculously turned to wine—and not just ordinary wine, but the very best! (v. 10)

Jesus' first recorded miracle proved to be unusual indeed, because most of his subsequent miracles met deep human need, while this one only spared social embarrassment. But we can see symbolic significance in it. Wine in the Old Testament often signified prosperity, life, and joy (Psalms 104:14; Amos 9:13-15), and in changing water to wine Jesus transformed the water of legalistic ritual into the sparkling wine of new life. This pictured what he was to do with the lives of his disciples and many after them.

No slight of hand or trickery could explain this inaugural miracle. In a few seconds 120 gallons of water had become 120 gallons of wine. Jesus' disciples were awed, his mother was astonished, the young couple could hardly believe it, and the whole village was dumbfounded. Yet this was only a small preview of things to come.

FOOTNOTES FOR CHAPTER TWO:

[1] See 2 Kings 1:8, which scholars consider a reference to a hair garment. Also compare Zechariah 13:4.
[2] The final fulfillment of Malachi's prophecy is probably realized in the coming of the two witnesses of Revelation 11:3-11. Elijah's return hearlds both the first and second coming of Jesus.

THREE

◆ ◆

The Gentleman
and the Lady

◆ ◆

The magnificent Jerusalem temple with its glistening gold domes, creamy white exterior, and gigantic walled courtyards stood there in all its glory. Through its gates multitudes of Jewish pilgrims trecked annually for the great holy days—Passover, Pentecost, *Yom Kippur*. It was the most sacred spot on earth to Jews. They built their synagogues facing Jerusalem and the temple. They prayed toward the temple. To profane this holy place was an unspeakable crime.

Jerusalem and the temple was Jesus' goal as Passover time approached. He and his disciples left Cana and visited briefly in Capernaum on the Sea of Galilee before joining throngs coming to Jerusalem (John 2:12, 13). As things turned out, Jesus came to the temple for more than worship.

The temple was governed by a Jewish sect named the Sadducees. As the aristocrats of Israel, they gave allegiance to Rome in return for financial and political favors. These greedy men had set up businesses in the temple courtyards which charged exorbitantly for exchanging pilgrims' money into local currency, and sold animals for sacrifice at many times the fair price. Priests in league with the merchants would accept only these over-priced animals. These "bazaars of the sons of Annas," as they were called, were so hated that public indignation finally swept them away in A.D. 67.

When Jesus entered the temple area his eyes lit upon these bazaars where the merchants were noisily haggling over prices as they defrauded their irate customers. Jesus quickly grabbed some cord, looped it into a small whip, and started overturning money tables while he flailed the merchants with his homemade weapon. "Stop making my Father's house into a place of business!" he furiously shouted as he kicked them out (v. 16).

The artist's brush often paints Jesus as meek and mild. But here he was full of fiery indignation over such injustice and hypocrisy. Yet his anger was properly restrained. He used a little whip, not his fists; he fought with daggers of truth, not of steel; and he even died for these Sadducees instead of leading an armed rebellion against them. His anger, like his love, was perfect.

ONE FATEFUL SENTENCE

Disturbance of temple operations meant immediate arrest, but the crowd that celebrated Jesus' heroics would not allow such retaliation. Another way must be found to humiliate Jesus. "Show us a miracle which gives you the right to do this," demanded the religious leaders (v. 18). Anyone who called the temple "my Father's house" and asserted Messianic authority by disrupting temple business ought to support his claims with miraculous deeds!

"You destroy this temple and in three days I'll raise it," Jesus retorted (v. 19). The challenge was more than the Sadducees could handle.

"It took forty-six years to build this temple, and *you* will rebuild it in three days?" they answered mockingly. They thought Jesus referred to the Jerusalem temple, but John explains in his Gospel that Jesus spoke "concerning the temple of his body. When he was raised from the dead, his disciples remembered what he had said" (vv. 21, 22).

Just three years later Jesus would stand before some of these same men on trial for his life. And the accusation they would hurl at him was Jesus' statement that he could "destroy the temple of God and rebuild it in three days" (Matthew 26:61). Though these greedy men daily desecrated the temple with their business ventures, they now tried to charge him with profaning that holy location. Even as he hung on the cross, the crowds mocked "you who destroy the temple and rebuild it in three days, rescue yourself!" (Matthew 27:40) His enemies used to the hilt this one fateful sentence.

THE NIGHT VISITOR

After the temple confrontation Jesus remained in Jerusalem ministering for many weeks, but as he was preparing to leave the city, a secret admirer appeared out of the darkness to question him: "There was a man of the Pharisees, named Nicodemus, a ruler of the Jews. He came to Jesus at night and said 'Rabbi, we know you have come as a teacher sent from God, for no one can continue to do these miracles you do unless God is with him' " (John 3:1, 2).

To become a card-carrying Pharisee, you had to promise to observe a mass of Jewish traditions relating to ceremonial purity and tithing. This mountain of rules went far beyond the requirements of Moses' law and proved so formidable that the number of Pharisees was only about six thousand, though their influence extended far beyond their membership.

Nicodemus was also a "ruler," which meant he was a member of the Jewish Sanhedrin, the seventy religious elders of the nation. Jesus later called Nicodemus "the teacher of Israel," which implied he was one of the great rabbis of his day, perhaps the most popular teacher in Jerusalem. So far as we know, Jesus never encountered a more prestigious, knowledgeable, refined representative of Judaism than Nicodemus.

THE ULTIMATE SHOCK

Jesus' blunt reply to Nicodemus' statement was, "Unless one is born anew he cannot see God's kingdom" (v.

3). This was the ultimate shock to Nicodemus, who believed as a Pharisee that Jewish birth and rigid observance of Jewish laws and traditions opened the door to heaven. Jesus swept all this away as he informed one of Israel's greatest rabbis that he was unqualified without a new birth.

The shaken rabbi questioned the possibility of a second birth. He could only compare it with a physical birth as he objected: "Can a man be born when he is old? Certainly he can't enter his mother's womb a second time" (v. 4).

But Jesus persisted: "Unless one is born of water and spirit, he can't enter God's kingdom. Human nature gives birth to human nature; God's Spirit gives birth to spirit. Don't be surprised that you have to be born anew. The wind blows where it wishes; you hear its sound, but don't know where it comes from or where it's going. So is everyone born of the Spirit" (vv. 5-8).

He now explained to Nicodemus that he must be born of water and spirit. Jesus probably meant that the repentance which John's water baptism symbolized was necessary for entering God's kingdom along with spiritual birth, both of which would repel a Pharisee. A physical birth gives us a physical nature, Jesus pointed out, and a spiritual birth is necessary for a spiritual nature. A spiritual birth comes like the wind which is invisible and mysterious, yet which exists and shows visible effects. Without this spiritual experience, Jesus declared, Nicodemus cannot understand Jesus or his message.

THE IGNORANT THEOLOGIAN

"How can these things happen?" the nonplussed Nicodemus replied (v. 9). "You are the teacher of Israel, and don't know these truths? . . . If I have told you earthly things and you don't believe, how will you believe if I tell you heavenly things?" Jesus answered with a mild rebuke (vv. 10-12).

The Old Testament taught that human nature is limited and sinful, and that God must give his people a new heart and put a new spirit within them (Ezekiel

36:25-27). If Nicodemus rejected this basic "earthly" truth of the Old Testament, Jesus questioned whether he would move on to more advanced "heavenly" truth.

Then Jesus staggered Nicodemus with the most startling revelation yet, as he moved on to such heavenly truth: "No one has gone into heaven except the Son of Man who has come out of heaven. And just as Moses lifted up the snake in the wilderness, so must the Son of Man be lifted up that whoever believes in him may . . . have eternal life" (John 3:13-15).

Jesus claimed to be the Son of Man, the Messiah, who existed in heaven before he came to earth! Furthermore, in some strange way this Son of Man will be lifted up for the salvation of believers as Moses once lifted a bronze snake on a pole so that snake-bitten Israelites could look on it and be miraculously healed.

A COWARD BECOMES COURAGEOUS

Nicodemus was probably never so speechless! He came expecting rabbinic dialogue, and in a few minutes his philosophy of a lifetime was overthrown and his theological system shattered at the hands of a man probably half his age, untrained in rabbinic schools, who claimed to be the Son of Man from heaven! But the more Nicodemus thought on Jesus' words, evidently the more glimmers of truth he saw, and when Jesus was raised up on a Roman cross Nicodemus must have recalled that phrase "The Son of Man must be lifted up," for he and Joseph of Arimathea courageously stepped forward to bury Jesus (John 19:39-41).

Nicodemus originally came at night probably out of cowardice—a prestigious Sanhedrin member could not afford to be seen consulting a radical, unschooled rabbi. But the once cowardly Nicodemus boldly declared his faith by burying Jesus when Jesus' own disciples had fled in fear. Jesus' words about the new birth finally bore fruit in the life of the prestigious Pharisee.

LIFE'S GREAT ISSUE

Instead of completing Nicodemus' conversation with Jesus, John apparently inserts his own mature reflections at this point in the Gospel narrative. "For God so loved the world," he wrote, "that he gave his only Son in order that whoever believes in him may not perish but have eternal life. For God did not send his Son into the world to condemn the world, but that the world might be saved through him" (3:16, 17).

In those days, the Jewish teachers never taught that God loved the whole world, but John asserts it here. But as there is love, so is there judgment. "Whoever believes in him is not condemned; whoever does not believe has already suffered condemnation because he has not believed in the name of the only Son of God" (v. 18). John makes belief in Jesus the central issue of life: trust in him brings salvation and eternal life; rejection of him seals one's doom. Then John explains the reason why people reject Jesus.

"This is the verdict: the light has come into the world and men loved darkness rather than the light, because their works were evil. For everyone doing evil hates the light and does not come to the light so his works won't be exposed, but the one doing the truth comes to the light that his works may be shown to have been wrought in God" (vv. 19-22).

John pinpoints the problem as moral, not intellectual; good versus bad, not enlightenment versus ignorance. Coming to Jesus is coming to moral light which exposes our sinfulness. Nicodemus had to struggle to come to that light—others prefer to slumber on in darkness unexposed but finally ruined.

WHO IS THE BEST BAPTIZER?

Jesus left Jerusalem for the Judean countryside close by, where he continued to preach about the kingdom of God, and his disciples began baptizing people who wished to confirm their repentance from sins. In the meantime, Pharisaic harassment apparently drove John the Baptist into Samaria (v. 23), but to the Pharisees' consternation, Jesus picked up where John left off. Some of the Pharisees now further harassed John by trying to set him against Jesus. They began to question John's disciples about whose baptism is best—Jesus' or

John's, and the prophet's disciples now came to their teacher complaining, "Rabbi, the one who was with you beyond the Jordan, to whom you bore witness, now he is baptizing and everyone is coming to him" (v. 26). They saw Jesus as John's competition and resented that Jesus took away from his following.

John's response revealed a different spirit. "You yourselves know that I said I am not the Messiah. . . . The bride belongs to the bridegroom, but the best man stands and hears him and rejoices over the voice of the bridegroom. He must increase; I must decrease" (vv. 28-30).

John referred to the Jewish wedding custom of the best man guarding the bridal chamber and opening the door only at the voice of the groom. He pictured Jesus as the Messiah-groom, Israel as the bride, and himself as the attendant of a proper marriage, after which he fades from the scene.

Jesus later said that a greater prophet had never been born than John the Baptist (Matthew 11:11). He stirred the Messianic hopes of Israel and began a revival which produced Jesus' first disciples and many of his followers. He baptized Jesus and proclaimed him as Messiah. Within a few weeks of this renunciation of fame, John was destined to go to prison and then to a grisly death. His ministry was brief—no more than two years—but what he did, he did well. His mission was accomplished.

RED-HOT PREJUDICE

Jesus' popularity was now arousing hostility from the Pharisees, so he headed north for the more tolerant atmosphere of Galilee (John 4:1-3). But between the provinces of Judea and Galilee lay Samaria—an area avoided by devout Jews.

The Samaritans were only half-Jews, and they accepted only the first five books of the Old Testament as their Scriptures. For over five hundred years Jews and Samaritans had despised and tricked each other. Jews had burned the Samaritan temple and Samaritans had desecrated the Jewish temple by littering it with human bones at Passover. Sometimes Samaritans murdered small caravans of Jews traveling through their territory, but unperturbed by all this, Jesus led his startled disciples right through the heart of Samaria, since it was the shortest route to Galilee (vv. 4-6).

At mid-day, Jesus stopped beside an ancient well to rest while his disciples went into town to buy food. A Samaritan woman approached the well as Jesus waited there, and he startled her with the request: "Would you give me a drink?"

"You're a Jew and I'm a Samaritan woman—how can you ask me for a drink?" she replied incredulously (v. 9).

Jesus understood her surprise. Jewish men typically looked down on women in those days. A rabbi was forbidden to speak with any woman in public—even his wife. To teach a woman the Law was considered a waste of time. But the lowest of all women in Jewish eyes was a Samaritan. It was forbidden to touch any utensil she touched, yet here was a Jew asking for water from her hand.

His next words surprised her even more. "If you knew God's gift and the one who is asking you for a drink, you would have asked him and he would have given you flowing water" (v. 10). This ancient well dug by Jacob was like a national monument to the Samaritans, yet this Jew was telling a Samaritan he could provide flowing water, as from a spring, far superior to the supply from Jacob's well!

"You have no pail and the well is deep, so where would you get this flowing water? You're certainly not greater than our father Jacob who gave us this well, are you?" she quipped sarcastically (vv. 11, 12).

THE FOUNTAIN THAT NEVER RUNS DRY

"Everyone who keeps drinking from this water will be thirsty again, but whoever drinks the water I give him will never thirst. In fact, the water I give him will become in him a fountain of water springing up into

33

eternal life," Jesus answered (vv. 13, 14). He told her he would quench the thirst of her parched soul and even enable her to spread the same satisfaction to others. But she still thought he was talking about literal water.

"Give me this water so I won't be thirsty and have to come here to draw," she said, half-mockingly (v. 15).

FIVE PLUS ONE EQUALS MISERY

"Go call your husband and come here," Jesus directed, looking her in the eye.

"I don't have a husband."

"You're right. You've had five husbands, and the man you live with now isn't your husband. You told the truth, for sure, when you said that!" (vv. 16-18)

Something undefinable intrigued her about this Jew. The women of her town gossiped about her. She had probably even come the half mile to this well alone to avoid their usual sneers and dirty looks. Yet he was willing to drink from her bucket; he talked about the gift of God, flowing water, never thirsting, and now he shows he knows all about her unsavory past! She was flooded with conflicting feelings. This man must be a prophet of God. Yet how could she surrender the religion of her forefathers and adopt the faith of those hated Jews?

Looking toward the ruins of a temple on nearby Mt. Gerizim, the woman parried: "I can see you're a prophet. Our fathers worshiped on this mountain, but you say that it's necessary to worship in Jerusalem" (v. 20).

Jesus' reply was as profound a statement as she had ever heard: "Believe me, a time is coming when neither on this mountain nor in Jerusalem will you worship the Father. You don't know what you worship. We know what we worship, for salvation comes from the Jews. But the time is coming—it is here now—when the true worshipers will worship the Father in spirit and truth, for the Father seeks such to worship him. God is spirit, and those worshiping him must worship in spirit and truth" (vv. 21-24).

Jesus affirmed that the Messiah would be a Jew, not a Samaritan. Then he explained God is not localized but is looking for true worshipers wherever they are. God is spiritual, not material, and cannot be contained in a building. A spiritual God for the whole world, not tied to a country or a temple, was undreamed of and unheard of then. The concepts were revolutionary!

"I know that Messiah is coming," she said. "When he comes, he will tell us everything." Her soul seemed to stand on tiptoe as she waited almost breathlessly for his reply.

"I who speak to you am he," Jesus answered, the words dropping like bombshells.

At that moment Jesus' disciples returned from town staring hard at the sight of Jesus talking with any woman—especially this one. But the woman hardly noticed them as she forgot her bucket, her waterpot, everything, and ran back into town where she quickly gathered a crowd and began announcing she had found the Messiah! When such a woman as this, probably called a whore to her face by the townspeople, suddenly starts announcing she has met the Messiah, curiosity alone would empty the whole place and send them out to the well.

THE FOOD THAT IS NOT BREAD

The puzzled disciples, meantime, laid out a spread of food. "Rabbi, eat!" they implored, wondering at his disinterest.

"I have food to eat you don't know of," Jesus replied.

"Did anyone bring him food?" they wondered aloud.

"My food is to do the will of the one who sent me and to finish his work. Don't you say, 'Four months and then harvest comes'? I tell you, lift up your eyes and look on the fields for they are white for harvest already. The reaper receives wages and harvests the crop for eternal life, that sower and reaper may share the joy together. . . . One sows, another reaps. I sent you to reap what you haven't worked for. Others have worked, and you have reaped the results of their labor" (vv. 34-38).

In these few sentences Jesus taught deep lessons to his followers. He told them that what truly satisfied him was not food, but doing God's will, as when he talked with the despised woman. Such words explode the fantasy that food, drink, and possessions guarantee happiness. He explained the harvest was not in four months, it was right then, and even a hostile, mixed-up people like the Samaritans were ready to believe in him. As he told his disciples to lift up their eyes and look on the white fields, he probably gazed up hill toward the town from which scores of Samaritans, clad in white clothing, were now coming. This was the field white unto harvest.

Sowers and reapers could rejoice together, Jesus said, because of the quickness of the harvest. Only shortly before, John the Baptist and his disciples had ministered not far from this area (John 3:23). Probably many of the citizens of this town—even this woman—may have heard him and marvelled at this devout Jew willing to preach to hostile Samaritans. Perhaps his call to repentance and his Messianic announcements had stirred spiritual longings in her soul. Jesus and his disciples could now capitalize on this sowing. While sowing material seed requires months for harvest, spiritual seed can blossom in weeks, days, even hours, as it did here.

THE FINAL OUTCOME

The harvest walked right into the reapers' hands as many Samaritans sought Jesus, listened to him speak, and affirmed: "This is indeed the Messiah, the Saviour of the world" (John 4:39-42). And this was only the beginning, for five years later a follower of Jesus named Phillip went to Samaria and received an enthusiastic welcome (Acts 8). Phillip took the fuller message of Jesus' death and resurrection, and the Samaritan woman and her friends then became foundation stones of the great spiritual movement which resulted there. John, the

Gospel author, joined Phillip in Samaria and may have learned then the details of Jesus' thirst-quenching conversation at Jacob's well.

TWO FROM OPPOSITE SIDES OF THE TRACKS

When Jesus left Samaria and went on to Galilee, the stark contrast between Jesus' encounter with the Samaritan woman and the earlier exchange with Nicodemus must have stuck with John. Nicodemus was among the highest of the high—wealthy Jew, Pharisee, teacher; she was the lowest of the low—Samaritan, harlot, ignorant. The elite Jew was startled to find his goodness so inadequate that he needed a new birth; the disreputable Samaritan was just as startled to find that her wasted years did not bar her from the spiritual water. Nicodemus took three years to muster the courage to proclaim his belief. She started a revival that hour.

That Jesus satisfied both individuals, each so prejudiced in different ways, shows his universal appeal. He and his message cross barriers of sex, race, and religion. His followers have been guilty of prejudice against fellow human beings all too often.

But no one could ever accuse Jesus of such prejudice.

FOUR

◆ ◆

The Taste
of New Wine

◆ ◆

Green, luxuriant hillsides funneled down to the fresh blue waters of the Sea of Galilee. The lake swarmed with fish, and the fertile fields around it, enveloped in a near tropical climate, were the richest in all Israel. The rest of Galilee was not quite so favored, but still fared well.

Galilee's bustling populace was a mixture of Jews and Gentiles, with international highways channeling citizens of many nations across its borders. Constant influx from the Gentile world made Galileans more tolerant than the provincial Judeans around Jerusalem. Jesus now left Samaria and settled down in Galilee for the next year. That move made Galilee the most important spot on earth for a time. Here Jesus would perform most of his spectacular miracles, here he would give eloquent discourses to hushed multitudes, and here he would appoint twelve apostles who would carry his message to the world. The dramatic events would cause Matthew, a one-time tax collector, to recall Isaiah's prophecy: "Galilee of the Gentiles—the people sitting in darkness saw a great light, and on those sitting in the land of the shadow of death light dawned" (Matthew 4:15, 16; Isaiah 9:1, 2).

Galilee is not finished as a center of world events

either. On its southern edge lies the fateful valley of Megiddo—better known as Armageddon, the scene of history's final blood-drenched battle (Revelation 16:16).

The Galileans now feverishly anticipated Jesus' return. They had a sharp eye for miracles and many of them had seen Jesus' miracles in Jerusalem. The stories of famous rabbis throbbed with miracles and the most dazzling display of all was expected from the Messiah when he came. Unlike secular men today, the Galileans looked for a miracle under every bush and now expected a rash of wondrous works from this unorthodox rabbi who had challenged the temple authorities.

HEALING AT A DISTANCE

Jesus had stopped in Cana when a Jewish government official came there from Capernaum to request healing for his dangerously ill son. Knowing what miracle mongers the Galileans were, Jesus tested him: "Unless you people see miracles and wonders you absolutely refuse to believe" (John 4:48).

Jesus' initial refusal stirred the faith of the distraught father and he begged, "Come down, before my son dies!" (v. 49)

Compassionately, Jesus directed: "Go, your son lives."

It was "the seventh hour," or about 1 P.M. when Jesus said this, notes John, and the father could not cover the twenty miles back before nightfall. But the next day he met his servants hurrying to tell him that yesterday at 1 P.M. his son's fever had left. John tells us that the man and all his household then believed in Jesus (v. 52).

This government official was evidently employed by Herod Antipas, king of Galilee and son of Herod the Great. Luke records that Joanna, the wife of Chuza, manager of Herod Antipas' household, later helped support Jesus and his apostles financially (8:3). Perhaps these were the grateful parents of the healed son. Jesus appealed to the poor and downtrodden. But here, a rich and powerful family, brought low by impending tragedy, found Jesus could meet their need too.

FROM CARPENTER TO MESSIAH

Jesus now left Cana for Nazareth. Probably while at Cana he had begun to teach and perform miracles, so his fame was spreading rapidly. How would his hometown react? On the Sabbath, the local citizens gathered for worship at their synagogue. There was only one national temple, of course, where Jews offered sacrifices and observed holy days. But there were many local synagogues where they could worship weekly as on this Sabbath in Nazareth.

As synagogues had no professional ministers, noted visitors were often invited to read the Scripture and address the assembly. Discussion and questions followed. The place was packed and every eye was riveted on Jesus as he stood up and read from Isaiah, "The Spirit of the Lord is upon me; therefore he designated me to evangelize the poor, commissioned me to proclaim freedom to prisoners and give sight to the blind, to release the oppressed, to proclaim the acceptable year of the Lord." He then sat down and began his sermon by announcing, "Today this Scripture has been fulfilled in your hearing" (Luke 4:18-21). What else he said, we don't know, but just interpreting these verses as he did was enough to shock the whole synagogue. This was Isaiah's prophecy of the Messiah, and Jesus had announced *he* was the fulfillment!

Perhaps very few noticed, but he also stopped reading Isaiah in the middle of a sentence. Isaiah had written that the Messiah would preach "the favorable year of the Lord and the day of vengeance of our God" (Isaiah 61:2, *NASB*). Plainly Jesus left out the words "day of vengeance of our God" because he did not view his coming as a proclamation of judgment. He had come as the lowly savior to heal and liberate. Later he spells out that he will come a second time as a conquering judge. In the middle of that sentence is a gap between his two comings now almost two thousand years long.

When Jesus' sermon concluded the audience was ready to explode. His wisdom left them spellbound, but his Messianic claim ignited fury. The Messiah was to be a great conqueror who fashioned far-reaching miracles. In their minds this man was once a carpenter, born of a shot-gun wedding. In thirty years he hadn't been known to heal a common cold, and didn't even keep his own father from dying. Suddenly he announces he is Messiah, and marches through Israel working wonders. Instead he should come home to Nazareth, perform miracles for his friends and neighbors, and bring the obscure place some deserved fame!

THE UNFRIENDLY FOLKS AT HOME

But Jesus was more than a match for them. "I tell you for sure, that no prophet is acceptable in his hometown. I tell you there were many widows in Israel when the sky was shut for three and a half years, when great famine covered the land, but not to one of them was Elijah sent. He went to a widow in Zarephath in Sidon. And many lepers were in Israel in the time of Elisha the prophet, but he cleansed none of them. He cleansed Naaman the Syrian" (Luke 4:24-27).

This was the final put down. Not only was the carpenter comparing his actions to those of Elijah and Elisha, the great Old Testament prophets, but he was likening the Nazarenes to their faithless ancestors who proved so unworthy of the prophets' miracles that they went to despised Gentiles like the widow of Tyre and Naaman the Syrian. Israel of that time was so prejudiced against her own great prophets that she forced them to minister to Gentiles. Now a greater than these prophets had come to Nazareth and they also were forcing him elsewhere. A prophet is without honor in his own home.

The crowd now turned into a lynch mob, threw Jesus out of the city, and took him to a cliff to hurl him off. Evidently as they approached the cliff, cooler heads protested such rash action. The crowd became divided, and as they argued, Jesus calmly walked away (vv. 28-30).

So ended Nazareth's opportunity—betrayed by its own preconceived notion of what the Messiah should be like. Jesus didn't fit their ideas and they were not willing to consider change. He had helped build their houses and repair their furniture and they assumed that's all he could do. Tragically, it was all—for them.

FROM FISH TO MEN

Jesus left Nazareth behind and headed to Capernaum on the Sea of Galilee. His mother may have already moved there, and most of Jesus' remaining time in Galilee was centered in this lakeside town.

About a year has passed since Jesus first met Peter, John, Andrew, and the other three disciples. Since then these and others had accompanied Jesus off and on. But now he decides to call some to accompany him full time, and he extends the call in a most profound way.

Multitudes flocked to Jesus as soon as his power to heal disease and exorcise demons became known. One day, to alleviate the pressure of the crowds, Jesus stepped into Peter's boat and asked him to move it a short way from the throngs on shore so he could preach. When he finished speaking, Jesus asked Peter to put his fishing nets into the deeper water for a catch. Peter and his companions had fished all night and caught nothing, and he knew the futility of fishing for large catches in the day. But reluctantly he obeyed Jesus.

Imagine his surprise when the nets were so bulging with fish that it required two boats to bring them in! Probably during Jesus' discourse Peter's fatigued mind had thought only of their failure to make a catch the night before. He had cast in the nets at Jesus' direction only to be polite. Now he realized his lack of faith and how little he and Jesus were on the same wave length. What place did a supernatural Messiah like Jesus have for a bumbling fool like him?

"Leave me, Lord, I'm a sinful man," Peter implored.

"Don't be afraid," Jesus replied, comforting him. "From now on you'll be catching men" (Luke 5:10).

At that James, John, Peter, and Andrew decided to

leave the fishing business and follow Jesus wherever he went. The great catch of fish, which probably brought in several weeks income, was their fond farewell.

What a strange moment Jesus chose for calling these men! They did not display strong faith, reckless dedication, or profound spiritual insight, but looked inept and bewildered. But Jesus' call was based on what he could do for them, not what they could do for him. It was a gift of his grace, not earned by their efforts. How different history might be if they had spent the rest of their days toiling for fish and money instead of for men and the richer rewards in Jesus' kingdom!

A DEMON IN THE SYNAGOGUE

Jesus now received an invitation to speak in the Capernaum synagogue. But as he was in the midst of his discourse, Mark's Gospel records that "a man in their synagogue with an evil spirit shouted 'What do you have to do with us, Jesus of Nazareth? Did you come to destroy us? I know who you are, holy one of God!' " (1:23, 24) The alarmed worshipers were probably ready to bolt for the door! The evil and mocking demonic voice sent chills up their spines.

Jesus responded instantly to the challenge. "Be quiet! Come out of him," Jesus commanded, and the evil spirit shook the man and exited with a blood curdling shriek (vv. 25, 26).

The people were amazed and frightened. Who was this man Jesus, that demon-possessed people were beginning to draw a bead on him? Where did he get such absolute authority over these demons? Others went through endless incantations and magical rites in uncertain attempts to cast out demons—Jesus did it in five words!

The twentieth century has ridiculed such tales of demon possession, claiming these people were all psychotic. But horrifying movies like *The Exorcist,* plus similar unnerving case histories, have now given second thoughts. The Gospels soberly tell us Jesus encountered real demon possession.

Ancient peoples, in contrast to the secular westerners, lived in daily fear of demon possession. They believed that thousands of demons populated the air about them, waiting to attack travellers, women in child birth, children, newly married couples, and any unwary person. They believed demons could enter the body through food, and they scattered amulets and charms all over their houses to ward off demons.

Such people did not ridicule the Gospel record of Jesus casting out demons; it gave them peace. They were thankful to learn Jesus was more powerful than Satan, and that they could rely on him instead of superstitious charms and formulas. Secular scholars have concluded that these Gospel stories did far more to set the western world free from superstition than the brilliant discourses of Greek philosophers. Unfortunately, under the influence of occult movements many are now returning again to the slavery from which Jesus freed us.

A JOYOUS MOTHER-IN-LAW

Jesus left the stunned synagogue to eat and rest at Peter's house. Upon arriving he found Peter's mother-in-law prostrated by a burning fever. This is one of the few occasions when the disciples' families are mentioned—here we see Peter was married.

Peter's decision to leave the secure family fishing business to tour with this unrecognized rabbi may have disturbed Peter's mother-in-law. She had always thought him unstable and this proved it! But Jesus clasped her hand and gently raised her to her feet—and the fever was instantly gone! Luke adds, "Right away, she got up and began to serve them" (4:39). So miraculous was the cure that her body didn't require recovery time—within a few minutes she was hard at work. She probably never complained about Peter's new career again.

A WHOLE TOWN HEALED

As the sun set that Sabbath day, the news of this miracle worker had swept over Capernaum and into surrounding towns. It may have reached nearby Tiberias, a health resort filled with the sick. As the Sabbath ended, crowds converged on Capernaum with their sick and demon-possessed loved ones. Matthew, probably an eyewitness, reports that "Jesus drove out the evil spirits with a word, and healed all the sick" (8:16).

Scores of people received instant deliverance and healing regardless of their affliction! Never before had Earth witnessed a scene like this. Moses, the Old Testament miracle worker, had brought numerous plagues upon the Egyptians, but a greater than Moses now lifted severe physical maladies from his people. The equivalent to such a scene today would be for someone to walk in and heal in one evening every bed-ridden patient in a vast medical center.

But after this exhausting effort, Mark reports that "very early in the morning, before dawn, Jesus got up and went to an isolated spot, where he prayed" (1:35). Despite his incredible success, Jesus did not rest on his laurels. He sensed he was in an unrelenting conflict with evil forces, and sought the strength only prayer could provide.

THE DISOBEDIENT LEPER

Jesus began several weeks of preaching and healing throughout Galilee, and during this time encountered a "leper" (Mark 1:40-45). The biblical term for leprosy described a wide range of chronic skin diseases, not just the disfiguring illness which bears this name today. Old Testament laws had made these skin diseases symbolic of sin, so people afflicted with them were considered ceremonially unclean. This limited but did not totally prevent their social contacts with others. When the disease went away, which could happen with the non-fatal types, the Mosaic law prescribed a strict ritual which the priests performed to celebrate the cure and the man was restored to the community once more. These Mosaic regulations helped prevent the spread of contagious infections and morally instructed the people as well.

45

To these rules the scribes had added their own traditions. They said people must stay six feet from a leper, and on a windy day one hundred feet. If a leper passed a person standing under a tree, that person was defiled. One scribe boasted he threw rocks to keep a leper away from him.

Jesus did not look like the typical scribe, and this leper plaintively requested, "If you want to, you can cleanse me" (v. 40).

Jesus responded by stretching out his hand, grasping the man firmly (as the Greek original implies), and healing him. Whereas other rabbis usually avoided these poor beings, Jesus laid his hand on him and cured him!

To keep the throngs from seeking him only for physical health and to show the priests he observed the law, Jesus sternly warned the man to keep quiet about his healing and to obey the Mosaic ritual for cleansing. Instead, the unthankful former leper broadcast his healing all through the city and made it impossible for Jesus to enter the cities any more because of the wonder-seeking throngs.

SIN AND SICKNESS

Jesus returned to Capernaum where he probably stayed at Peter's house. Soon curious crowds filled every room and Jesus began to teach them. He was interrupted by four men who were unable to get near because of the crowds, so they dismantled the mud, straw, and tile roof to lower their paralyzed friend down in front of Jesus. Instead of resenting the intrusion, Jesus welcomed the determined faith of these men who would go to such efforts on behalf of their friend.

But before healing the helpless man, Jesus shocked even his disciples by declaring, "Son, your sins are forgiven" (Mark 2:5).

Moses' law promised that obedience to God's commands would bring health and prosperity to Israel, while disobedience would bring sickness and adversity. Unfortunately, what the Old Testament applied to Israel's general welfare, the scribes of Jesus' time applied with vengeance to the condition of each individual. Behind every illness lurked a specific sin, they asserted. Lists of sicknesses and the sins which caused them were drawn up. Crippled children could be caused by parental adultery; leprosy could result from blasphemy, murder, or perjury; death from childbirth might strike the woman who was careless about Sabbath traditions. Consequently multitudes of sick people staggered under an agonizing load of guilt in addition to their physical maladies. Furthermore, the scribes emphasized that until the sufferer's pain atoned for the sin, or God forgave it, healing was impossible.

Jesus' spontaneous declaration of forgiveness to this man lifted off the load of guilt heaped on unnecessarily by the traditional teaching. But the theological experts in the crowd were enraged: "Why does this man speak this way? He's blaspheming! Only God can forgive sins" (v. 7). They believed God had heaped the punishment on this paralytic and only God could lift it off. Jesus was interfering with divine retribution.

MORE THAN THEY BARGAINED FOR

Jesus' response was more than the critics bargained for. "Which is easier: to say to the paralytic, 'Your sins are forgiven,' or to say, 'Get up, pick up your stretcher and walk'?" he asked.

The scribes could only answer that forgiveness and healing were equally difficult to grant because they were equally acts of God. They taught that one included the other. But Jesus gave them no chance to answer: "That you may know the Son of Man has authority on earth to forgive sins . . ." and he turned to the paralytic . . . "I say to you, 'Get up, pick up your stretcher and go home" (v. 10).

As the crowd watched in disbelief the deformed legs gradually become whole and a man probably bed-ridden for years leaped up and began to walk. What could the religious experts say? They taught that healing followed forgiveness, so according to their own theory Jesus had proved he could forgive sins. Instead of being a blasphemer, he had proved he possessed the authority of God! The crowd was stunned, the scribes dumbfounded, the man and his friends overjoyed. The evidence before their eyes was incontrovertible—this man healed more than visible bodies—he healed invisible souls.

I.R.S.—ROMAN STYLE

Not long afterward the scribes got another jolt. Jesus already had several full-time followers, but now he recruited one that no self-respecting Pharisee would talk to. Mark reports: "As he walked along, he noticed Levi the son of Alphaeus sitting at the tax collectors' office. 'Follow me,' Jesus told him, and Levi got up and followed him" (2:14).

Tax collectors have never been popular, but they were especially hated in the Roman Empire. Originally they were paid on a commission basis, so the more taxes they could collect the more they could keep for themselves. As a result they badgered the public and extorted money over nearly every transaction. Jews who became tax collectors were considered traitors because they took money from their own people in the service of pagan Rome. Tax collectors were called "wild beasts in human shape" and classed with assassins and robbers. They were forbidden to enter a synagogue, their money was considered unclean, they could not be witnesses at trials, sacred promises to them could be broken without penalty, and for all practical purposes they had committed an unforgivable sin. For Jesus to add such a man to his team was akin to a Billy Graham enlisting a Mafia mobster to help in an evangelistic campaign.

KEEPING BAD COMPANY?

Of course, this was not the first meeting between Jesus and Levi, also called Matthew, the future author of the Gospel. Levi had doubtless heard Jesus teach often. Perhaps they had personally talked together. Perhaps Levi was in the audience when Jesus forgave the paralytic's sins. The forgiveness the scribes denied to Levi, Jesus seemed to offer.

Yet that fateful day, seated in his tax office, he still heard the call to follow Jesus with disbelief. A Jewish untouchable was invited to personally accompany Jesus! When Levi recovered from the shock, he was so overjoyed that he threw a big party and invited all his friends.

The whole scene was revolting to the Pharisees. Israel's six thousand Pharisees and several thousand associate Pharisees restricted their social involvement to their own Law observing group, and labeled everyone outside this elect circle a "sinner." Jesus utterly scandalized the Pharisees by attending a large party populated by these supposed spiritual rejects.

When the Pharisees complained to Jesus, he replied: "Those who are healthy don't need a doctor, those who are sick do. I didn't come to call the righteous, but sinners" (v. 17).

He accused the Pharisees of being like doctors afraid to visit the sick because they might get infected. He announced that his lot was cast with the vast majority of the nation whom they wouldn't touch. He sarcastically labeled the Pharisees "righteous" and implied *they* are the ones he'll avoid!

Shortly after, Jesus was questioned as to why his disciples banqueted at feasts like Matthew's instead of fasting as the Pharisees and the disciples of John the Baptist. The Old Testament commanded only one day of fasting per year, but the Pharisees, not satisfied with Moses' law, increased the requirement to twice a week. Jesus replied, "While the bridegroom is with them, the wedding party does not fast, do they?" (v. 19) Jesus is the bridegroom savior. This was no time for sorrow and fasting—they should join the celebration!

THE NEW WINE

Jesus then further illustrated his mission: "No one sews a patch of unshrunk cloth on an old garment.

Otherwise, the new will pull away from the old and make the tear worse. And no one pours new wine into old wineskins. Otherwise the wine will break the wineskins and the wine and wineskins will be lost. He pours new wine into new wineskins" (vv. 21-22).

Everyone knew that unshrunk cloth could not be sewed on a frequently washed garment, or the first laundering would tear the reparied material. Likewise, as new wine fermented it produced gases which would split wineskins already stretched.

The revolutionary truths in these illustrations would not dawn on his followers for years to come. Jesus was new cloth and new wine; the Pharisees were worn garments and stretched wineskins. Their religion rewarded the "righteous," he saved the sinner. He was faithful to Moses' law and the fulfillment of its prophecies. They set aside that law for their treasured traditions and opposed the Messiah of whom Moses wrote. Between what Jesus was and what the Pharisees stood for stretched an unbridgeable chasm.

Jesus' veiled prediction was that a new movement beyond what these ritual-laden leaders could ever envision was necessary to contain the new wine. That new movement was born on Pentecost two years later.

FIVE

The Day
You Could Never Rest

Over one hundred years before Jesus was born, Israel experienced a terrible tragedy. Syrian persecution of the Jewish faith drove one thousand men, women, and children from Jerusalem to caves outside the city. When Syrian scouts discovered the hideaway, they offered amnesty if the Jews would come out and surrender their weapons.

It was Saturday, the Jewish Sabbath, and the refugees agreed that walking out of the caves was "work." Resisting the Syrians was also work, which was prohibited on the Sabbath under traditional interpretations of the Mosaic Law. Immobilized by their misguided zeal, one thousand Jews refused to accept the amnesty, refused to fight, and on that Sabbath refused life itself as they were slaughtered to the last man!

Jewish history records other such misfortunes. In 320 B.C. Ptolemy Lagos captured Jerusalem while its able-bodied defenders watched passively because they refused to fight on the Sabbath. In 63 B.C., Pompey and the Romans conquered Jerusalem because, though Jews would now fight on the Sabbath, they would not oppose Pompey's construction of a mound outside the walls on the Sabbaths from which he could bombard the city. Gentile armies blinked in disbelief at this strange

51

devotion to the Sabbath which lost wars and sacrificed lives.

How did such excessive zeal originate? Since the ancient world knew nothing of a forty-hour week, and relentless, back-breaking labor burned out many a life before age thirty-five, the ten commandments mercifully made each Saturday a day when the people and animals *must* rest. But not content with this simple, life-sustaining rule, Jewish scribes tried to spell out the command in detail by categorizing every conceivable action and decreeing whether it was permissable. They divided all types of forbidden work into thirty-nine categories, then divided each category into multitudes of sub categories.

Ploughing was a major category of forbidden work. Sub-classified under ploughing was digging. But digging must be defined. They decided that dragging a chair along the ground could make a rut, which was digging, so chairs must be left in place on the Sabbath. Similarly, if you spat on the ground you might rub it into the dirt, which would also be digging, so no spitting on the ground was permitted on the Sabbath. On the other hand, spitting on the pavement was permissible.

FIDDLING WHILE YOUR HOUSE BURNED

Carrying certain objects was another forbidden work. If your house burned on the Sabbath, carrying water to extinguish the blaze was forbidden. You were provided a list, however, of what belongings you could and could not carry out as your home was consumed. You could lift your little child on the Sabbath, though debate flared over this action if the child held an object which could not be carried on the Sabbath.

Sabbath rules became so burdensome that the scribes had to devise ways of sneaking out from under their own unbearable system. Since a devout Jew could only walk three thousand feet from his dwelling on the Sabbath—a "Sabbath days' journey"—relief was gained by moving food for two meals away from the home on

Friday and then measuring travel distance from the food instead of the house.

The simple Sabbath day command thus grew into a mountain of complex traditions. Jesus' repeated attacks on these traditions so enraged the leaders that they actually began plotting his death. As much as any other issue, Jesus' humane disregard of Sabbath legalism etched his death sentence in Pharisaic hearts.

The clashes began on a trip to Jerusalem for one of the Jewish festivals, possibly a Passover celebration. If so, it marked one year of Jesus' public ministry—beginning and ending in conflict with religious authorities.

ONE IN A CROWD

John records: "Now there is in Jerusalem near the sheepgate a pool . . . called Bethesda, surrounded by five covered colonnades. Here a multitude of sick, blind, lame, and paralyzed lay" (5:3). Apparently this multitude superstitiously believed an angel would stir up the water, and whoever stepped first into the pool after this was healed. Jesus walked among this mass of sufferers and stopped beside a man whose ailment had hindered him for thirty-eight years.

"Do you want to become well?" Jesus asked.

"I have no one, when the water is troubled, to put me in the pool, but while I am coming someone else always gets there first" he answered.

"Get up, pick up your stretcher, and walk," Jesus commanded. Immediately the man was well; he picked up his stretcher and walked away a picture of health.

The miracle opens a pandora's box of questions about God's mysterious ways. Why did Jesus choose this man out of all the needy, when he evidenced no faith and didn't know who Jesus was? Why did Jesus not heal all the sick that day as he did earlier in Galilee? Why does he heal some and not others? Why does God permit some to suffer much and others little? Why are some born in palatial Beverly Hills and others in squalid Harlem? Such mysteries are not completely unraveled in

Scripture. Perhaps Paul was thinking of their final resolution when he wrote "Now I know in part, then I will know fully" (I Corinthians 13:12).

CAPITAL PUNISHMENT FOR CARRYING A STRETCHER

The healed man picked up his stretcher and started toward home when some of the scribes accosted him. "It is the Sabbath, and you are not allowed to carry your stretcher," they objected (John 5:10).

"The man who healed me—he told me to pick up my stretcher and walk," explained the transgressor.

What an amazing exchange! The miraculous healing of a thirty-eight-year-long invalid would have made headlines any place else in the world, but the Jerusalem Pharisees' only concern was a little stretcher carried under his arm on the Sabbath!

Later Jesus encountered the man in the temple and said, "You are made whole, give up your sin lest something worse come on you" (v. 14).

Jesus did not link all sickness to personal sin as his later teaching makes clear, but this man's sin evidently did play a part in his illness. Perhaps he was injured during a drunken brawl or while committing a crime. Jesus challenged him to give up his sinful ways, trust in God, and begin a new life. Unfortunately, the words had little effect on the one-time cripple, for he immediately told the Pharisees that Jesus had ordered him to pick up the stretcher. Sabbath violations could incur the death penalty, so the desperate man, fearful for his life, pointed the accusing finger at Jesus. But in sparing himself, he lengthened the shadow over Jesus' head.

AN AMAZING DISCOURSE

"The Jews kept persecuting Jesus because he kept doing these things on the Sabbath," John reports (v. 16). Since Jesus made a habit of such Sabbath infractions, the Jewish leadership now organized a campaign to harass the troublesome Galilean.

But Jesus didn't shrink from the challenge. "My Father is working until now and I myself am working," he said. By again using the Messianic term no Jew would use, "My Father," he stirred the leadership into such frenzy they began to plot his death (v. 18), for now they view him as guilty of blasphemy as well as Sabbath breaking. Shortly after this, Jesus was accosted again by the Pharisees, and he elaborated on his unity with God in one of the most stupendous claims ever to come from human lips.

"The Son can do nothing on his own, except what he sees the Father doing, for whatever he does, the Son does also. . . . Just as the Father raises and gives life to the dead, so the Son gives life to whomever he wills. For the Father judges no one, but has given all judgment to the Son, that all may honor the Son just as they honor the Father. Whoever does not honor the Son does not honor the Father who sent him. I tell you the truth, whoever responds to my word and believes the one who sent me has eternal life and will not come to condemnation, but has passed out of death into life" (vv. 19-24).

The Nazareth carpenter asserts that he does only God's works, that he raises the dead, that he gives life, that he should be honored the same way as God, and that whoever rejects him rejects God also! In their wildest dreams, most Jewish people never believed that even the Messiah would do all these things. Jesus is claiming to be God in human form! And there is more.

"For as the Father has life in himself, so he granted to the Son to have life in himself. And he granted him authority to judge because he is the Son of Man. Don't be surprised at this, because an hour is coming when all who are in their graves will hear his voice and will come forth—those who have done good to a resurrection of life, and those who have done evil to a resurrection of judgment" (vv. 26-29).

Most Jews believed in a final resurrection when all people would stand at the divine judgment bar. But they didn't picture the Messiah as the one who would resurrect the dead or judge the righteous and the wicked. Yet Jesus claims both for himself.

REJECTED WITNESSES

Jesus went on to rebuke the Jewish leaders for rejecting various witnesses to his identity. He pointed out that John the Baptist acclaimed him the Messiah, but they listened to him only momentarily (vv. 33-35).

Jesus' miracles and words also attested his Messiahship, yet they scorned these (v. 36). God himself has certified Jesus, yet they reject this as well.

Finally, he made his most scathing denunciation of all:

"You search the Scriptures, because you think you possess in them eternal life, and these Scriptures are testifying of me. Yet you will not come to me to have life. . . . I have come in the Father's name, and you don't receive me. If another comes in his own name, you receive him. How can you believe, if you accept praise from each other and don't seek the praise which comes from the only God? Don't think I'll accuse you before the Father; the one accusing you will be Moses, on whom you set your hope. For if you believed Moses, you'd believe me, because he wrote of me. But since you don't believe his writings, how will you believe my words?" (vv. 39-47)

Jesus denounces the Jewish leaders for spending their lives studying Scripture and ignoring the very prophecies of Scripture which identify him. Jesus warns that others would come on their own authority, with spurious claims and no commission from God, and they would be welcomed. The tragic fulfillment of these words is written in Jewish history, which records that sixty-four false Messiahs have so far led the Jews astray, with the greatest false Messiah of all yet to come—the anti-Christ.

Jesus concluded by charging the leaders with a rejection of Moses and his prophecies. Jesus aligns God, himself, and Moses on one side—the tradition-bound leaders of first-century Judaism on the other, as he claims to be the Messiah of whom Moses wrote (Deuteronomy 18:18).

Nothing could insult these Jerusalem Pharisees more! Their every waking moment was devoted to following

Once a Carpenter

Moses' teachings; they established their Sabbath traditions to guarantee strict observance of Moses' law—now Jesus tells them he is faithful to Moses and they are not, he is the true Jew, and they are apostates! The gulf between him and them was now impassable. The final outcome could only be his crucifixion.

ANOTHER ENCOUNTER

Jesus returned to Galilee and quickly landed in another controversy. He and his disciples were walking through a grainfield, and they plucked some heads of grain, rubbed them in their hands, and ate them. The Mosaic law allowed hungry travelers to gather a meal from someone else's field—but this was a Sabbath day, and the thirty-nine categories of the scribes prohibited this "work." Picking the grain was harvesting, rubbing it in your hands was threshing, blowing away the chaff was winnowing, and the whole process was preparing food on the Sabbath. In addition, the group had probably walked farther than "a Sabbath days' journey"—so they have logged five separate violations.

Eagle-eyed Pharisees instantly accused Jesus of breaking the law. He replied: "Didn't you read what David did when he and those with him got hungry? How he entered God's house and ate the showbread, which wasn't lawful for him or the ones with him to eat, but only for the priests? Or didn't you read in the law that on the Sabbath the priests in the temple break the Sabbath and are guiltless? I tell you that someone greater than the temple is here. If you had known what these words mean, 'I desire mercy, and not a sacrifice,' you would not condemn the guiltless. For the Son of Man is Lord of the Sabbath" (Matthew 12:3-8).

Jesus humiliated the Pharisees by exposing their rejection of scriptural principles. David had desperately needed food as he tried to escape being killed by Saul, and his life was more important than the rule conventionally restricting the tabernacle bread to priests. Israel needed to worship on the Sabbath day, and this required "work" by some of the priests. People were more

57

important than rules, Jesus tried to tell the Pharisees. The Sabbath was made for man and not man for the Sabbath.

Jesus' teaching has been ignored by more than the first century Pharisees. Usually the state does not serve man, but man the state. The church too often has tyrannized men rather than freeing them. Humanity creates institutions to be its servants but they inevitably become its masters. Jesus' words here challenge all traditionalism legalism, institutionalism, ritualism, and bureaucracy which lord themselves over humanity rather than serving its needs.

A WITHERED HAND MADE WHOLE

The Sabbath storm boiled anew when Jesus entered a synagogue and encountered a worshiper with a deformed hand. The Pharisees taught that healing such a man violated Sabbath ritual. They even debated whether you were guilty of Sabbath violation if you took some vinegar with a meal and unintentionally healed your toothache!

Mark reports that Jesus told the man to stand in front of the assembly, and, looking at his critics, Jesus asked, "Is it lawful on the Sabbath day to do good or to do harm? To save life or to kill?" Then, boiling with anger toward them, he miraculously restored the man's hand (3:1-6).

They were speechless. Obviously it is wrong to do evil on the Sabbath, but if they answered it is wrong to do good, Jesus would accuse them of prohibiting good works. They could only remain silent as the gaping congregation watched the hand miraculously become whole.

The infuriated Pharisees left the synagogue and went straight to the Jewish politicians of the Herodian party to plot Jesus' execution (v. 7). The Herodians were their natural enemies, since they endorsed loyalty to Rome while the Pharisees hated Rome. But both could unite over ridding themselves of Jesus!

A MOTLEY CREW

Jesus had engaged in a public ministry for over a year, and the nation was divided into enthusiastic followers and bitter antagonists. Much of the religious leadership had rejected him and secretly schemed to kill him, but his great popularity with miracle-hungry masses frustrated the execution of their plot.

Jesus knew that his death was inevitable, yet his mission was world wide. To accomplish his ultimate goal, he must train those who would become future leaders of a great new people movement. So from his many followers he selected twelve men: Peter, James, John, Andrew, Philip, Bartholomew (also called Nathanael), Matthew (also called Levi), Thomas, James the Son of Alphaeus, Thaddaeus (also called Judas, brother of James), Simon the Zealot, and Judas Iscariot.

They were a motley crew. Peter, James, John, and Andrew had been commercial fishermen. Matthew, a tax collector. Judas evidently was called "Iscariot" because he was from a Judean town of that name—he was probably the only Judean of the group. They were apparently not wealthy, brilliant, or outstanding. Simon the Zealot was probably even a member of a fanatic band of super patriots called the Zealots, who later fomented war with Rome.

That Jesus could take men like Matthew, servant of Rome, and Simon the Zealot, Rome's sworn enemy, and forge them into a unity was remarkable. That a group so average and mistake prone would one day shake the world was almost inconceivable. Jesus, with uncanny ability, could refine and develop the potential of even the most ordinary person.

A PAUSE FOR THOUGHT

The events of this chapter give pause for thought. The ancient world overflowed with vice and immorality. Over against this stood the most outwardly moral and religious men of Jesus' day—the Pharisees. Yet the religious Pharisees, not the pagan Romans, engineered Jesus' crucifixion. Underneath their outward good lurked an arrogance, pride, and self-righteousness which offended God more than all the ills of pagan society, and is at the core of human sin itself. This spirit of arrogance and self-righteousness was a curse to ancient Judaism, has since cursed the church, and should be avoided by every true follower of Jesus.[1]

FOOTNOTE FOR CHAPTER V

[1] For a discussion of the psychological causes of the Pharisees' attitudes and how they appear today, see my book, co-authored with Bruce Narramore, *Guilt and Freedom,* (Vision and Harvest House Publishers), Chapters Ten and Eleven.

SIX

They Never Heard it Like This Before

A distinguished Princeton psychologist used to tell his students that the Sermon on the Mount was "the most effective propaganda in history." He defined propaganda as information that influences and controls opinion for good or for bad, and then demonstrated that the Sermon on the Mount probably contained the most compelling and powerful words ever uttered.

No words of Jesus are more famous. No words spoken by anyone have attracted such universal admiration. Yet the Sermon on the Mount, in the form we have it, is but fifteen minutes long and only a sample of many such talks Jesus gave. Matthew and Luke both record the sermon, but their reports differ from each other at some points because they translated Jesus' remarks from spoken Aramaic into written Greek, and they condensed differently for their particular readers.

Jesus spoke from a level spot on a grassy hill overlooking the Sea of Galilee. Grouped closely around him were his twelve apostles, while some of the curious populace sat attentively behind the disciples. On the edge of the crowd, no doubt, were the scribes and Pharisees who had committed themselves to keeping their prey under surveillance.

61

TRUE HAPPINESS

Jesus began with what are called the Beatitudes:

"Happy are the poor in spirit, for theirs is the kingdom of heaven. Happy are the mourners, for they shall be comforted. Happy are the self-controlled, for they shall inherit the earth. Happy are those hungering and thirsting after righteousness, for they shall be satisfied. Happy are the merciful, for they shall obtain mercy. Happy are the pure in heart, for they shall see God. Happy are the peacemakers, for they shall be called God's Sons. Happy are those who are persecuted because of righteousness, for theirs is the kingdom of Heaven. Happy are you when they insult you, and persecute you, and speak all kinds of evil against you falsely because of me. Rejoice and be glad, because your reward is great in heaven, for this is how they persecuted the prophets before you" (Matthew 5:3-12).

The poor in spirit are those who recognize they suffer spiritual poverty. The mourners are those who, like King David, deeply regret their own sins and the sins of their nation. The self-controlled (usually translated "meek") are those who control their anger and submit to God and the circumstances he allots them. The word was used of an animal who submitted to its master. Jesus exercised such self control when he submitted to the cross.

The pure in heart possess inward purity, in contrast to those who seek purity through observing external rituals. The peacemakers do more than live peacefully; they promote peace among others and restore harmony between former enemies. The persecuted are those who suffer rejection because of their devotion to Jesus. They should feel privileged, Jesus said, to follow in the great tradition of their spiritual ancestors like Elijah, Isaiah, and Jeremiah who were also persecuted.

To speak of happy mourners and rejoicing sufferers must have startled Jesus' audience! His words grated on self-satisfied success-types who trampled on others to attain status. How many of the rich, famous, and powerful in his audience were sensitive, submissive, and merciful? Jesus' words reverse the world's values—the arrogant, cold-blooded successes become eternal failures, and the truly meek inherit the earth.

SALT AND LIGHT

Looking directly at his disciples, Jesus informed them:

"You are the salt of the earth, but if the salt loses its flavor, how can it become salty again? It is good for nothing but to be thrown out and trampled under foot. You are the light of the world. A city built on a hill cannot be hidden, nor do people light a lamp and put it under a basket, but on a lampstand so it lights the whole house. Let your light shine before men in such a way that they see your good works and honor your Father in heaven" (vv. 13-16).

Jesus' pungent and earthly illustrations drew from the daily life of his audience. The Israelis used salt to preserve and flavor food, but the salt they gathered from Dead Sea marshes was often contaminated by other substances which rendered it tasteless. Such salt was commonly tossed into the street. Israeli cities were built on hills for defensive purposes and their lights were visible for miles through the clear night air. Most houses had a single light, centrally located on a high lampstand, which lit up the entire dwelling. Like salt and light, Jesus' disciples were to purify and enlighten a corrupt world by living in its midst, instead of retreating to Dead Sea caves to pursue sainthood, like the Qumram community.

WHO ARE THE ORTHODOX?

The positive encouragement to his followers then shifted to a stinging denunciation of the twisted teachings and practices of the scribes and Pharisees.

"Don't suppose that I came to abolish the Law or the Prophets; I didn't come to abolish but to fulfill," he thundered. "Anyone who breaks one of the least of

63

these commandments and teaches this to others will be called least in the kingdom of heaven, but whoever practices and teaches them will be called great in the kingdom of heaven. For I tell you that unless your righteousness more than surpasses that of the scribes and Pharisees you absolutely can't enter heaven" (vv. 17-20).

Once again Jesus turned the tables on his foes, who labeled him as a rebel against Moses' law. Jesus claimed to uphold Moses' law to the letter and fulfill its Messianic prophecies, while he charged them with being the rebels! He represented true orthodoxy, while they were the apostates. How shocking for this unschooled rabbi to charge Israel's religious leaders with heresy, when they labored to observe every detail of the law!

SIX TELLTALE EXAMPLES

To illustrate his point, Jesus cited six examples of the scribes' inadequate or erroneous teachings. "You have heard that it was said by the ancients, 'You shall not murder, and whoever murders deserves judgment.' But I tell you that everyone who is bitter with his brother shall be punished, whoever says to his brother 'Raca' shall be guilty before the supreme court, and whoever says 'You fool' shall be cast into the hell of fire" (vv. 21, 22).

Jesus accused the scribes of warning against acts of murder while allowing attitudes of murder. He says that continued anger (as the Greek original implies), or calling another "Raca," which meant "idiot," or "you fool," will also bring judgment, because God judges attitudes and words as well as actions. The judgment Jesus warns of, "the hell of fire," described the valley of Hinnom, the city dump outside Jerusalem's walls where maggots continually crawled over garbage and fires incessantly burned—a graphic picture of eternal judgment.

Next he attacked their view of immorality. "You shall not commit adultery," they said, again with emphasis only on the outward act. He taught, "Anyone who looks at a woman in order to lust after her has already committed adultery in his heart" (v. 28). His words distinguish between a passing glance which arouses temporary sexual fantasy and the indulgent gaze aimed for the express purpose of lust.

Whatever ensnares us into sin, Jesus went on to say, should be cut out of our lives. It may seem as precious as an eye or a hand, but we should be willing to sacrifice it because suffering for a brief time now is better than suffering forever in hell (vv. 29, 30). The Jews were accustomed to exaggerated figures of speech, and even spoke figuratively of cutting off their arms or plucking out their eyes, so the audience did not interpret Jesus' words as recommending literal mutilation.

A FIRST CENTURY DIVORCE MILL

The scribes went back on the hot seat as Jesus took up the subject of divorce. They maintained that "anyone who divorces his wife should grant her a divorce certificate," basing their decree on Moses' teaching (v. 31). Moses was actually attempting to discourage divorce by regulating it, but many of the scribes insisted the divorce certificate was intended to facilitate marriage dissolution instead. They said, "Moses intended for us to divorce our wives or he never would have commanded a divorce certificate." They taught that God gave the Jews the privilege of divorce but denied it to the Gentiles. They said a husband could divorce his wife if she spoiled his dinner. One scribe even taught divorce was permissible if the husband simply met someone more attractive. Another scribe, when he visited a strange town, would advertise for a wife while he visited there, then divorce her when he left. As long as the certificate was in order, divorce was fine!

But Jesus condemned this: "I tell you that anyone who divorces his wife except for unfaithfulness exposes her to adultery, and anyone who marries a divorced woman commits adultery" (v. 32). He teaches that divorce is tragic. It puts the rejected wife in desperate need for support and companionship which can only be relieved by remarriage. But in such cases the remarriage

65

is really adultery, Jesus said. So while these scribes condemned adultery their twisted teachings on divorce actually promoted it.

BROKEN PROMISES

Solemn oaths have always been used by society to reinforce honesty. Today we hear them mostly used in courtrooms and swearing-in ceremonies. Ancient societies used them in everyday transactions to guarantee fulfillment of promises.

The scribes taught that oaths sworn in God's name were binding because God was part of the transaction. But they ingeniously added that oaths not sworn in his name were not binding, since God was not involved in the transaction. Jews could solemnly swear by heaven, earth, Jerusalem, or even their own head, and break their promises with the scribes' approval. It reminds us of the little children who make promises to each other but cross their fingers behind their backs so they don't have to keep them.

Jesus said that God was part of every oath, even though his name was not used—for heaven and earth were parts of his kingdom, Jerusalem was his city, and he alone could determine even the color of the hair on our head (vv. 33-35). Furthermore, Jesus taught we should not need oaths in daily life to prove we are truthful. Our "yes" should mean "yes" and our "no" should mean "no" (v. 37). It's easy to see who really valued truthfulness.

EVEN-STEPHEN SYNDROME

The Law of Moses commanded "an eye for an eye, and a tooth for a tooth" as the basic principle of public justice. This figurative expression taught that major crimes merit serious punishment (eye for eye), while minor crimes merit light punishment (tooth for tooth). But the scribes applied the public law to private revenge. Since tax collectors cheated you, you could cheat them; if others lied to you, you could lie to them without committing sin.

Jesus not only rejected this perversion, but replaced it with a revolutionary standard: "Don't resist the evil doer—to him who slaps you on the right cheek, turn the other also. And if anyone sues you for your tunic, give him your outer cloak also. And whoever forces you to go one mile, go with him two" (vv. 39-42).

To slap the cheek was a scathing insult. Lawsuits for clothing in lieu of debt payment were common. Soldiers could force citizens to carry burdens, mail, or messages against their will. Jesus used these vivid illustrations to teach a course of non-resistance instead of bitter revenge.

Jesus' sweeping ethical pronouncement raises the question of how literally he meant us to follow his words. Obviously, he intended us to use common sense, and not copy the fanatic literalism which the Pharisees displayed over the principle of Sabbath-day rest, as we saw in the last chapter. Jesus plainly condemns vengeful schemes in personal relationships, but his words do not oppose proper use of force by police, armies, courts, and other instruments of public justice.

LOVE ON THE HIGHEST LEVEL

Jesus' last attack on the scribes' teaching zeroes in on love. "Love your neighbors and hate your enemies" was their official version of God's word (v. 43). They rationalized that Moses command to "love your neighbor" logically implied "hate your enemy"! Jesus corrected them by telling them to love their enemies and even pray for their persecutors (v. 44). He explained that God loves his enemies by sending rain and sunlight on all peoples—even those who reject and despise him (v. 45). Jesus pointed out that if the Pharisees only like their friends their love rises no higher than that of godless pagans.

Jesus utterly exposed the superficial and erroneous teachings of Israel's vaunted scribes. Then he replaced their misconceptions with such challenging and profound commands that we still marvel at his words. "Turn the other cheek," "love your enemies," and "pray for those persecuting you," were given to the conscience of the world by the rabbi from Nazareth. His conclusion to this section: "Be perfect therefore as your heavenly Father is perfect" is a fitting climax (v. 48).

MADISON AVENUE RIGHTEOUSNESS

As examples of what not to do, the Pharisaic practices now came under fire. "Be careful not to practice your righteousness before people only to be noticed by them, otherwise you'll have no reward from your Father in heaven", Jesus warned (Matthew 6:1). Many Pharisees ordered their behavior to gain human acclaim instead of divine approval.

"When you give to the poor, don't announce it with a trumpet blast, as the hypocrites do in the synagogues and in the streets so that people will admire them. I tell you they've already got their reward in full" Jesus said (v. 2). Religious Jews were often generous donors, but many made a Madison Avenue production out of giving. They advertised it all over. Jesus' description of them as blowing a trumpet probably sent gales of laughter through his audience. He said human acclaim was their only reward because God had none for them.

"Whenever you pray," Jesus continued, "don't be like the hypocrites, for they love to stand in the synagogues and on the street corners so that they will be seen by people. I tell you they have their reward in full" (v. 5). The Pharisees had established set hours of prayer, and some of them would place themselves in public locations so everyone could see them piously reciting prayers. Again, their only reward was human recognition, not divine response.

Jesus further instructed, "when you pray, don't repeat empty words like the pagans, for they imagine they will be heard because of their volume of talk" (v. 8). Jesus condemns the pagan practice of chanting—repeating words and phrases over and over, often until a trance-like state occurs. This useless praying is unfortunately surfacing on American street corners today as Hindu devotees with shaved heads chant and dance.

A MODEL PRAYER

In contrast to this Jesus offered a simple, but profound example of prayer at its best: "Our Father in heaven, may your name be honored. Let your kingdom come, your will be done on earth as it is in heaven. Give us today food for the coming day, forgive us our debts, as we also have forgiven our debtors. And don't bring us into temptation, but rescue us from the evil one" (vv. 9-13).

Jesus did not intend this to be repeated in a rote, unthinking way as if the recitation had magic in itself. Rather he simply taught the majestic character of God and four basic requests his followers could make of him.

Jesus says to call God "Father." He is a person who lovingly cares for us, not a blind force, an impersonal principle, or a mystical "ground of our being." Jesus directs his followers to ask their heavenly Father to bring his kingdom to earth, so his will can be done all over this earth, just as it is done all over heaven. Second, we are to ask God for physical needs, like daily food. God wants to supply these basic needs to people who trust him. Third, Jesus says to request daily forgiveness, and be willing to forgive others as well. The word he uses for sins here is "debts"—the moral obligations we owe God and cannot pay him. Fourth, aware of our weakness and proneness to fail, we are to pray that God will keep us from temptations we feel we can't handle, and thus protect us from Satan, the evil one.

FURTHER LIGHT

Jesus gave this model prayer, of course, before his disciples understood that he would die on a cross and that the Messiah would come a second time. Today we read this prayer and realize that God's kingdom will come in its fullness at Jesus' return. We also understand that believers now possess final and eternal forgiveness through Jesus' death, whereas the prayer spoke only of obtaining the daily temporary forgiveness which Moses' law offered (see Hebrews 10).

Jesus' concluding remark after the prayer, that God won't forgive us unless we forgive others, shows the importance he attached to God's forgiveness (Matthew 6: 14, 15). He did not mean that we are to forgive others to earn God's forgiveness. A forgiving spirit shows we have accepted God's forgiveness, while a bitter spirit reveals an unbelieving heart. This was probably directed at the Pharisees who claimed salvation for themselves despite their unbelieving, bitter attitudes.

Jesus next mentioned a final example of Pharisaic hypocrisy—fasting: "When you fast, don't be gloomy like the hypocrites, for they disfigure their faces to appear to people to be fasting" (v. 16). Each Monday and Thursday the Pharisees ritualistically fasted, and some donned pained expressions to make sure their sacrifice was observed. Jesus' description of this grotesque ritual probably amused his audience—except for the guilty parties.

TWO KINDS OF TREASURE

Jesus now broke off his attack against the Pharisees to focus on one of the most gnawing problems of human existence—money. "Don't store up treasures on earth, where moth and rust corrupt and thieves break in and steal," he urged, "but store up treasures in heaven where moth and rust don't corrupt and thieves don't break in and steal, for where your treasure is, there your heart will be also" (vv. 19-21).

"Moth and rust" picture whatever eats up and corrodes material wealth. In ancient times, clothing handed from one generation to another was an important segment of wealth—styles rarely changed! Yet moths often devoured these garments. Today, inflation and world economic ills gobble up material possessions. One way or another material wealth disappears, but spiritual treasure lasts forever.

Jesus' linking of ones' heart and his treasure highlights the tragedy of ultimate devotion to money. The person who devotes himself to a treasure which is here today and gone tomorrow is an inevitable pauper. The

heart devoted to moth-proof, rust-p[...]
spiritual possessions has security e[...]
wealth vanishes.

DEVOTION AND POSSESSION

Jesus added two more illustration[...]
body is the eye; if therefore your e[...]
whole body will be full of light. [...]
unhealthy, your whole body will be [...]
one can be the slave of two masters. Either he will hate
one or love the other. . . . You cannot be a slave to God
and money" (vv. 22-24).

The ancients believed that eyes were like windows
through which light entered the body. Good eyes
brought in the health and benefits of light and bad eyes
shrouded the body in darkness which produces disease.
Jesus revealed the spiritual truth that devotion to God
will make our whole life bask in light, but devotion to
material values will plunge us into darkness and confu-
sion. Our attitude toward money reaches into every
corner of our existence.

Jesus used the anology of slavery to show that as a
slave cannot devote himself to two masters, so we cannot devote ourselves to piling up material and spiritual
wealth at the same time. Either God or money will
enslave us. Jesus attacks *devotion* to wealth, not *possession* of it. We may possess wealth without devotion to it
(though this is regrettably rare), or we may lack wealth
entirely and yet be devoted to a desire for it.

CARE-FREE LIVING

Jesus moved on to examine the underlying anxiety
which often stimulates devotion to money. A flock of
birds may have flown over the audience at this time, as
this was a crossroads of bird migration. Jesus said:
"Look at the birds of the air—they don't sow or reap or
gather into barns, and your heavenly Father feeds them.
Aren't you worth more than they? Which of you by
worrying about it can add eighteen inches to your

And looking around the Galilean hillsides, with bright wild flowers, he added, "Consider ld flowers how they grow—they don't toil or spin, I tell you Solomon in all his glory was not clothed ke one of them" (vv. 28, 29).

Probably two more memorable illustrations never fell on human ears. His audience was spellbound. The illustrations do not imply, of course, that *work* is unnecessary. Birds work for their food. But Jesus teaches *anxiety* is unnecessary. God cares for the birds and flowers which are here today and gone tomorrow—"Will he not do much more for you, O you of little faith?" (v. 30).

These people weren't anxious over payments on the color TV. They worried whether they would starve or freeze that year! But Jesus tells them to trust a loving Father. He adds that since worry can't add five minutes to our life span, it is utterly useless. He concludes this magnificent section of the sermon with the famous words: "Seek first God's kingdom and his righteousness, and all these things will be added to you. Don't worry about tomorrow, tomorrow will have its own worries. Each day has enough trouble of its own" (vv. 33, 34).

Anxiety over money has always hounded us. Here Jesus dispenses a cure—trust in the loving Father who cares for nature and will care much more for us. A corollary of such trust is a proper order of priorities: it is not money first and God on the side, but God and his kingdom first. This is the way to freedom from financial worry.

Jesus' was not denouncing planning for the future, but worrying over the future. He advises us to shrink our burdens to those of the present moment rather than weight ourselves down with imagined problems of tomorrow.

BLIND EYE DOCTORS

Jesus began the final part of his sermon with a warning against self-righteous criticism of others. With a glint of humor he said, "And why do you keep seeing a speck in your brother's eye, but you don't consider the beam of lumber in your own eye? Or how will you say to your brother, 'Let me pick the speck out of your eye,' and behold the beam of lumber in your own eye!" (Matthew 7:3, 4).

The ludicrous exaggeration struck home the truth. An overly critical spirit usually covers blindness to one's own faults. The Pharisees were so intent on catching violators that they never looked at their own shortcomings.

Then Jesus quoted a proverb which flashed the other side of the coin: "Don't give what is holy to the dogs, or cast your pearls before swine" (v. 6). Despised packs of wild dogs roamed the streets of ancient cities, and pigs were unclean animals to Jews. Here they symbolize not the sinner or outcast, but those who mock and scorn God's truth. Jesus' followers need not feel obligated to present the truth to such. At his trial the depraved King Herod Antipas hoped to see Jesus perform a miracle—he got not even a word from Jesus (Luke 23:8, 9).

Jesus gave encouragement to prayer by telling us not to give up, but to "keep on asking, keep on seeking, keep on knocking," as the Greek original implies (Matthew 7:7, 8). The reason, he explained, is the loving character of God. "Which of you, if his son asks him for bread, will give him a stone? Or if he wants some fish will give him a snake? If you, being sinful, know how to give good gifts to your children, how much more will your Father give good things to the ones asking him?" (vv. 10, 11). The way to receive from God is to ask, not simply wish; and we may be sure God will respond only with *good* gifts—though they may be different from what we ask!

THE GREAT SUMMATION

Jesus summed up much of what he had said in what has come to be known as the "Golden Rule." "Whatever you wish that people should do to you, do this also to them—for this is the law and the prophets" (v. 12). Jesus masterfully captures the personal ethics of the Old Testament in less than twenty-five words. Confucius and the great Jewish teacher Hillel had stated this in negative form—"Don't do to others what you don't want them to do to you." But the positive form Jesus gives requires not simply refraining from harming others, but a positive, costly, and rewarding expression of love.

TWO GATES, TWO WAYS, TWO HOUSES

The climax of the sermon was a sobering exhortation to choose Jesus' way and enter his kingdom. He spoke of the wide gate and popular road that leads eventually to destruction, and the narrow gate and lightly traveled road that leads to life (vv. 13,14). The image was·suggested by gates in walls of ancient cities that were wide for heavy traffic, whereas occasional small doors off the beaten path were used only by a few. In spiritual matters, the majority are often wrong, Jesus indicates. Throughout most of its history much of Israel had turned against its true prophets, and the prophets began to say that only a "remnant" would believe and find deliverance from God. A minority of the Jewish people believed in Jesus when he came, and only a remnant know their Messiah today.

Jesus warned the listeners about false prophets who are like "wolves in sheep's clothing" (vv. 15-20). He makes the astonishing claim that he personally will keep these false leaders from entering the kingdom of heaven (vv. 21, 22).

Dramatizing man's two destinies, Jesus described two houses, one built on the sand, the other on rock (vv. 24-28). Israel had two seasons—wet and dry. During the rains some areas would be flooded and the swamped houses built on rock would stand, while those on a sand base would collapse. Jesus and his words are the rock which will support when the storms of life come, while other foundations can only erode and disintegrate.

THE PROPHET LIKE MOSES

As Jesus finished, the crowd was shocked because he "taught as one having authority and not as their scribes" (v. 29).

The Jewish scholars constantly appealed to teachings of earlier great rabbis. Tradition was everything. Jesus referred to no other authority but himself, and on this basis he boldly set aside traditional interpretations. Such innovation frightened them. It seemed safer to stick with the old traditions than to follow this radical new teacher into uncharted waters. What they overlooked, of course, was that his teaching unveiled as never before the great spiritual truths of the Old Testament which their tradition obscured.

Jesus' disciples must have been perplexed. All that Jesus said had the ring of truth, but the standards he set that day were so high that if a man must keep them to enter heaven, who was qualified? Later they would understand that his death for them, not their keeping the unkeepable Sermon on the Mount would bring them acceptance with God.

Perhaps someone listening that day remembered what God had told Moses, "I will raise up a prophet . . . like you, and I will put my words in his mouth, and he shall speak to them all that I command him" (Deuteronomy 18:18 *NASB*).

From Mount Sinai Moses had unveiled God's law to his people. From a mountain in Galilee Jesus now unveiled a higher law to their descendents. For centures Israel had yearned for the prophet like Moses to come. That day had finally arrived.

◆ ◆

SEVEN

The Prophet
Without Honor

◆ ◆

From the midst of Capernaum's silent ruins rise the remains of a once fine synagogue. Built of white limestone, colonnaded on three sides, the now empty house of worship was evidently built on top of the synagogue of Jesus' time. In that original synagogue Jesus inaugurated his Capernaum ministry by casting out a ferocious demon on the Sabbath. In that synagogue he preached a memorable discourse on the bread of life before a hushed audience. The actual builder of that synagogue now enters the Gospel records.

Jesus came down the hill after the Sermon on the Mount, and perhaps as he entered Capernaum, the Jewish elders of the synagogue approached him with a plea for help. A Roman army officer, called a centurion, owned a slave who was paralyzed, suffering intense pain, and on the verge of death (Matthew 8:6). The centurion had sent Jewish elders to intercede for his slave. How strange that a Gentile Roman soldier should fraternize with Jewish synagogue elders! But they informed Jesus, "He is worthy for you to do this, for he loves our nation and he built the synagogue for us" (Luke 7:4, 5).

The centurion evidently possessed a private fortune and financed the beautiful structure. The present ruined synagogue in Capernaum is unusually decorated with some Gentile and Roman ornamentation, in opposition to Jewish custom. Some scholars speculate that its art work is copied from the original synagogue, which was so adorned because a Roman had built it!

A GREAT FAITH

Jesus immediately headed for the centurion's home, even though religious Jews were prohibited from entering a Gentile residence. But the centurion sent messengers to intercept Jesus with the words: "I don't deserve for you to come under my roof, but only speak a word and my slave will be healed. For I also am a man under authority, having soldiers under me, and I say to this one, 'Go' and he goes, and to another 'Come,' and he comes. . . ." (Matthew 8:8, 9)

Here was a Roman who loved Jews and even had compassion for a slave whom most Romans considered only a piece of property. He even believed that Jesus has such authority over the forces of nature that he can command diseases to depart like a centurion commands soldiers!

"From no one in Israel have I found such faith!" Jesus exclaimed. "I tell you that many will come from the east and west, and will banquet with Abraham, Isaac, and Jacob in the kingdom of heaven, but the sons of the kingdom will be thrown outside into the darkness where there will be crying and grinding of teeth" (vv. 10-12). Then he healed the slave from afar.

Religious Jews never ate with Gentiles. The Pharisees believed the Messiah would sponsor a great banquet for all of Israel to feast at while the Gentiles only looked on. But the faith of this Gentile soldier caused Jesus to tell the real story. Despised Gentiles—full of faith—will come from east and west to banquet with the Jewish believers while many descendants of Abraham suffer in pain outside. They will be in darkness, which the ancients feared terribly, and they will weep and grind their teeth in anguish. This is another vivid and terrifying description of hell. Ironically, it came from the lips of a Jew who loved his nation as no other Israeli ever had.

A DEAD MAN RISES

Shortly afterward Jesus traveled to the city of Nain, some twenty-five miles southwest. As he approached the city, he saw a funeral at the local graveyard—a widow's only son had died. Without husband or son, a widow's plight could be grievous in those days. Furthermore, she would leave no heir—considered a dire fate in Israel. Luke reports that Jesus felt great compassion for her, and he went over and commanded the dead son to arise—he did! (7:13-15)

This was a miracle done in the absence of faith. Jesus spontaneously performed the great wonder out of his compassion for the widow's need. Only three times do the Gospels report that Jesus raised a dead person, and each time it was because of deep human need. Yet the need was not of those who died, for they may have been destined for a far better place than this world. The need was among the grieving left behind.

Nothing could be more spectacular than raising the dead, so the watching crowd proclaimed, "a great prophet is arisen among us!" Understandably, Jesus' fame spread even more.

A PUZZLED PROPHET

In the meantime John the Baptist, who had been imprisoned by Herod Antipas, sent a delegation to Jesus with the question, "Are you the coming one or should we expect someone else?" (Matthew 11:3) John had already proclaimed Jesus as Messiah at his baptism, but now he was torn by doubts.

John had predicted that the Messiah would "thoroughly cleanse his threshing floor, gather his wheat into the barn, but consume the chaff with unquenchable fire" (Matthew 3:12). This was a picture of the Messiah coming in judgment and separating the evil from the good. Now where was this judgment? John was suffering in prison while the cruel reign of King Herod Antipas and Queen Herodias flourished. John's predicament was

that he didn't know the Messiah would come twice—
first to die, then to root out injustice.

As John's delegation watched him, Jesus began to
perform miraculous healings among the crowds (Luke
7:21). Then Jesus told John's friends, "Go, report to
John what you hear and see. The blind see, the lame
walk, lepers are cleansed, the deaf hear, the dead are
raised, and the poor receive good news, and happy is the
man not offended because of me" (Matthew 11:4-6).
This is almost an exact description of what the prophet
Isaiah said the Messiah would do (35:5, 6; 61:1), except
it was even better, for Isaiah didn't predict raising the
dead!

THE GREATEST EXCEEDED BY THE LEAST

But Jesus used John's question to teach the crowds
more about God's kingdom. "What did you go into the
wilderness to see? A reed shaken by the wind? . . . a
man in luxurious clothing? Those in luxurious clothing
are in king's houses. But why did you go out? To see a
prophet? Yes, I tell you and more than a prophet!"
(Matthew 11:7-9) Jesus described John as a steadfast
prophet who, unlike a reed, never wavered in the face of
fierce gales of opposition. Nor did he flatter Israel's
leaders as officials in king's households do to keep their
positions.

Jesus continued: "He is the one about whom it is
written, 'I will send forth my messenger ahead of you
who will prepare your way before you.' I tell you
among those born of women a greater has not arisen
than John the Baptist. But the least in the kingdom of
heaven is greater than he" (vv. 10, 11).

John's privilege of introducing the Messiah to Israel
was greater than any Old Testament prophet ever
achieved, or any man born of woman. Yet, ironically,
the least participant in Messiah's kingdom was more
privileged than John, for John announced Messiah's
kingdom, but never shared in it. Jesus' disciples now

experienced the power of that kingdom while John only heard about it from his jail cell. John was like the top step on a first flight of stairs—higher than all the other stairs, but lower than the bottom step of the next flight.

"From the days of John the Baptist until now," Jesus concluded, "the kingdom of heaven forces its way powerfully, and forceful men seize it. For all the prophets and the Law prophesied until John. And if you will accept it, he himself is the coming Elijah" (vv. 13, 14).

In the year since John began to prophesy, the kingdom of heaven had rapidly and powerfully spread, forcing its way into one city after another. Determined men were earnestly seeking entrance. This marked the close of the Old Testament era and the beginning of a new age. As a pivotal figure of history John had started all this. He was the first fulfillment of Elijah's return, for whom every Jew looked! (See Chapter Two)

This generous praise of John informed the Pharisees that Jesus and John were united. Jesus' tribute came when John was discouraged and doubting, because Jesus wanted to assure the prophet that his greatness was not blotted out by this one low moment. John had done his task well, and Jesus never forgot it. No doubt when the delegation took back these glowing words to John's cell, his discouragement lifted, and even as his horrible death approached, the words kept ringing in his ears.

THE CHILDREN WHO WERE NEVER SATISFIED

As the common people listened to Jesus they began to praise God they had responded to John's baptism, but the Pharisees began to sneer (Luke 7:29, 30). Jesus, reaction was that the Pharisees were like little children who didn't want to join in a happy game of "wedding" because it was "too happy!" But when their friends said, "Let's play funeral and pretend we're mourning," they objected, "That's too sad!" (Matthew 11:17) Nothing satisfied them but criticism.

"John came neither eating or drinking, and they say, 'he's got a demon!' ", Jesus continued. "The Son of Man came eating and drinking, and they say, 'a glutton, a drunk, a friend of tax collectors and sinners!' " (vv. 18, 19)

The ascetic John lived in the desert, while Jesus dined and drank wine with sinners. The Pharisees pronounced John a demon-possessed maniac for being too ascetic, and Jesus a profligate drunk for being too social. In whatever garb the message came they rejected it, because the message was the real offense, not the messenger's life style. Yet Jesus concluded, "Wisdom is vindicated by her works" (v. 20). Both John and Jesus successfully fulfilled their appointed missions and demonstrated the wisdom of God's plan, regardless of Pharisaic rejection.

THE LOST OPPORTUNITY

As Jesus' opposition grew steadily fiercer, he announced the consequent ruin facing the cities of Galilee where he had performed such miracles. "Woe to you Chorazin! Woe to you Bethsaida! If in Tyre and Sidon the mighty miracles happened which occurred in you, they would have repented long ago with sackcloth and ashes! I tell you, it will be more tolerable for Tyre and Sidon on Judgment Day than for you. And you, Capernaum, will you be exalted to heaven? You shall go into the depths. It will be more tolerable for Sodom on Judgment Day than for you!" (vv. 21-24)

Tyre was the original home of the legendary Queen Jezebel, who corrupted Israel with Phoenician Baal worship, a religion centered around sex and child sacrifice. Sodom's vicious sexual perversion is still proverbial, yet Jesus said God would blast the Galilean cities with a heavier judgment than descended on those pagan centers of vice. Why? Because the revelation of truth to the Galilean cities was so great even Tyre, Sidon, and Sodom would have been brought to their knees by it.

Today these three Galilean cities stand in deserted ruins. They are silent monuments to one of the great lost opportunities of history. The ruins testify that Tyre's orgiastic worship and Sodom's gross perversions were not the final depths of human sinfulness. The final depths were plumbed by the moral and religious citizens of Galilee when they rejected Jesus.

THE GREAT INVITATION

Yet the rejection of Jesus was not universal, and to those who would receive him, Jesus now turns. He thanks God for revealing the truth to these simple, humble believers while bypassing the arrogant and learned scribes. He declares that God has deposited all spiritual truth with him, and asserts that only the Father fully knows him, and only he fully knows the Father; yet he will reveal this knowledge of the Father to whomever he chooses (vv. 25-27).

"Come to me all who are toiling and burdened and I will refresh you," Jesus calls. "Take my yoke upon you and learn from me because I am gentle and humble in heart and you will find rest for your souls. For my yoke fits well and my burden is light" (vv. 28-30).

Jesus invites those saddled with unkeepable Pharisaic traditions, and beyond that, those burdened with sin, to come to him. He asks them to take his yoke upon them, a rabbinic phrase meaning "become my disciple." Those who become his disciples will find he is gentle and humble, not harsh and arrogant like many of the scribes. His yoke will fit comfortably on each disciple and enable him to bear life's burdens without exhaustion. As a carpenter, Jesus once made oxen yokes which were custom fitted to each individual animal, and a legend says they were the finest in Galilee.

Jesus' great invitation called Israel to come to her greatest rabbi. He would teach her the depths of God instead of endless traditions. He would forgive and fellowship with her sinners instead of banishing them to outer darkness. He would lift her heavy load instead of doubling its weight. Doubtless it was an offer that some could not refuse.

THE PROSTITUTE WHO CAME TO DINNER

A rare confrontation soon followed when a Pharisee named Simon invited Jesus to dinner. Jesus had dined with many tax collectors, but few, if any, Pharisees. At special meals such as this, guests reclined to eat, leaning on one elbow with their feet stretched out behind. When rabbis such as Jesus were honored guests, outsiders could enter the open courtyard and listen to the instructive conversation.

As Jesus was eating at Simon's, a "sinful woman," which here meant a prostitute, entered the dining area and began weeping by Jesus' feet. As the tears trickled down, she dried his feet with her hair, kissed them fervently, and began to rub them with the sweet perfume Jewish women carried in small containers around their necks (Luke 7:37, 38). For a prostitute to enter a Pharisee's home, then to untie her hair as respectable women never did in public, and to pour out her emotions at Jesus' feet required phenomenal courage. But Simon was offended. He reasoned that if Jesus were a true prophet he would know she was a prostitute and never allow her to touch him.

A CASE OF BAD MANNERS

Jesus, unruffled by the embarrassing yet tender scene, told Simon this story:

"A lender had two debtors, one owed him ten thousand dollars, the other, one thousand dollars. As they each had nothing he forgave them both" (vv. 41, 42). Jesus then asked, "Which of them will love him more?" Simon's obvious answer was that the one who was forgiven the most would love the most.

Jesus told Simon: "You see this woman? I entered your house; you gave me no water for my feet, but this woman with her tears wet them and wiped them with her hair. You gave me no kiss, but this woman . . . has not stopped kissing my feet. You did not rub my head with oil, but this woman rubbed ointment on my feet. Therefore, I tell you, her many sins have been forgiven, because she loved much. But to whom little is forgiven, he loves little" (vv. 44-47).

It was Simon's turn to be embarrassed. The host's duty was to greet his guest with a kiss (a customary greeting in those days), to have his guest's feet washed, and to rub the guest's face with a soothing oil. Simon had deliberately ignored these amenities to hand Jesus a social snub.

As the prostitute left for home a new woman, Jesus' final words to her, according to the Greek original, were "Go *into* peace" (v. 50). For her a life of guilt and turmoil was over. Simon, the distinguished Pharisee, probably went to bed without peace. He perhaps questioned within himself whether this rabbi he had scorned was not right after all.

THE WOMAN'S LIBERATOR

Jesus and his disciples began to travel once more through Galilee. Luke reports that several women—Mary Magdalene, Joanna the wife of Herod's steward, and Susanna—also accompanied him and his disciples, and helped with financial support (8:1-3). This too was revolutionary in Israel. Though Jews treated women far more humanely than most Gentiles, their men were taught to pray, "Blessed are you, O Lord . . . who has not made me a woman."

Jesus practiced his own brand of women's liberation, and the Gospel writers note repeatedly that he was not an ally of the prejudice against women which marred that society and has much of the world since.

Though some Pharisees like Simon may have had second thoughts about Jesus, most Pharisees became more hostile than ever. When he cast a demon out of a blind and dumb man, and observers hinted that Jesus might be the Messiah, some Pharisees had a ready and horrible explanation. "This man only expels demons by Beelzebub, ruler of the demons" (Matthew 12:24).

Jesus' reaction was slashing. "Every kingdom divided against itself comes to destruction . . . and if Satan keeps casting out Satan, he is divided against himself. How therefore can his kingdom stand? And if I by Beelzebul cast out demons, by whom do your followers cast them out? Therefore they will be your judges!" (vv. 25-27)

Satan would have to be in civil war with himself, and

his kingdom in a state of collapse for the Pharisees' view
to be true. Furthermore, the Pharisees' boast that their
followers also exorcised demons made their actions suspect in the same way they accused Jesus.

THE UNFORGIVABLE SIN

Jesus then declared the real truth of the conflict. "If
by the Spirit of God I cast out demons, then God's
kingdom has come upon you. How can anyone enter a
strong man's house and take his possessions unless he
ties up the strong man?" (vv. 28, 29) Jesus claimed to
be the ultimate exorcist. Satan is the strong man, but
Jesus is stronger and has broken into his house, tied him
up, and begun to plunder his goods.

If Jesus was bringing God's kingdom, the Pharisees
committed a graver error than they could imagine by
rejecting him. Jesus warns them clearly: "The one who
is not with me is against me.... I tell you, all sin and
slander will be forgiven people, but the slander against
the Spirit will not be forgiven.... Either make a tree
good or its fruit good, or make a tree bad and its fruit
bad, for the tree is known by its fruit. You deadly
snakes! Since you're evil, how can you speak good? For
out of the abundance of the heart the mouth speaks"
(vv. 30-34).

Neutrality is impossible where Jesus is concerned. He
must be welcomed or he is rejected. In rejecting Jesus,
the Pharisees slandered God's Holy Spirit, for they saw
God's works and credited them to the devil! A man can
descend no deeper into evil that to call God the devil.
Such men, Jesus indicated, have crossed a line of no
return. They had so hardened their hearts that belief
was now impossible and forgiveness was no longer available.

Is this "unforgivable sin" possible today? Yes and no.
All who persist in rejecting the gospel throughout life
commit in one sense the unforgivable sin, for this is the
one sin which separates a person from God. Yet no one
today has so full a revelation as these men who faced
Jesus. We read only what the witnesses tell us Jesus said

and did, but the Pharisees saw with their own eyes and heard with their own ears all this and more.

No men on earth had seen a more blazing revelation, and no men had less excuse for their blindness. Jesus said that they were sons of snakes, bad trees with bad fruit whose mouths only revealed the evil of unbelieving hearts. They were inwardly corrupt and proved his pronouncement right by never resting until he was crucified.

THE FINAL MIRACLE

Jesus' scathing rebuke aroused even more opposition. "Rabbi, we want to see a miracle from you," the Pharisees said (v. 38).

They had already watched miracle after miracle, yet they felt the Messiah should perform additional spectaculars like making the sun stand still or dividing the Dead Sea waters. These would really prove he was the Messiah! But Jesus refused such requests. His miracles nearly always met deep human need and never catered to the spectacular just for the sake of the spectacular.

"An evil and unfaithful generation looks for a sign, but no sign shall be granted it except that of Jonah the prophet. For as Jonah was in the stomach of the great fish three days and three nights, so also shall the Son of Man be in the heart of the earth three days and three nights," Jesus replied (vv. 39, 40). Jesus again predicted his coming death and resurrection, of which Jonah's experience was a prophetic picture. This is the great sign for Israel—a crucified and resurrected Messiah. Rejection of this sign meant there would be no more.

Jesus intensified his warning by declaring the men of pagan Nineveh who repented at Jonah's preaching will rise up at Judgment Day and condemn these Pharisees. Likewise the pagan, legendary "Queen of Sheba" who came to see Solomon will do the same. The Ninevites repented at the words of a minor prophet who was himself foolish and rebellious, had done no miracles, and showed no love. The Queen of Sheba trusted in God because of the wisdom of an imperfect Solomon. The

Pharisees were rejecting one greater than Jonah and wiser by far than Solomon. How his references to these Gentiles must have grated on these proud Pharisees!

Jesus' final accusation is that they resemble a demon-possessed man from whom the demon has gone out, but who becomes possessed again by even worse evil because his life is a vacuum. His last state is worse than his first (vv. 43-45). Centuries before the Israelites had turned from paganism, but instead of filling the vacuum with worship of the true God, the Pharisees loaded the people with rituals and traditions. Ultimately, this is worse than paganism, for it led them to crucify their Messiah.

THE FINAL BLOW

While Jesus was expressing these solmen realities, his mother and his brothers stood outside trying to get his attention. They could not understand his attacks on Israel's prestigious leaders. Their once normal son and brother was a source of turmoil and agitation to all Israel, and they evidently concluded that he had suffered a breakdown and lost his mind, so they came to take him home (Mark 3:21, 22). This was the final blow. His enemies called him the devil, his family and friends pronounced him insane. He was truly a prophet without honor. But Jesus told the crowd he has a new family: "Who is my mother and who are my brothers? Whoever does the will of my Father in heaven, he is my brother, and sister, and mother" (Matthew 12:46-50).

Unperturbed by misgivings of friends or threats of foes, Jesus declares that the great spiritual family of God consists of all who do the Father's will. And what is the Father's will? To believe that Jesus is the Messiah!

EIGHT

◆ ◆

The Great Delay

◆ ◆

The land of Israel, small and vulnerable, was flanked by powerful, aggressive neighbors. Years of peace and freedom were few as Gentile armies trampled Galilee's fertile fields or climbed up Judaea's rocky hills. Yet a dream burned in every Jewish heart, and the more she was besieged by armies, the brighter that dream blazed.

The dream was that Messiah would suddenly appear, drive off Israel's conquerors, and make her chief among the nations, ruling from Jerusalem over his worldwide kingdom. Israel's great prophets had predicted this, but the prophets also envisioned Messiah as a righteous king who demanded holiness from his people—and many of the dreamers of glory were blind to this reality. When John the Baptist announced the kingdom was at hand and called for repentance, feverish excitement gripped Israel at the prospect of Messiah's appearance, but the leaders' self-righteous hostility rejected the demand for repentance.

As Jesus emphasized the spiritual character of his kingdom, resistance grew until he was slanderously accused of being the devil's henchman. At this point Jesus' message took on a new slant. Instead of speaking to the crowds about the kingdom being near at hand, he described a kingdom with a new form, unforeseen by those prophets who foretold Israel's great deliverance and era of magnificence.

What Jesus began to unveil more clearly was the twofold appearance of the Messiah—first to suffer, second to reign—with an indefinite time period between. Jesus' revelation was cloaked in his great and famous parables of the kingdom.

POINTLESS PARABLES?

Matthew tells us that on the same day when some Pharisees committed the "unpardonable sin," Jesus began to teach great crowds from a boat anchored a little way from shore (13:1, 2).

Instead of the clear declarations characteristic of the Sermon on the Mount, he began to tell apparently pointless stories:

"A farmer went out to sow, and as he sowed, some seeds fell beside the path and the birds came and devoured them. Others fell on rocky places, where they didn't have much soil, and grew quickly because there was no depth of soil. But when the sun came, they were burned up and withered because they had no root. Others fell on good soil, and produced a crop, a hundred, sixty, or thirty times more than were sown" (vv. 3-8).

Puzzled, Jesus' disciples asked why he should tell parables which, though interesting, had no obvious point (v. 10).

STORIES WHICH REVEAL AND CONCEAL

"Because to you it's been given to know the mysteries of the kingdom, but to them it has not been given," he answered. "For whoever has, it will be given to him, and he will have an abundance, but he who has not, even what he has will be taken from him. Therefore, I speak to them in parables, because though they see, they don't see, and though they hear, they don't hear, or understand. And with them Isaiah's prophecy is fulfilled, 'You hear indeed, but don't understand, you see indeed but don't perceive. For the heart of this people is dull and they barely hear with their ears and they close their eyes so they won't . . . turn back and have me heal them' " (vv. 12-15).

Jesus discloses that his parables are a form of judgment! Israel, as in Isaiah's time, is so dull spiritually that she refuses to respond to God's message. Her leaders plot to murder their Messiah, while the masses seek food and military conquest instead of personal righteousness. Because of their callousness, Jesus will no longer shower truth upon them; instead he will speak so that genuine seekers will discern the truths of the parables and pursue entrance into the kingdom, but the hard-hearted will puzzle over the meaning of the stories.

The ancient saying, "Light rejected brings night" described Israel's situation. Unbelievers would sink further into skepticism and lose the gleams of light they once possessed. Yet the believers would gain even more faith and understanding, especially as Jesus interpreted the parables to them. The parables were a double-edged sword—they concealed and revealed truth at the same time.

THE KINGDOM WINS NO POPULARITY CONTENTS

Jesus interpreted the parable of the sower for his questioning disciples (vv. 18-23). In those days farmers sowed their seed first, then plowed it in. Some, blown by wind, fell on hard paths at the edges of the field and were never ploughed into the soil. Other seed fell on soil with rock near the surface. After ploughing, it grew rapidly because the shallow soil was warm, but when long, hot days came it was scorched and died. Another portion of seed was choked by the thistles left by farmers to burn as summer fuel. But the remaining seed fell on good ground and produced a crop of varying proportions.

Jesus said he is the sower, his words are spiritual seed, and the different kinds of soil are human hearts giving different responses. The roadside represents *indifferent* hearers in whose hearts his message takes no root. Stony soil stands for *impulsive* hearers whose quick enthusiasm vanishes when persecution comes. The thistle-bearing soil pictures *distracted* hearers who choke the seed with materialistic preferences. The good soil portrays *true* hearers who bear, in proportion to their gifts, much fruit.

This opening parable taught that Messiah's longed-for kingdom would assume an unexpected form in this age. Instead of being suddenly established by the Messiah-king and universally received by Israel, the kingdom would be preached to a widespread audience over a length of time and receive a mixed response. The conflicting reactions were already occurring in Jesus' ministry, and unknown to his disciples then, they would extend beyond Israel to the Gentile nations.

Clearly, the deficiency was not with the message, pictured by the seed, but with the condition of the hearers, pictured by the soil. Yet Jesus encouraged generous and universal sowing of the message. Farmers had to expect they would lose a certain percentage of seed, but they knew the more seed they sowed, the greater the crop. As the disciples later spread Jesus' message to every city and synagogue they could get to, they saw similar spiritual results. And when many hearers were indifferent, superficial, or half-hearted in response, the disciples didn't blame themselves. Jesus himself achieved only a mixed response.

SILENT MARCH TO HARVEST

Jesus continued to illustrate from the familiar world of agriculture.

"So is the kingdom of God like a farmer planting seed in the soil, and he sleeps at night and gets up in the day, and the seed sprouts and grows, but he doesn't know how. For the soil by itself bears fruit—first the blade, then the head, then the mature kernel in the head. And when the wheat is ripe, he puts forth the sickle because the harvest has come" (Mark 4:26-29).

To the discerning listener this parable reveals that Messiah's kingdom will grow gradually of its own power over its appointed time until maturity and future harvest. Perhaps some of Jesus' disciples, like Simon the Zealot, still had thoughts of bringing in the Messianic reign through violent revolution against Rome. Inflamed fanatacism did sweep the nation and doom it to destruction within a generation of Jesus' words. But Jesus taught his followers to await God's slower, but inevitable steering of history to its appointed end.

MYSTERIOUS MIXTURE OF GOOD AND EVIL

Jesus next related a parable of a farmer who sowed good seed in his field, but at night an enemy secretly sowed tares in the same field. As the wheat grew up, the tares grew alongside. The farmer's servants then wanted to uproot the tares, but he said to wait so they wouldn't uproot the wheat before it was grown, and at harvest the two would be separated for their different destinies (Matthew 13:24-30). In Palestine grew a poisonous weed called bearded darnel, the "tares" of Jesus' story. Darnel closely resembled wheat in its earlier stages, and its roots would intertwine with the wheat. Romans passed laws against sowing darnel in another's field.

Jesus is again the one who sows the good seed, who are believers. The field is the world. The enemy is the devil, who sows the tares, which are his children. The harvest is the end of the age and the reapers are the angels who will separate God's followers from the devil's followers. The burning of the tares pictures hell, where the devil's followers will go (vv. 36-43).

This parable was another surprise package. John the Baptist had taught that Messiah would separate the wheat from the chaff and cleanse Israel and the world of evil. Here Jesus teaches that evil will flourish alongside good until the end of history. Since the tares are called sons of the devil, they were probably not ordinary unbelievers. They include false prophets, heretics, and fake spiritual leaders of every kind.

Jesus' words have proved all too true. Counterfeit spiritual leaders have plagued the world since Jesus' days on earth. The movement which claims to follow Jesus has sometimes built corrupt institutions, aligned itself with oppressive governments, trampled down the poor and helpless, persecuted Jews, maligned true believers, and promoted every kind of error. And, of course, the age began when corrupt religious leaders crucified Jesus.

FROM SMALL BEGINNINGS . . .

Next, Jesus said the kingdom of heaven is like "a mustard seed which a man sowed in his field, which is the smallest of seeds, but when it grows is the greatest of the herbs and becomes like a tree so that the birds of heaven come and nest in its branches" (vv. 31, 32).

The mustard seed was proverbially the smallest of seeds, yet it grew into a towering shrub. This parable teaches that Messiah's kingdom, though its beginnings are small and obscure, will become gigantic. From Jesus and the few he gathered around him has grown a movement with more adherents in more lands than any other faith in history. The Old Testament prophets foresaw the eventual size of Messiah's kingdom, but not its gradual growth from obscure beginnings.

The final installment of God's kingdom, of course, which Jesus will establish at his second coming, will be the greatest, most powerful, most enduring kingdom of all time.

Jesus followed this with a similar parable. "The kingdom of heaven is like yeast, which a woman mixed in a bushel of meal until the whole was penetrated" (v. 33). This described what occurred frequently in every household where bread was made. Leaven, or yeast, usually symbolizes evil in Scripture, so this could be teaching that the kingdom will eventually become permeated with evil. But since it parallels the parable of the mustard seed, which carried no evil connotation, it seems best to interpret it in the same way. Jesus is teaching that though the kingdom begins small, it will finally permeate the whole world. This ultimate conquest will only come, however, when the king returns to establish his worldwide authority.

As Jesus' disciples later reflected on the parables of

the mustard seed and the leaven, they undoubtedly felt encouraged. They were but a small band with limited resources, hounded from city to city by their enemies and eventually by the Roman government. They were continually swimming against an overwhelming tide. Yet Jesus predicted the eventual outcome of their labors would be a great spiritual movement and total victory over evil by the all-conquering Messiah. They might appear losers now in the battle, but they would be eventual winners of the war.

Jesus called his followers to a cause which would one day triumph. No doubt this has attracted many contemporary youth to Jesus. They have found following him a thrilling alternative to the despair and purposelessness which grip the world.

A TREASURE AND A PEARL

The kingdom sparkles with other facets, Jesus revealed. "The kingdom of heaven is like treasure buried in a field, which a man found and hid, and from joy goes and sells his possessions and buys that field. Again, the kingdom of heaven is like a businessman seeking beautiful pearls and finding one pearl of great value, he went away and sold all that he had and bought it" (vv. 44-46).

Treasures of gold coins and other valuables were buried in the earth by ancient people who lacked vaults and other places of safekeeping. A man might die without revealing the location of his buried treasure, and a later purchaser of his land might stumble on the unexpected wealth. Pearls were costly in ancient times, and an especially beautiful one would have enormous value. Jesus indicated that his kingdom would be different in its early stage from anything his disciples expected. They looked for spectacular display. These stories depict the kingdom as invisible to the average person, but a shining reality to the believer who gladly gives up everything for it.

The man who found the treasure seemed to stumble on it by accident. Some of Jesus' disciples probably came upon him "by chance." The Samaritan woman, who went out to Jacob's well to fill her waterpot and returned an hour later a citizen of God's eternal kingdom, is an example of this. Others were like the pearl buyer—they were seeking earnestly for truth and knew Jesus was the answer when they found him. Probably the Apostle John, who first followed John the Baptist and later found Jesus, was an eager seeker. Believers discover the kingdom in a variety of ways.

THE GREAT DRAGNET

The final parable describes a great dragnet cast by fishermen into the water which pulls in fish of every kind. The fishermen, after pulling it to shore, keep the edible and useful fish and throw away the worthless ones (vv. 47-50).

Again, this pictures our present age as allowing the good and the bad to exist side by side until a future separation and judgment. Peter and Judas, Paul and Nero, Pharisee and disciple are next-door neighbors for this era. But whereas the parable of the wheat and tares emphasized false spiritual leaders beside the true, the dragnet seems to focus on the believer intermingled with the unbeliever.

Jesus' conclusion to his parables is that the wise teacher in his kingdom is like "the owner of a house who brings out of his collection of valuables new and old things" (v. 52). Jesus drew on the picture of a wealthy man who had many possessions, some new, some old, but all valuable. New and old truths are combined in Jesus' presentation of the coming kingdom. The old truth of Messiah's irresistible reign and final judgment is joined to the unperceived truth of the delay of that reign and judgment.

THE GREAT DELAY

The Pharisees expected Messiah to immediately appear, and to exalt the Jews and punish the Gentiles. John the Baptist waited for Messiah to suddenly unleash his power to save believers and to condemn unbelievers—regardless of race.

But Jesus' parables taught a momentous delay of God's judgment. During the delay Messiah's quiet reign would receive only a mixed response and would spread gradually, allowing wheat and tares, good fish and bad, to co-exist temporarily, though the final triumph of Jesus' kingdom is certain. In the meantime, Messiah's reign would advance without pomp and display—but believers would discover and give their all to it.

How Jesus' disciples longed for the abolition of evil, and how humanity has longed for it since! John the Baptist desired to see the corrupt Jewish leaders, the evil King Herod, and cruel Rome toppled immediately by Messiah. We long for poverty, sickness, oppression, war, and injustice to disappear. Yet Jesus taught that God's program would flow slowly and patiently toward its appointed victory rather than to burst through like a flood and instantly sweep away all obstacles in its path. This mysterious program demands of Jesus' followers faith and patience which sometimes are tested to the extreme.

Yet finally the kingdom will arrive in all its majesty! The poor soil, worthless fish, and posionous tares will be gone. The wheat will be in the barn, the mustard tree will be full grown and the bread wholly leavened. The treasure will no longer be hidden in the field and the priceless pearl will be on display. Then the long wait, now nearly two thousand years, will have been worth it all.

The great dream will have come true.

NINE

The Miracle Worker

It was only three in the afternoon, but already Jesus was exhausted. Crowds had begun to pour into his lodgings shortly after sunrise, hounding him like fans after autographs from their favorite star.

In the midst of the turmoil, Mary and Jesus' step-brothers arrived, fearful that his strenuous pace had pushed him to the breaking point. But they were unable to get near him because of the throngs. Then Jesus had cast the demon from a deaf and dumb man, only to have the Pharisees attribute the healing to Satan. Before a shocked audience, Jesus had accused them of committing the unpardonable sin. Then he went outdoors and taught the parables to the crowds, which he interpreted privately to his seemingly forever dense disciples.

Jesus decided to retreat for some peace and quiet, so he and the disciples climbed in a boat, probably Peter's, and began rowing across the Sea of Galilee toward the hills on the eastern shore. The fatigued teacher soon went to sleep in the stern of the boat, his head resting on the steerman's pillow, while the others continued to row. Incidentally, this is the only time the Gospels mention Jesus being asleep.

A SUDDEN STORM

The Sea of Galilee lies seven hundred feet below sea level, and cold air from nearby hills frequently funnels down to it, creating unpredictable and violent storms. Such a storm suddenly engulfed the boat, yet Jesus' exhausted form remained motionless in the stern. The agitated disciples finally awakened him: "Rabbi, don't you care that we're perishing?" (Mark 4:38) They had no idea what Jesus might do, but unless he did something they were done for!

Jesus stood erect and rebuked the wind and shouted at the sea: "Silence; be still!" (v. 39) At his words the wind ceased and the water became glassy smooth. Mark says a great calm developed. Jesus' disciples could hardly believe their eyes. Before they could express their astonishment, Jesus turned to admonish them for their rude insinuation that he could care less if the boat went to the bottom. "Why are you so afraid? How come you still have no faith?" (v. 40)

They were almost more afraid in the calm than they were in the storm. "Who is this man? Even the wind and waves obey him!" they whispered to each other (v. 41). They believed he was the Messiah; they had witnessed his healings and his exorcisms. But their understanding of the Messiah was pitifully limited. The fullness of his divine grandeur had not yet dawned on them.

A TERRIFYING WELCOME

But the long day was not yet over. They arrived on the eastern side of the sea perhaps as night was descending, and were greeted by a scene as terrifying as any in the Gospels. They had pulled the boat to shore close to a kind of graveyard—some caves used as tombs, and out of these caves rushed two demon-possessed men. Mark mentions only one, but his vivid description sends chills down the spine:

"He lived among the tombs, and no one was able to tie him up, even with a chain, for he had often been tied with chains, hand and foot, and he tore the chains in pieces and shattered the shackles on his feet. And no one was able to subdue him. And constantly, night and day, he was among the tombs and in the mountains crying out and cutting himself with stones" (5:3-5).

The disciples, with nerves already jangled by the storm, probably heard the men's haunting howls over the quiet waters as the boat approached shore. When the wild-eyed demoniacs then began running toward them in the night, they probably were ready to risk the waves again! But Jesus was unperturbed, and he directly addressed the demon in the man:

"What is your name?"

"Legion," the demon revealed, "for we are many" (v. 9).

A legion was six thousand Roman foot soldiers plus 120 cavalry and additional technical personnel. The demon pictured himself as head of a powerful demon army. No wonder the man couldn't be bound!

DEMON-DRIVEN PIGS

Fearing judgment, the demons began to beg Jesus not to send them out of the country, but to let them enter a nearby herd of two thousand pigs. Jesus gave them permission and Mark reports "the evil spirits came out and entered the pigs, and the herd rushed over the precipice into the sea . . . and drowned in the sea" (v. 13).

Quickly a crowd gathered from the surrounding countryside to gape at the dead pigs in the water and at the demon-possessed men, now clothed and sane. The floating pigs were concrete evidence that the men were not psychotic. The dead creatures showed the terrible power of the demon army. Unfortunately the crowd did not welcome this dramatic invasion of light into their dark world. They pleaded with Jesus to leave (v. 15). They had grown accustomed to those shrieking maniacs and a strange new force, even though it shattered the chains of evil, was more distressing than the demons.

The freed man, however, was so grateful that he wished to become a disciple of Jesus and return with him to the other side of the lake. But Jesus sent him back to his family, which no doubt had suffered terribly during the ordeal of his possession, and told him to tell them and his friends what God had done.

The man was from Decapolis, a Gentile area (v. 20). This man followed the Roman centurion in becoming the second Gentile in the Gospel record to believe in Jesus. As he returned to his pagan, idol-ridden community, his story evidently made a great impact. Jesus later had a significant ministry in the Decapolis area, and the miraculous feeding of four thousand people took place in that region (Mark 7:31-8:9). This former demoniac, like one returned from hell, served as Jesus' missionary to his people in preparation for thousands of later converts.

A DESPERATE MAN

The hectic day finally ended, and early the next morning Jesus and his disciples returned across the lake, probably to Capernaum. Again crowds swarmed around him. Suddenly a synagogue elder named Jairus broke through the crowd and asked Jesus to come and heal his twelve-year-old daughter, an only child who was on the verge of death. If this was in Capernaum, then not only the synagogue builder but now one of its elders is touched by Jesus' ministry. Perhaps Jairus had watched Jesus from a distance in the past, but an impending tragedy drives him to seek help now, regardless of criticisms from fellow Pharisees.

AND A DESPERATE WOMAN

As Jesus, surrounded by the crowd, headed toward Jairus' home, a woman pushed close behind him. She was a twelve-year victim of what is now called menorrhagia—almost continuous uterine bleeding. Caused by a hormone imbalance, this condition made her permanently unclean under Old Testament ceremonial rules— she could not engage in temple worship or enjoy sexual fulfillment in her marriage.

Mark adds she "had suffered much at the hands of many physicians, and had spent all she had, and was not even helped, but rather grew worse" (5:25). Luke, himself a doctor, simply says "no one was able to heal her" (8:43).

Mark's accusation against medical ineptness was fully justified. The Jewish Talmud lists eleven treatments for this common ailment, among them the carrying of ostrich egg ashes in a linen rag and carrying a barley grain recovered from the dung of a white female donkey! The Talmud also had a saying, "The best of doctors is ripe for hell." An old Roman proverb cynically stated that a doctor is worse than a robber because a robber takes your money or your life while a doctor takes both. Such doctors, with their superstitious remedies, made this woman's plight even more miserable.

"WHO TOUCHED ME?"

The woman, embarrassed over her illness, perhaps thought she could get secret healing by simply touching Jesus' clothing, so she reached out to one of the tassels which hung from a corner of his garment. Immediately she sensed she was healed—but Jesus also sensed that his healing power had surged forth.

"Who touched my clothing?" Jesus asked as he stopped and turned around (Mark 5:30).

"You see the crowd pressing upon you, and you say, 'Who touched me?'" said his disciples with a grin (v. 31). But Jesus was serious. He looked around the crowd and refused to go on. Finally the woman, perhaps afraid the healing would not last unless she confessed, knelt before Jesus and blurted out her story.

"Daughter, your faith has saved you," Jesus assured her. "Go into peace, and be healed of your plague" (v. 34). The poor woman had touched his garment, half in faith, half in superstition. Jesus made her come out with her story and instructed her that faith in him, not some magic power in his clothing, had been the real channel of healing.

A FATEFUL DELAY

During this episode Jairus had probably been in a nervous sweat because Jesus was delaying. Then his worst fear was confirmed when someone hurried up and announced: "Your daughter is dead; why bother the rabbi any more?" (v. 35)

But the perceptive carpenter-teacher overheard and said to Jairus, "Stop being afraid; only believe" (v. 36).

Jesus then took Peter, James, and John with him to witness a stupendous event. They came to Jairus' house, where the mourning had already begun. Typically, the mourning started with an eerie death wail which could be heard for blocks. Then relatives and hired female mourners gathered. The mourners began a macabre "dance of death," probably to the accompaniment of flutes, loud wails, and weeping. When Jesus broke into this dismal scene and told them the child was not dead, but only asleep, the mourners and relatives heaped scorn on him. He refused to act amidst such unbelief and expelled them all.

Then Jesus entered the child's room with Jairus, his wife, and the three disciples. Mark tells us: "Taking the child's hand, he said to her, 'Talitha kum,' which translated means, 'Little girl, I say to you, arise' " (v. 42). The mention of Jesus' taking her hand, plus the recalling of his exact words in Aramaic, are signs this is an eyewitness account. Many scholars believe Peter was Mark's source of information (cf. I Peter 5:13). No doubt as Peter told Mark this story he could still recall the moment Jesus took her hand and his exact tone of voice as he pronounced those memorable words.

The girl immediately got up and began to walk around. Jesus cautioned them to give her some food and to keep quiet about the miracle (Mark 5: 42, 43). He wanted no more publicity in Capernaum, and he knew the miracle would soon enough get Jairus into trouble with the Pharisees.

This was his second recorded raising of a dead person, done again from compassion for the sorrowing loved ones. That Jairus once ignored or opposed Jesus did not matter now—tragedy, turned to joy, made them friends.

THE GROWING REALIZATION

Rampant nature, Satanic spirits, dread diseases, and ultimately death are mankind's great external enemies. Yet these relentless powers had yielded instantly to Jesus' word and touch! Slowly the staggering truth would dawn on Jesus' disciples: they were walking with one more exalted than the Jewish Messiah—this man was wielding authority held by the creator alone; they were face-to-face with Jehovah!

When this realization later gripped them, and other first-century believers after them, their lives were transformed. Underneath the peasant garb of a Galilean laborer was the Caesar excelling all earthly Caesars, the king of all history, the controller of all circumstances, the creator of all matter and spirits—God in human flesh. As they faced an uncertain, hostile world where their cause often appeared hopeless, they did so courageously, for the greatest power in existence was on their side!

Jesus left Jairus' house and returned to his lodgings, but two blind men followed him and kept yelling, "Have mercy on us, Son of David" (Matthew 9:27, 28). They did more than beg for healing—they called him by the Messianic title, "Son of David."

Jesus questioned them: "Do you believe that I am able to do this?"

They replied in the affirmative, and Jesus healed them. As with the leper healed earlier, Jesus directed them not to spread the news of his healing, but they also disobeyed (v. 31).

As the two men imprisoned so long in darkness headed out into new light, a demon-possessed man unable to speak was brought in. Jesus also healed him, and the fame of the Nazareth carpenter surged again. But the Pharisees renewed their bitter counter attack that Jesus cast out demons by Satanic power (vv. 32-34).

FAREWELL—FOREVER

Jesus then made his last known visit to his hometown of Nazareth. His previous visit, about a year earlier, had ended riotously in their attack on him in the synagogue. This visit encounters no violence, but the same stubborn opposition. "Isn't this the carpenter, Mary's son, the brother of James, Joses, ahd Judas, and Simon? Aren't his sisters here with us?" they again muttered (Mark 6:3).

They cannot get beyond the recognition that Jesus was a carpenter, an unschooled manual laborer, from an unprestigious family. They call him "Mary's son" to show their contempt, for Jews commonly referred to a man as his father's son. Their words clearly imply that Joseph is not his father and therefore he is illegitimate, as we saw in Chapter One. In the midst of these insults at Jesus and his godly parents, he could do only a few miracles. Mark reports that their blind unbelief amazed him (v. 6).

The response to Jesus' miracles demonstrated Israel's unwillingness to come to terms with its Messiah. The blind men believed in his power but refused to obey him and helped to increase the people's craving for spectacular feats. When he healed the demon possessed, religious leaders gave credit to Satan. When he went to Nazaraeth to minister to hometowners, they ridiculed him because of his humble background. Only a few, such as the demoniac who returned to Decapolis, the woman delivered from a twelve-year illness, and Jairus the synagogue elder, accepted the full benefit from Jesus' power.

SHEPHERDLESS SHEEP

Jesus then embarked on another tour of Galilee. Despite the fierce hostility of synagogue leaders, Jesus' popularity with the masses was approaching its zenith. As Jesus entered town after town, he was grieved by the dire physical and spiritual needs he saw. Matthew says, "He felt deep compassion for them because they were harassed and worn out, like sheep without a shepherd" (9:36).

Like shepherdless sheep harassed by the wild animals of sickness, demon possession, and sorrow of every kind, the people were worn out. Yet the very shepherds who should have been guiding, comforting, and protecting them were not only increasing their burdens but even resisting the one shepherd who could really save them. Stirred by the plight of spiritually straying people, Jesus told his disciples, "The harvest is great, but the workers are few. Therefore, ask the Lord of the harvest to send out workers into his harvest" (vv. 37, 38).

He pictures the nation as a great harvest field, with only a few laborers prepared to bring in the crop. This always seems to be true. Fake religions and false hopes lead shepherdless masses to destruction, while truly spiritual shepherds seem to number only one in a million. The harvest always outnumbers the workers.

THE APOSTLES GET THEIR FEET WET

Looking over the hapless crowds and his own disciples, Jesus appointed his followers as laborers in the national harvest field. This was a momentous step for them. As sideline spectators they had watched Jesus in action; now they were to get their own feet wet. They couldn't know, of course, that within eighteen months the leadership of this revolutionary movement would rest fully in their hands.

Before Jesus sent them out, he prepared them with careful instructions. In the Sermon on the Mount he had described standards set for citizens of his kingdom. Now he gives marching orders for workers on behalf of that kingdom.

"Don't go to the Gentiles and don't enter a Samaritan city, but go instead to the lost sheep of the house of Israel. And when you go, proclaim that the kingdom of God has arrived. Heal the sick, raise the dead, cleanse the lepers, exorcise the demons. You received without charge; give without charge" (Matthew 10:5-8).

The Messianic promises were primarily to Israel, and Jesus directed that the descendants of Abraham have full opportunity before the message is taken to the rest of the world. Jesus authorizes them to do the same miraculous works they have seen him do, which implies he can transfer some of his great power into human hands. Evidently they were to go to areas where the message was yet unknown and preach that God's kingdom had arrived.

Next, Jesus instructed them on their preparation: "Don't provide money for your wallets, or a bag for the trip, extra tunic or extra sandals, or a club for protection, for the workman is worthy of his food" (vv. 9, 10). Desiring to build their faith, Jesus commanded them to take nothing for emergencies. They are to go with only the clothes on their backs and trust God to provide their needs through the local populace. As kingdom workers they are worthy of such help and they will receive it.

DIVINE REPRESENTATIVES

The all-important approach to each village was spelled out. "Into whatever city or village you enter, seek out who is worthy in it. Stay there until you leave. When you enter the home, greet it. If the home is worthy, let your peace come upon it. But if not, let your peace return to you. And whoever does not receive you or listen to your words, when you leave that home or city, shake the dust off your feet. Truly, I tell you it will be more tolerable for Sodom and Gomorrah on judgment day than that town" (vv. 11-15).

The disciple-apostles could expect home hospitality since there were few public inns and providing for travelers was considered a sacred duty. But the apostles must carefully choose where they stayed—a family favorable to their message would recommend a hearing by other villagers. And they must not waste time and fragment their impact by moving around, but remain in one house until leaving the area.

On entering various homes, they were to pronounce the customary sacred blessing on the home and pray for God's peace on it. But if the home rejected them, they were to retract the blessing as a witness against the family. If a town rejected them, the apostles were to dramatically shake their feet at the border—a Jewish custom signifying denunciation and separation from evil. As Jesus' representatives, they were welcomed or repelled in the place of Jesus and ultimately of God. This was a deadly serious mission.

A LEAP INTO THE FUTURE

Jesus' discourse then took a prophetic leap. Old Testament prophets had frequently jumped from statements about local events to similar events of worldwide magnitude that occurred hundreds or thousands of years later. For example, Joel spoke of God's judgment by a plague of locusts in his own lifetime, then envisioned calamities at the end of the world (Joel 1, 2). Jesus spoke here in the same now-later style.

"I send you out as sheep in the middle of wolves. Therefore be as shrewd as snakes and innocent as doves. And beware of people, for they will deliver you up to councils and beat you in the synagogues. And you will be brought before kings and rulers because of me, as a witness to them and to the Gentiles" (Matthew 10:16-18).

The analogy with gentle and fierce animals fit the disciples' immediate situation, but not until after Jesus' resurrection were the apostles delivered to Jewish councils, flogged in synagogues, and, as the book of Acts records, hailed before Gentile rulers. In the midst of hostility, they were to be as shrewd as the proverbial snake yet harmless as doves, the beloved birds of Palestine that were always allowed to nest unmolested.

AN EVEN GREATER LEAP

Jesus' warning then vaulted farther into the future. "And brother will deliver up brother to death, and a father, his child, and children will stand up against parents and put them to death and you will be hated by everyone on account of my name, but the one enduring to the end will be saved. But when they persecute you in this city, run to another. I tell you, you will not finish going through the cities of Israel until the Son of Man comes" (vv. 21-23).

Though harsh persecution besieged Jesus' followers at various times, the explicit setting of this intense attack is Israel, and it ends with the coming of the Son of Man—Jesus' first clear reference to his second coming. He predicts that before his second coming, his Jewish followers will be so persecuted that even in the tightly knit Jewish families they will suffer betrayal from their loved ones. But Jesus encourages these believers by promising their patient endurance will result in salvation. As he taught in the parable of the sower, false faith withers under pressure, while genuine faith flourishes. Jesus also orders these followers to flee from their opposition rather than to battle it because they will still not have time to evangelize every city of Israel before he returns.

The Old Testament prophesied Messiah's coming to deliver Israel in the midst of world turmoil centered in Palestine. Jesus' contemporaries expected this immediately and fomented a revolt against Rome. The Jewish rebellion was crushed in A.D. 70 and the people expelled to distant countries for centuries of exile. In recent decades Israel has returned to its homeland, and again she is the center of world turmoil. Meanwhile Jews worldwide are becoming open to the gospel of Jesus. The real-life actors are now taking their places and the world stage is being set for Jesus' far-seeing prophecy. He would have much more to say about this later.

PRESCRIPTION FOR PERSECUTION

Jesus shifted his perspective to persecuted believers in any time and place to counsel:

"A disciple is not above his teacher, nor a slave above his master. . . . If they called the head of the house Beelezebub, how much more the members of his household! So don't be afraid of them, for nothing is covered which won't be uncovered. . . . What I say to you in the darkness, say in the light, and what you hear in your ear proclaim from the housetops.

"And don't fear those who kill the body but can't kill the soul. Instead, fear the one who can destroy both body and soul in hell. Aren't two sparrows sold for a dime? Yet not one of them will fall on the ground without your Father. But even the hairs of your head are all numbered. Don't fear them, for you're worth more than many sparrows" (vv. 24-31).

If the disciples' leader was slandered, his followers cannot expect to escape the same. Yet God has determined their message will get out: the truths heard in private will be broadcast publicly, as if by town criers on housetops in Israel's villages.

And persecutors are not to be feared, for they can only bring victims to the grave. God is the one to be feared, for he can send individuals to heaven or hell beyond the grave. Not even a sparrow, sold as food for a nickel, can die unless God permits it. How much more carefully will God guard believers. The Father is so interested in each believer that he notices what the believer never thinks of—the exact number of hairs on his head. With such omnipotent companionship, the dread of their persecutors should vanish!

THE ULTIMATE PRIORITY

Knowing persecution can pressure people into compromising their convictions, Jesus bluntly states life's ultimate priority in soul-shaking terms:

"Whoever confesses me before people, I will confess him before my Father in heaven. But whoever denies me before people, I will also deny him before my Father in heaven. Don't think that I came to bring peace on earth; I didn't come to bring peace but a sword. For I came to set a man against his father and a daughter against her mother. . . . Whoever loves father or mother more than me is not worthy of me. . . . Whoever finds his life will lose it, whoever loses his life for my sake will find it" (vv. 32-39).

Jesus tells his disciples *he* is life's ultimate priority. Affirmation of him means heaven; denial of him means hell. Yet faith in him will divide some of the closest families. True followers willing to lose family and everything else for Jesus will find new life here and eternal life hereafter, but those who clutch life and lose Jesus will eventually lose it all.

Every encounter and association of the messengers would be noted, Jesus assured them:

"Whoever welcomes you welcomes me, and whoever welcomes me welcomes the one who sent me. Whoever welcomes a prophet because he is a prophet receives a prophet's reward. . . . whoever gives a drink of cold water to one of these little ones because he is a disciple, I tell you he absolutely will not lose his reward" (vv. 40-42).

Jesus completed his instructions with stirring words of encouragement. God will note carefully what treatment the world gives his followers. Those who welcome them and their message will find that welcome meant as much to God as if they had welcomed Jesus himself! Whoever befriends one of Jesus' prophets because he is such a prophet will end up sharing the prophet's eternal reward. In fact, just as God notices the hairs on their heads, he will note and honor even a cup of cold water given to an obscure disciple ("little one").

During persecution, those courageous enough to help Jesus' followers really identify with Jesus and his cause and thus become believers themselves. The apostles would soon discover this, for during their missionary labors after the resurrection, those who welcomed them became believers while those who persecuted them, as Paul once did, found that persecuting Jesus' representatives was persecuting Jesus himself.

FAR-FETECHED, AND YET . . .

This may have been the most amazing talk Jesus' apostles had ever heard him give. He began with instructions for their upcoming tour, moved on to warn of perils for the next half century, and then concluded with advice for their spiritual offspring who would spread the same message, in the same country, generating the same persecution at least two milennia later. He called on contemporary and future followers to disdain fear, to love him more than anyone else, and to anticipate rewards for everything done to help Jesus' cause.

On that day in this obscure corner of the world the unschooled carpenter spoke such words to twleve ordinary working men who had no position, no money, and no weapons. He spoke as if they were the most important people on earth. They would stir a whole empire to persecute them. They would appear before kings and emperors. Almighty God would count the hairs on their heads and record every cup of cold water given them. This carpenter must mean more to them than wives, children, parents, or life itself.

Who was he to demand more devotion than wives or children? Who were they to dream that they could turn a world upside down? What was tiny Israel, that she should become the final center of world events? It was all ridiculously far-fetched . . . yet it wasn't after all.

TEN

—————◆ ◆—————

Free Bread

—————◆ ◆—————

Five miles east of the Dead Sea lie the lonely, wind-
swept ruins of Machaerus. Here, on a lofty hilltop, perch
great stones which once were the walls of Herod
Antipas' castle retreat. Late one night in A.D. 29 those
stones witnessed a gruesome murder.

That evening King Herod Antipas, son of Herod the
Great and ruler of Galilee and Perea (the eastern bank of
the Jordan), celebrated his birthday. For the occasion
he invited leading dignitaries of his kingdom and as the
hours wore on, the majority of the all-male celebrants,
including Herod, probably became drunk. At the height
of the revelry Herod's stepdaughter entered the hall half-
naked and began twisting and swaying through the
seductive motions of a sensuous dance. Such perfor-
mances were reserved for women of questionable
morals; for a king's daughter they were unheard of!

But the crude, drunk king and his guests roared their
approval. "Ask me for whatever you want, and I'll give
it to you—up to half of my kingdom!" Herod blurted
out (Mark 6:22, 23). Then he confirmed his rash offer
with a solemn oath.

This was the moment she had waited for. She immediately exited and asked her mother, Queen Herodias,
what to request. "The head of John the Baptist on a

112

plate," came back the ghastly answer (Matthew 14:8). John was imprisoned in this very castle, so probably within the hour, as the guests continued to feast on the king's delicacies, they saw John's bloody head carried in—one of the most revolting scenes in all literature.

A WOMAN'S SCORN

Behind the events of that terrible evening was an evil and calculated plan. Herodias originally had been married to Herod Antipas' half-brother, Philip, whom she had left for Antipas. Since the Herod family, though of Idumean descent, were professing Jews, John the Baptist had repeatedly condemned this violation of Old Testament law. This infuriated Herodias, who relentlessly pressured her husband to execute John. Antipas put John in prison, but hesitated to put him to death, and even called him to preach before his court.

Eventually, Herodias had all of this she could take, so she devised the plan which doomed John that night. Mark says Herod was "extremely grieved" over having to execute John, but refused to renege on his promise to Herodias' daughter, because he might lose face before the dignitaries (6:26). He was so degenerate that pleasing drunken nobles outweighed preserving the great prophet's life.

When he heard of Jesus' astounding deeds in Galilee, the superstitious monarch would later fear that John the Baptist had returned to life (Mark 6:14). One year later he faced Jesus, who was on trial for his life. Instead of redeeming himself by securing Jesus' freedom, the shameless king and his soldiers mocked the weary, bleeding Galilean (Luke 23:6-12). Following the crime strained footprints of his father Herod the Great, who slaughtered Bethelehem babies attempting to exterminate the newborn Jesus, Antipas executed John and tried to make Jesus a laughingstock. Herod Agrippa, a brother, later executed the Apostle James and tried to kill Peter (Acts 12). Few families in history have been such a curse to the people of God.

NO REST

When Jesus learned of John's execution, the apostles had just returned from their preaching mission. Seeking relief and rest, they retreated again to an uninhabited area on the eastern side of the Sea of Galilee. But the crowds followed in hot pursuit.

Though the mobs had hounded Jesus almost daily for two years, he didn't resent this intrusion into his well-earned rest. Luke says he "welcomed them, spoke to them about the kingdom of God, and healed those who needed healing" (9:11).

Jesus was also sensitive to their need for food and asked Philip; "Where should we buy bread for them to eat?" (John 6:5)

Philip quickly calculated that two hundred denarii—equivalent today to three thousand dollars in purchasing power—could not buy enough food (v. 7). Andrew checked to see how many had brought food with them, and discovered only one small boy who had brought a lunch of five pieces of barley bread and two small pickled fish! (v. 9)

The apostles advised Jesus to send the people into town (Luke 9:12), but Jesus insisted, "You give them something to eat."

MIRACULOUS MULTIPLICATION

While they stared blankly at Jesus, he commanded the apostles to make the crowd sit down in groups of fifty and one hundred. By this time their numbers had swollen to five thousand men, plus probably an additional thousand women and children. Jesus thanked God for the boy's food, asked his blessing on it, and began distributing the boy's lunch to the apostles to give to the six thousand people.

The apostles must have thought he was crazy! Yet as each one took bread and fish from Jesus' hands, miraculously additional bread and fish were in his hands. Soon they had fed all six thousand and gathered up enough scraps to fill the twelve wicker traveling baskets the apostles carried with them (John 6:13).

As when he transformed water into wine, so Jesus again demonstrated powers possessed by the creator alone. Earlier he had altered quality—dead water became living wine. Here he showed he could alter quantity—a little food became an abundance. The two miracles proved Jesus could provide every material need his followers would require.

A TALE OF TWO KINGS

The meal on the hillside was a stark contrast to Herod's birthday feast. Herod fed nobles rich food in a palace, while Jesus fed common people barley bread in a wilderness. Herod provided sensuous entertainment, while Jesus prayed and gave thanks. Herod got drunk with his guests, while Jesus taught and healed his. Herod extinguished the first prophetic light Israel had seen in four hundred years, while Jesus unveiled the glory of God as Israel had not witnessed in fifteen hundred years. Herod's banquet demonstrated he was a worthless leader of Israel. Jesus' compassionate miracle showed he was Israel's true shepherd and worthy to be her king.

The crowds now wanted Jesus to be their king, but their motives were disastrously perverted (vv. 14, 15). They believed that Messiah's miracles would surpass those of Moses, whose greatest feat, according to Jewish tradition, was providing Israel with bread for forty years. Jesus' miraculous ability to multiply bread convinced the crowds he is the Messiah whose miracles will even excel those of Moses.

They thrilled at the propsect of marching to Jerusalem for Passover with Jesus at their head, ready to unleash his powers to break the Gentile yoke. With his kingdom established, he could miraculously fill their stomachs every day as he did that afternoon in the wilderness. They hungered for a political Messiah who brought free bread, but they lacked any appetite for his spiritual qualities which their own Scripture so emphasized.

Fearing his disciples would catch the crowd's revolutionary fever, Jesus retreated from the frenzied mob and sent the apostles back by boat to Capernaum. He went alone to a hilltop to pray, probably burdened more than ever for his stiff-necked people (Matthew 14:23).

ANOTHER STORMY CROSSING

Unfortunately, the apostles faced another stormy crossing. Their boat made little progress against a strong headwind, and by 3 A.M., after probably nine hours of rowing, they had covered only three miles. Near exhaustion and probably uneasy over Jewish superstitions of demonic spirits inhabiting the waves and manifesting themselves at night, the lonely crew suddenly saw a distant figure approaching the boat on the waters. Their panic was indescribable. They screamed with fear, certain a demon was descending on their doomed craft.

"Take courage, I am he; don't be afraid!" came reassuring words from the figure (v. 27). They could now see the figure looked like Jesus.

"Lord, since it's you, command me to come to you on the water," Peter yelled, hardly aware of what he was saying (v. 28).

"Come on!" the figure encouraged.

Peter stepped out of the boat and began walking, but as he sensed the immensity of the miracle he panicked and started to sink. "Lord, save me!" he yelled (v. 30).

Jesus reached out and pulled him up, gently chiding him, "You of little faith, why did you doubt?" They walked to the boat and got in, and suddenly the storm stopped. In a short time the craft arrived south of Capernaum, in Genessaret (v. 34).

This miracle reasserted Jesus as master over nature. During the first stormy crossing he had quieted the hostile waves. Here he defied them even more by walking over them. When he called to his disciples, "I am he," he was using an expression the Old Testament equated with diety. He had also told the Samaritan woman, "I am he" (John 4:24), and later he would tell his opponents the same (John 8:58).

But the disciples' hearts were still oblivious to the full significance of his identity (Mark 6:52). They knew he was the Messiah. They recognized his stunning miracles. But that he was the God of creation, the "I am he" of Old Testament majesty, their human comprehension could not yet grasp. It would take his resurrection from the grave to pierce through their prejudices. Then the words "I am he" in the midst of adversity would finally assure them of his supreme control of life.

IN PURSUIT OF A KING

After healing numerous men, women, and children that morning in Genessaret (Matthew 14:34-36), Jesus and his disciples went to nearby Capernaum where he entered the synagogue again—perhaps for the last time.

It was probably an informal week-night service, and perhaps scattered among the crowd were trophies of his Capernaum ministry—Jairus and his only daughter, the woman with the twelve-year hemmorhage, the centurion and his servant, Herod's nobleman and his son. But most of the audience relished thoughts of free food supplied the day before. Curious as to how Jesus had returned unnoticed, they asked as he prepared to speak, "Rabbi, when did you come here?"

"I tell you, you seek me not because you saw miracles, but because you ate the bread and were satisfied. Don't work for the food which perishes, but for the food which endures to eternal life, which the Son of Man will give you, for he is the one on whom God the Father has put his stamp of approval" (John 6:25-27).

He had read their minds like a book. They were captives of the lavish, materialistic dream of Messiah's reign then current in Israel. Their scribes pictured a kingdom of overflowing banquets, fruit trees which bore daily, wheat fields thirty feet high which could be harvested without labor, and winds which would miraculously convert grain into flour and deposit it in every home.

Picking up Jesus' mention of spiritual work, the listeners asked, "What must we habitually do to perform works pleasing to God?" (v. 28) Since Jesus had exhorted them to work for the food of eternal life, they now wanted a list of the best works to do. This typified their approach to God.

His simple answer must have dumbfounded them. "This is the work pleasing to God, to believe in the one whom he has sent" (v. 29).

TWO KINDS OF BREAD

Stubborn and persistently materialistic, the crowd raised a feeble challenge. "What miracle do you do that we may see and believe you? Our fathers ate manna in the wilderness, just as it stands written, 'He gave them bread out of heaven to eat.' "

To these cynical kingmakers, Jesus' innumerable healing miracles meant nothing. They wanted miracles like Moses' daily provision of manna, and if Jesus was truly the Messiah he must outdo that feat to gain their devotion.

Jesus tried again to focus their spiritual vision. "I tell you, Moses hasn't given you the bread out of heaven, but my Father gives you the true bread out of heaven, for God's bread is the one coming down out of heaven and giving his life to the world" (vv. 32, 33).

"Sir, give us this bread permanently," they replied (v. 34). Like the woman at the well who could not visualize spiritual water, they could not fathom spiritual bread. They thought he was talking about an exalted food akin to manna, and wanted him to provide it continuously.

Jesus responded with one of his most sublime revelations: "I am the bread of life. Whoever comes to me will never hunger, and whoever believes in me will never, ever thirst" (v. 35). He identified himself as the spiritual food and water which alone can satisfy man's spiritual cravings. Then he went on to expose their unbelief and its cause.

"But as I told you, you have seen me and yet you don't believe. All that the Father gives me will come to me, and whoever comes to me I'll never send away. . . . And this is the will of him who sent me, that I should lose none of those he has given me, but raise them up the last day" (vv. 36-38).

Once a Carpenter

In contrast to most of this Galilean audience, true believers, as God's gifts, come to him, Jesus revealed. They remain loyal to him and can never be lost. These Galileans were not to prove such gifts of God, for though they proclaimed him king one day they would reject him the next.

UNCONQUERED RESISTANCE

His words simply heated up the debate. They began to criticize him for claiming to be the heavenly bread of life. He's only the son of Joseph and Mary! (vv. 41-42)

But he continued, "Stop murmuring to each other. . . . No one can come to me except the Father who sent me draws him, and I will resurrect him on the last day. It stands written in the prophets, 'They will all be taught from God.' Everyone who listens to the Father and learns comes to me. Not that anyone has seen the Father except the one who is from God; only he has seen the Father" (vv. 41-46).

Such words could be misunderstood only by people who refused to listen. Obviously God was not "drawing" them—a word which described a pulling against resistance, as when a net draws a fish. Their resistance kept them as far as ever from God, despite the Old Testament prophecy that Israel eventually would respond. Only Jesus had seen the Father face-to-face and could tell what God is like, but they refused to listen.

Once again Jesus put God and himself on one side, his audience on the other. He told people who prided themselves in their faith, who despised pagan temples, that they didn't know God at all; for if they did, they would believe in Jesus!

THE AUDIENCE DIVIDED . . .

Now he took another swipe at their obsession with the material:

"I am the bread of life. Your fathers ate manna in the wilderness, and they died. This is the bread coming down out of heaven, that anyone may eat of it and not die. . . . If anyone eats of this bread he will live forever, and this bread is my flesh, which I will give for the life of the world" (vv. 48-50).

The audience began to argue among themselves—some in support, but most in opposition. The meaning of Jesus' word "flesh" caused the fiercest dispute (v. 52).

"I tell you, unless you eat the flesh of the Son of Man and drink his blood, you have no life in you. . . . For my flesh is real food and my blood is real drink. Whoever eats my flesh and drinks my blood remains in me and I in him. As the living Father sent me and I live because of the Father, so the one who eats me will live because of me" (vv. 53-56).

Jesus' expression was obviously figurative. He compared himself to food which must be eaten and incorporated into the body to sustain life; so he must be believed and incorporated into the human spirit to impart spiritual life. God the Father was in Jesus and sustained him; Jesus must be incorporated into human life to sustain us. No half-hearted attachment or conditional allegiance would suffice. The words describe a complete absorption into Jesus and Jesus into the believer.

AND REPULSED

But the audience by now was repulsed. "This is a harsh message, who can respond to it?" even some of his supporters said (v. 60).

Jesus prodded them, "Does this offend you? Then what if you behold the Son of Man ascending where he was before? The Spirit gives life, the flesh profits nothing. The words I have spoken to you are spirit and life. But there are some of you who don't believe" (vv. 61-64).

Jesus challenged his hearers to grasp the spirit of his words. If they were repelled by his claim to be the bread from heaven they would be convinced when they saw him resurrected and returning to heaven, Jesus said. The Holy Spirit gives life, he told them; matter, whether Moses' manna or Jesus' flesh, cannot give life, so they must see the spiritual nature of his words and not stumble over a literalistic approach.

Despite his plea, the majority of the crowds who had once followed him left that day. Jesus' claims and demands were too extravagant for them. They walked away, perhaps wondering when the fanciful Messiah of their dreams would come.

THE FEW WHO REMAINED

But the twelve apostles remained.

"Don't you also want to go?" he said to them.

"Lord, to whom shall we go? You have words of eternal life and we have believed and know that you are God's Holy One," Peter answered.

Jesus replied soberly: "Did not I choose you twelve? Yet one of you is a devil" (vv. 67-70).

This first prophecy of his betrayal applied to Judas, though the other apostles only realized it later. Jesus' words had aggravated Judas more than anyone knew. One door in his heart was closing, as he shut God out. But another door was opening. The first suggestions of betrayal were planted by Satan that evening as Judas, deeply disturbed, heard about the bread of life in the Capernaum synagogue.

This discourse precipitated Israel's third great rejection of Jesus. First the Jerusalem Pharisees had plotted his death over violation of Sabbath traditions. Then they followed him to Galilee and accused him of being in league with Satan. Both of these rejections came from the Judean religious leadership. Now the Galilean crowds turned their backs on him, too. He offended them because he claimed to be straight out of heaven, demanded total committment to himself, and, perhaps most of all because he would not allow them to live on bread alone. He insisted that the spiritual took precedence over the material.

These people were poor, they lived in one room houses with dirt floors and earned a few cents a day. They had little more than the clothes on their backs. But in their own way they were as materialistic as any

American surrounded by gadgets and luxury in his plush suburban home.

Little wonder that Paul later wrote "The love of money is a root of all kinds of evil" (I Timothy 6:10).

ELEVEN

———◆——◆———

Traditions, Traditions. . .

———◆——◆———

Twenty-five miles downstream from where the Sea of Galilee empties into the Jordan, a jubilant band of Pharisees cautiously waded across the river and continued their trek up the valley toward the cities of Tiberias and Capernaum. News that crowds were deserting the Galilean prophet had filtered to Jerusalem. This delegation, one of so many Jerusalem had sent, finally hoped to entrap Jesus; and with his popularity waning, they appeared at least to have a chance.

Not long after their arrival in Capernaum, an opportunity appeared. They observed that Jesus' followers, for whose actions he could be held responsible, violated one of the most sacred Pharisaic traditions—ritual handwashing.

The Old Testament taught that certain situations rendered an Israelite ceremonially impure, so he could not engage in temple worship. The pollution was removed through a prescribed washing of hands, the whole body, or an animal sacrifice. The priests also practiced ritual handwashing or bathing on specified occasions.

But from these comparatively simple instructions the ingenious Pharisees again built a mountain of rules which far surpassed anything their ancestors had

123

dreamed of. Israelites in good standing must wash their hands before, sometimes during, and after every meal in a carefully regulated fashion. They must use special water, usually preserved in large stone jars. At least one and one half eggshells of water were poured on the hands with fingers pointed upward so the water trickled to the wrists. With the hands wet, the palm of one was rubbed with the fist of the other. Then the hands were washed again to clean off the first water, now considered polluted. This time the fingers must be held down so the unclean water would not run back down the hands.

THE CLEANEST PEOPLE ON EARTH

Nor was this all. Mark's Gospel adds, "When they return from the market place they don't eat unless they wash, and they cling to many other traditions such as the washing of cups, and utensils, and copper vessels" (7:2, 3). At the marketplace an Israelite might accidentally touch a Gentile or an object owned by a Gentile. To remove contamination he had to go through an extremely thorough handwashing when he returned home. Furthermore, if a ceremonially unclean person, animal, or piece of food touched an object, the object must be discarded or cleansed according to strict rules. A hollow vessel of pottery which became contaminated, for example, must be broken, and no broken piece must remain which was big enough to hold enough oil to anoint the little toe!

All of this was done with the utmost seriousness. One rabbi was buried in excommunication because he questioned these rules. Another, imprisoned by the Romans, nearly died of thirst because he used his water ration for handwashing rather than drinking. The faithful were taught that to neglect handwashing opened them up to special attacks from a demon named Shibta; and the Talmud, reflecting the importance of such practices, warned: "He who lightly esteems handwashing will perish from the earth."

THOSE TRADITIONS . . .

"Why are your disciples not following the tradition of the elders, but eat bread with uncleansed hands?" the Pharisees demanded of Jesus (v. 5).

"Isaiah prophesied well concerning you hypocrites," Jesus retorted, " 'This people honor me with their lips, but their heart is far away from me. Their worship of me is useless. They teach what are only commandments of men.' "

Jesus accused the Pharisees of substituting tradition for Scripture—the voice of man for the voice of God. Their complex regulations sprang from human cleverness not divine revelation. What was worse, their traditions forced Israel to violate God's will, as Jesus proceeded to show.

"You beautifully set aside God's commandment that you may keep your tradition. For Moses said, 'Honor your father and your mother,' and, 'Whoever curses father or mother, let him die.' But you say that if a man says to his father or mother, "Whatever you might get from me is corban (i.e., devoted to God),' you no longer allow him to do anything for his father or mother, nullifying the word of God by your tradition which you received, and you do many similar things" (vv. 9-13).

Jesus referred to an ancient custom called "the ban." When someone wished to forbid usage of his property or goods to another, he placed them under a ban. Jews could pronounce a ban by declaring their property "corban," an Aramaic word which meant "dedicated to God." The property, of course, was not really dedicated to God. The owner continued to use it for himself—he simply had forbidden its usage by persons who were objects of the ban.

During heated family squabbles, grown children might resort to such bans to prohibit their parents from further use of the children's possessions. They might even forbid parents to come on their property. Pharisaic tradition taught that once such bans were pronounced, they could never be removed, even if the children later repented. They reasoned that vows should be kept, even they could never be removed, even if the children later repented. They reasoned that vows should be kept, even if keeping them violated the commandments of God! Jesus exposed their glaring hypocrisy. They carefully observed Scripture's minutiae while they casually violated its great commandments.

THE OUTSIDE AND THE INSIDE

Turning back to the crowd, Jesus added: "Nothing outside a man which enters him can pollute him. But what comes out of a man is what pollutes him" (v. 15). Later he spelled this out to his disciples:

"Nothing on the outside entering a man pollutes him because it enters his stomach, not his heart, and then leaves his body. . . . What comes out of a man pollutes him. For from within, out of peoples' hearts, come terrible thoughts, immorality, stealing, murder, adultery, greed, evil, deceit, lewdness, envy, blasphemy, arrogance, and stupidity. All these evils come from within and pollute a man" (vv. 18-23).

Jesus assaulted religious externalism—the twin brother of traditionalism. The Pharisees put excessive emphasis on dietary laws just as they did on purification rules. The dietary laws originally had certain health benefits, for they prohibited Jews from eating pork—a notorious vehicle of illness in those times. They also helped keep Israel a distinct people who could not easily intermix with pagan culture. But the zealous scribes found forty-nine different reasons for declaring each animal clean or unclean, and pronounced seven hundred species of fish and twenty-four kinds of birds unclean. Dietary laws became a national cause for which any good Israeli was expected to lay down his life, and many did.

Jesus ripped this mentality to shreds by declaring the obvious truth that the heart, not the stomach, is the source of evil, and that real pollution is moral and spiritual, not ceremonial and physical.

Once again Jesus and the Pharisees took irreconcilable positions. For them, piety was achieved by appearance,

ence to God's will from the heart. Jesus' determined opposition to their traditions made it clear to the Pharisees that they must destroy him before his teaching destroyed them. Unfortunately, the Pharisees' emphasis on traditions and externals was not unique to them, for most religions still dwell on outward forms.

THE LIGHT DEPARTS

Since the crowds had deserted him and the Pharisees were heightening their attacks, Jesus left Galilee for the Gentile area near Tyre and Sidon, on the Mediterranean Sea. His departure was a silent judgment on Galilee. During the remainder of his ministry he spent little time within its borders. He instead spent concentrated hours with the twelve, ministered to audiences of Jews and Gentiles on the fringes of Israel, and made strategic trips to Jerusalem for religious festivals. The Galileans who walked in spiritual darkness had seen the great light—but most preferred their darkness so Jesus left them in it.

In the vicinity of Tyre, Jesus and his disciples obtained the private use of a house. There a Gentile woman from the area kept badgering him and the disciples to heal her demon-possessed daughter. At first Jesus gave her a puzzling reply: "Allow the children first to be satisfied, for it isn't good to take the children's bread and throw it to the dogs" (v. 27).

He meant that he was called to minister to Israel—the children—and they must be fed first. Only *after* they were satisfied should the message be taken to the Gentiles, pictured as the household pets.

The ardent woman agreed and disagreed: "Yes, Lord; yet the dogs under the table eat of the children's crumbs" (v. 28). She refused to take no for an answer, and turned the illustration around to her own benefit, insisting he could meet her need *now.*

His temporary refusal drew out her persistence and faith, and Jesus granted her request. What a heart-warming contrast she was to the super-orthodox Pharisees

Jesus had just left! They relentlessly pursued him to trap him; she sought him just as earnestly out of faith. Jesus delighted in responding to the downtrodden, such as this pagan woman, while he resisted Israel's proud and self-satisfied religious leaders.

A SPECIAL TOUCH

Leaving the area of Tyre and Sidon Jesus went to Decapolis on the eastern side of the Sea of Galilee. There great crowds to whom he had not ministered before waited. They were a mixture of Jews and Gentiles. A deaf man who had an accompanying speech impediment was brought for healing (v. 32). Jesus took him aside, put his fingers in his ears, touched his tongue with saliva, and sighed toward heaven, "Be opened." Immediately the man heard and spoke normally. Jesus used touch—adapting his method to the need—since the man couldn't hear his words.

ANOTHER WILDERNESS BANQUET

The miracle only made the crowds grow. Jesus retreated from the towns to wilderness areas, but the crowds still swelled. After three days of teaching and healing in the wilderness, Jesus told his disciples, "I feel compassion for the crowd because they have stayed with me three days and have nothing to eat, and if I send them home without food, some of them will faint on the way, for some of them are from far off" (Mark 8:1, 2).

The disciples should have recalled his feeding of five thousand with a few pieces of bread and some fish, but perhaps they never dreamed he would repeat it, so they weakly replied, "Where in this wilderness can anyone get enough bread to satisfy them?" (v. 4)

Jesus saw that the disciples had small pieces of bread and a few fish, so he seated the crowd and proceeded to repeat his great miracle of multiplying food—this time four thousand were present (vv. 8, 9).

Why did Jesus repeat this miracle? Probably because

the first crowd was mostly Jewish and the second largely Gentile. Jesus wished his disciples to grasp that he was the bread of God for the whole world. He had undermined the dietary laws which separated Jews and Gentiles in his recent controversy with the Pharisees. Now he provided a whole meal for those normally considered unclean. Later the book of Acts records that God gave Peter a vision of food forbidden under the dietary laws but now pronounced clean (Acts 10:15), which symbolized that God had removed the barrier between Jew and Gentile. Probably this made Peter recall and finally understand this great Gentile feast in the wilderness.

BLIND AND DULL

Jesus and his disciples departed from the enthusiastic Gentiles for the Jewish side of the Sea of Galilee. There the Pharisees were waiting, ready to spring another trap. They demanded "a miracle out of heaven" to prove he is the Messiah (Matthew 16:1).

They considered all his miracles so far as only "earthly miracles." Now they wish a "heavenly miracle," such as Elijah's calling down fire from heaven. Jesus denounced their spiritual blindness. "When evening comes you say 'fair weather,' for the sky is red and clear, and in the morning, 'stormy weather,' for the sky is red and overcast. You know how to discern the appearance of the sky, but you can't discern the signs of the times" (vv. 2, 3). They understood the significance of weather signs, but not the significance of Messianic signs!

Leaving the Pharisees via the lake, Jesus pondered the animosity of his enemies. He told his disciples: "Beware of the yeast of the Pharisees and Sadducees" (v. 6). Since yeast or leaven usually symbolized evil, Jesus warned against the evils of his enemies, lest their viewpoints should infiltrate the disciple band.

But the disciples were anxious over another problem. They had forgotten to take food for the trip, so they supposed he was warning them not to purchase bread made with the same kind of yeast used by the Pharisees and Sadducees! Instead of absorbing his profound insights, they were worried over where they would get their next meal. Jesus reprimanded them.

" 'Don't you yet understand or realize? Have your hearts been hardened? Don't you see with your eyes and hear with your ears? When I gave the five pieces of bread to the five thousand, how many baskets full of fragments did you take?'

'Twelve,' they said to him.

'When I gave the seven to the four thousand, how many baskets full of fragments did you take?'

'Seven,' they said.

'Don't you yet understand?' he said to them" (Mark 8:17-21).

The miracles of the wilderness meals should have convinced the disciples they would never go hungry while traveling with Jesus. But they were too bound by the worries of everyday existence to rise to the higher, freer life he had for them.

THE TWICE-TOUCHED MAN

The boat docked at Bethsaida on the northeast corner of the lake, and Jesus was promptly confronted by men leading a blind man. They asked expectantly that Jesus heal him. Jesus took him outside of town, put saliva on his eyes, and touched them.

"Do you see anything?" Jesus asked (v. 23).

"I see people who are like trees walking" he replied. Jesus again touched his eyes, and then he saw clearly (v. 25). Jesus sent him home, directing him not to tell anyone in the village.

Jesus apparently was intent on avoiding the crowds who sought only physical well being. But he took time to minister to the needy man thrust in his path. On no other occasion did Jesus heal a man in two stages. His use of touch and saliva, and the two stages of healing probably helped to build the man's faith. He became vividly aware of Jesus' power as hope leaped with gradual improvement in his sight.

Perhaps Jesus also intended a lesson for his disciples.

In the boat he had accused them of being spiritually blind. As he restored this man's sight in stages, perhaps he was illustrating that they were only half tuned in spiritually. They needed a second touch from Jesus before they would clearly perceive truth. That touch would come at his death and resurrection, now less than a year away.

A HOTBED OF PAGANISM

Leaving the former blind man, Jesus and the twelve trooped straight north twenty-five miles, beyond the borders of Galilee to the environs of Caesarea Philippi. Here they were temporarily beyond reach of hostile Judean Pharisees and fickle Galilean crowds, for they were in the most pagan location the disciples had ever visited.

The area was dotted with Syrian temples of the god Baal, while from the midst of the city rose a great, gleaming white structure dedicated to the deity of Caesar. The Greeks considered a nearby cavern the birthplace of Pan, the mythological god of nature—so streams of Asian, Roman, and Greek religions converged here.

In a setting where such superstition reigned, the Galilean carpenter gathered his apostles around him and asked, "Who do people say the Son of Man is?" (Matthew 16:13)

"Some say John the Baptist; others, Elijah; and others, Jeremiah or one of the prophets," they answered, reflecting the current Jewish superstitions that Jesus was one of Israel's great heroes resurrected (v. 14).

"Who do *you* say I am?" he asked.

"You are the Messiah, the Son of the living God!" Peter blurted out (v. 16).

The apostle's first confession of Jesus as Messiah, two years before, had been tested to the limits because Jesus had behaved so differently from Peter's preconceived notions. Yet the seed of faith survived and Peter now confessed Jesus not only as Messiah but as the supernatural Son of the living God.

131

THE NEW COMMUNITY

"Happy are you, Simon, son of Jonas, because flesh and blood didn't reveal this to you, but my Father in heaven! And I also say to you, you are Peter, and on this rock I will build my community, and the gates of death will not conquer it. I will give you the keys of the kingdom of heaven, and whatever you bind on earth shall have been bound in heaven, and whatever you loose on earth shall have been loosed in heaven" (vv. 17-20).

Rarely did Jesus pack so much meaning into such few words. He told the apostles he would build a new "community." He had taught that he would delay bringing in his kingdom because of Israel's rejection, so it made sense for him to raise up a new community of followers during this delay, a community of followers beyond Israel. This new community, Jesus said, would be indestructible—even death could not swallow and hold its members. Later the apostles would understand that this new community was the church. As the New Testament uses the word church, of course, it never refers to a building or denomination, but simply to the people who trust in Jesus—whether Jews or Gentiles.

Then Jesus said that Peter, whose name meant "rock," would be the rock on whom the church rested. This did not mean that Peter was the only rock on which the church would rest, however, for Paul describes Jesus as being "the chief cornerstone" and the other apostles, as well as the New Testament prophets, as being part of the foundation too (Ephesians 2:20). Although Peter was not the only rock, he was a major one. The book of Acts records Peter's great Pentecostal sermon which ushered the church into existence, and throughout its early history he is one of its key leaders.

THE KEYS TO THE KINGDOM

Jesus also promised Peter the keys to the kingdom of heaven. In those times owners of large houses entrusted keys to house managers who would open doors to whomever the owner desired. On the day of Pentecost, Peter's bold sermon opened the doors of God's kingdom for three thousand Jews who believed in Jesus. Later, when Peter preached at the house of Cornelius the centurion, he opened the doors to the first of vast numbers of Gentiles. Today any believer also opens the doors of God's kingdom when he leads others to faith in Jesus.

Then Peter was told whatever he would bind or loose on earth would be bound or loosed in heaven. "Binding" and "loosing" were rabbinic phrases meaning to prohibit or permit. Peter would make decisions for God's new community which would prohibit or permit certain practices and determine its direction through the age. Later Jesus gave this power to the other apostles as well (Matthew 18:18). The book of Acts shows Peter and the other apostles making such important decisions under the guidance of the Holy Spirit. One of their key decision was that Gentiles did not have to follow the Jewish law (Acts 15).

Peter probably expected Jesus to commend him for his faith, but that such inestimable privileges should be heaped on him and the other apostles over this simple confession must have staggered him. Because of this they were utterly unprepared for Jesus' next announcement.

"From then on Jesus the Messiah began to show his disciples that he must go to Jerusalem and suffer many things from the elders and chief priests and scribes, and be killed and on the third day be raised" (Matthew 16:21).

THE NEW REVELATION

This was Jesus' first clear declaration of his coming death and resurrection. The idea was so foreign to these men that Peter instantly protested: "This won't happen to you!" (v. 22)

What a bundle of contradictions Peter was! One minute he confessed Jesus as Son of the living God. The next minute he thought Jesus didn't know what he was talking about. But Jesus, who had just lavishly praised Peter, now sternly rebuked him. He accused Peter of being the instrument of Satan himself by making such a

133

statement. Peter and the others still shared too much of the crowds' Messianic dream of glory. Jesus warned them to forget their visions of grandeur and face the cost of following him.

"If anyone wants to come after me, let him deny himself and take his cross and follow me," Jesus said. "For whoever wants to save his life will lose it, and whoever loses his life for me will find it. For what will it benefit if a man gains the whole world and loses his life? Or what will a man give as exchange for his life? For the Son of Man will come in his Father's glory with his angels, and then he will reward each man according to his conduct" (vv. 24-27).

As Jesus was willing to die to save his followers, so he demanded that they be willing to give up their own plans in order to follow him. As he had to carry the cross on which he was crucified, so they must be willing to carry whatever crosses God places on them. If such self-denial seems too much to ask, their self-indulgence can cause them to lose out forever in the future. Then he asked one of the most profound questions of all time: Can all the wealth of the world compensate for a life lost for eternity? When Jesus returns in all his glory and asks an accounting of every person, what will the one who rejected Jesus do then?

THE CENTERPIECE OF HISTORY

Again Jesus had spoken incredible truths to his followers. Surrounded by dead idols of the past, he assured them he was the Son of the living God. But he must die, then rise again, and establish a new community of God's people which they would lead. He warned them they must face sacrifice and death. He prophesied he would come a second time and hold all men accountable. Once more the carpenter of Galilee was claiming to be the centerpiece of history.

His words were either the words of the Son of the living God, or the words of a madman. His claims were so vast, his predictions so far reaching, his call to dedication so encompassing that nothing else could explain him.

TWELVE

— ◆ ◆ —

Lessons Never Forgotten

— ◆ ◆ —

The view was magnificent. Before them the whole land of Israel was spread out—the Sea of Galilee; the Jordan River twisting down to the Dead Sea, earth's lowest spot; the hills which stretched like a backbone down the center of the country; and the costal Plain of Sharon with beaches washed by the blue Mediterranean. Above them towered the nine thousand foot summit of Mount Hermon, dotted with patches of snow even in summer.

James, Peter, and John were accompanying Jesus from Caesarea Philippi part way up adjacent Mount Hermon. Even in Gentile territory, crowds had thronged Jesus and he felt the need for solitude. As the sun set that evening, the travel-weary disciples dozed off while Jesus devoted himself to prayer.

Suddenly the disciples awoke to a blaze of light. Jesus' body began to shine with blinding brightness. Two men appeared and began to talk with him. From the conversation, the amazed disciples learned he was talking with Moses and Elijah about his approaching death (Luke 9:31).

The disciples had witnessed many miracles of Jesus, but never had they beheld such a spectacular scene as this! Yet when Jesus finished his discourse at Caesarea Philippi a few days previously, he had mysteriously prophesied, "I tell you there are some standing here who will not taste death until they see the kingdom of God come with power" (Mark 9:1). The disciples, of course, thought he was speaking of the immediate establishment of his kingdom. But he was really prophesying that they would get a "sneak preview" of his second coming in this dazzling event, known as the transfiguration. Jesus later said that his second coming would be "with power and great glory" (Matthew 24:30), and that power and glory were manifest in miniature on lonely Mount Hermon this night.

A PREVIEW OF COMING ATTRACTIONS

What were Moses and Elijah doing on Mount Hermon? The book of Revelation, written by a witness of the transfiguration—John, describes two illustrious figures who arise in Israel at the end of history, just before the return of Jesus (Revelation 11:2-12). Their ministries resemble Elijah, because they prevent rain for three and one half years and call down fire from heaven as the rugged prophet did during his ministry. They also resemble Moses, because they turn water into blood and summon plagues, as the great lawgiver did in Egypt.

These two men will either be a literal reappearance of Elijah and Moses, or two figures like them, as John the Baptist was like Elijah. How appropriate that two of Israel's greatest heroes should appear at this preview of Jesus' second coming!

Peter, James, and John were overwhelmed. Peter, who usually spoke first and thought second, exclaimed, "Rabbi, it's good we are here. Let's make three shelters—one for you, one for Moses, and one for Elijah (Mark 9:5). Peter evidently thought that God was inaugurating his heavenly kingdom on earth at this moment. Since Moses had remained on Mount Sinai to receive visions and revelations, it seemed fitting that the six of them should remain on Mount Hermon for several weeks of heavenly visions, then return down the mountain to take over Israel and the world.

But Peter made two mistakes. He could not grasp that they were speaking of Jesus' actual death. The transfiguration was only a momentary display—before Jesus set up his kingdom he must *die*. Then Peter seemed to put Moses, Elijah, and Jesus all on one level—each was to have a shelter, each would have his say as the enraptured disciples listened.

Impulsive, wholehearted Peter was never allowed to bask long in his blunders. After his outburst a cloud enveloped them and a voice thundered, "This is my Son, whom I love, listen to him" (v. 7). Abruptly the cloud disappeared, Moses and Elijah vanished, and Jesus resumed his normal appearance.

JUST A CLEVER STORY?

This was probably the most "mind-blowing" experience the three disciples had ever known. Even as they walked down the mountain they must have pinched themselves to make sure it was real. Yet over thirty years later Peter wrote: "For we were not following cleverly devised tales when we made known to you the power and coming of our Lord Jesus the Messiah, but we were eyewitnesses of his majesty. For he received honor and glory from God the Father when the voice came to him from the Magnificent Glory, 'This is my Son, whom I love; with him I am pleased.' This voice that came from heaven we ourselves heard when we were with him on the sacred mountain" (2 Peter 1:16-18).

In Peter's two New Testament letters this is the only experience with Jesus that he mentions. It is so remarkable he could never forget it. Because it seems unbelievable, he assured his readers that it is not some clever story, but an actual event which he *saw* and *heard*. Especially vivid was that voice which said Jesus is God's Son to whom he should listen—for Peter had tried to put Moses and Elijah on Jesus' level. The transfiguration is one more event the Gospels recount to prove the supernaturalness of Jesus.

FROM MOUNTAIN TO VALLEY

As Jesus and the three disciples came down the mountain the next day, he warned them not to broadcast this experience until after his death and resurrection. He did not want to inflame the crowds with false hopes that the Messianic reign was just around the corner. He also explained again to them that John the Baptist was a preliminary fulfillment of the Old Testament prophecy about Elijah (Mark 9:9-13). But they grasped little of what he said about his death and resurrection. If anything, the transfiguration intensified their expectation for the all-conquering Messianic reign.

But when they reached the valley below, they were jolted back into reality. They found the other nine disciples surrounded by a crowd which included some scribes who had traveled into this despised Gentile area in another attempt to trap Jesus. In the midst of the crowd was a demon-possessed boy and his distraught father. The disciples had been unable to exorcise the demon, and the scribes were denouncing them.

As Jesus began to question the grieving father, he discovered another example of the ravages of the demonic. The evil spirit paralyzed the boy's speech and caused him to fall on the ground, foaming at the mouth in an epileptic type of fit. The demon's destructive power had driven the boy to attempt to burn or drown himself repeatedly.

When Jesus saw that his disciples were helpless before this demon, he exclaimed, "O faithless generation, how long shall I be with you?" (v. 19)

Then the father said,"If you can do anything, have compassion on us and help us."

"If you can?" Jesus replied. "Everything is possible to the one who believes" (v. 23).

"I believe, help my unbelief!" the desperate man pleaded.

Then Jesus cast out the demon and gave the boy, now whole, to the thankful father.

After the crowds departed, the disciples asked why they were unable to drive out the demon. "This kind

Once a Carpenter

comes out only by prayer" he answered (v. 29). In Matthew's account Jesus also said their lack of faith had hindered them (17:20).

The incident stresses the importance of a present, active faith in Jesus. When the father said *"If you can,"* he showed that he doubted Jesus could help. Jesus forced him to come up with at least a half-way faith. The disciples probably assumed they could help the man because they had cast out demons before. Though they had believed on those occasions, they did not have sufficient faith for this occasion, and failed. They were without excuse, for their previous successes should have increased their belief. Instead they rested on the laurels of the past and came up short in the present.

BACK TO CAPERNAUM

Jesus returned with the twelve to Galilee and again told them of his upcoming death and resurrection, which they again failed to understand (Mark 9:30-32). When they reached Capernaum, local tax collectors accosted Peter and asked if Jesus paid the annual "half shekel" tax—equivalent to about forty dollars in today's inflated economy (Matthew 17:24). The half shekel tax, collected by Israel to support the temple, was unrelated to Roman taxation.

Peter replied that of course Jesus did, then returned to the house where Jesus was staying. There Jesus told him this story:

"What do you think, Simon? Do the kings of the earth collect duties and taxes from their own sons or from outsiders?"

"From outsiders," Peter answered.

"Then the sons are free. But so we won't offend them, go to the sea, put in a hook, take the first fish that comes up, and when you open its mouth you will find a shekel. Take it and pay them for you and me" (vv. 25-27).

Matthew alone records this story, for as an ex-tax collector it especially caught his interest. In those days no son of a king ever paid taxes to his own father. Jesus informed Peter that as God's Son he was not expected to help pay for his Father's temple. But since Israel did not receive him as God's Son, his refusal to pay the tax would be taken as rebellion against his nation, so Jesus told Peter to pay the tax. Jesus did not hesitate to offend his nation when he encountered erroneous Pharisaic teaching, because he wanted to awaken them to the truth. But he did not oppose legitimate practices such as the temple tax, even though he did not approve of all that went on in the temple. His followers later faced heavy taxations by a corrupt Nero, but Paul, following Jesus' example, instructed them to pay (Romans 13:7). They were to be spiritual, not political revolutionaries.

"MAKE ME A CHILD AGAIN!"

Perhaps while Peter was gone to catch the fish, Jesus began discussing with the other disciples what was to them a crucial issue—which one of them would have the highest position in Messiah's kingdom. Obviously all that he had said about death for him and presecution for them had gone unheeded. The master teacher placed a little child on his lap and said:

"I tell you, unless you turn and become as little children, you absolutely can't enter the kingdom of heaven. Therefore, whoever humbles himself as this child is greatest in the kingdom of heaven. And whoever welcomes one such child in my name welcomes me. And whoever ensnares one of these little ones who believe in me, it would be better for him to have a great millstone hung around his neck and be drowned in the depth of the sea. Woe to the world because of its snares! For it is necessary for them to come, but woe to the man through whom they come. . . . See that you don't despise one of these little ones, for I tell you that their angels in heaven always behold the face of my Father in heaven" (Matthew 18:3-10).

Small children know little of the ambitions and prejudices of adult life. The child of a king will gladly play with the child of a beggar. Jesus strikingly sets this childlike helplessness and humility over against the arrogance and ambition of his disciples. Furthermore, Jesus says the disciples must welcome those believers who, like children, are weak and without social position, for to welcome such an insignificant believer is to welcome Jesus, and to lead such a one astray is disastrous. The great circular millstone Jesus referred to, used to grind grain, was so heavy only a large animal could turn it. Moreover, Jesus declared that these unnoticed, apparently insignificant believers even have angels assigned for their care. Such angels are among the most important in the angelic realm, for they are in God's presence continuously.

Wealth and social position loomed large in the ancient world, as in ours. Ambition and pride were admired while modesty and humility were despised. Yet Jesus spoke of a kingdom where the humble would be exalted and the proud would be excluded, where money would be meaningless, and earthly social divisions would vanish. His teaching was revolutionary in the deepest sense—the world's treasured values were overturned. Whether they knew it or not, the poor and helpless had found a true champion in Jesus.

GUILTY LOOKS AMONG THE APOSTLES

Jesus' warning against pride and ambition caused some guilty looks among the disciples. "Teacher, we saw someone casting out demons in your name and we stopped him because he wasn't following us," John confessed, suspecting they had made a mistake (Mark 9:38).

"Don't stop him, for no one who does a miracle in my name can the next minute speak against me. For whoever is not against us is for us," Jesus explained (vv. 39, 40).

The apostles dreamed they were an exclusive group. They couldn't imagine Jesus' power operating outside their select company, yet they were powerless to exorcise the demon from the boy, while this unknown believer was driving out one demon after another.

Jesus told them that anyone channeling his power

must be on their side. Those who encounter Jesus' claims and power in its fullness will either oppose him or follow him. Failure to oppose means they will follow. The apostles needed a more tolerant and perceptive spirit, devoid of selfish suspicion.

Jesus repeated some earlier instructions, then concluded by stating: "Everyone shall be salted with fire. . . . Have salt in yourselves and be at peace with one another" (vv. 49, 50). The Old Testament commanded that all animal sacrifices be salted before they were acceptable. Jesus described his followers as those whose lives would become acceptable to God as they were "salted with fire"—purified through trials and discipline from God. Suffering, not immediate rewards, lay directly ahead of them.

As salt was symbolic of purity, the disciples were to banish their self-seeking motives so they could cooperate and live in peace with each other. Before these men could lead Jesus' movement, their foolish pride must be purified. The events of the next year, unknown to them, would accomplish this, as they would be "salted with fire" more than once.

THE SINNING BROTHER

Jesus shifted from the sinfulness of his own followers to their treatment of sinning members in the new community he would establish. Whereas egotism foments harsh attitudes toward others, humility fosters a forgiving spirit.

"If your brother sins, go and correct him in private. If he listens, you have won your brother. But if he won't listen, take one or two with you. . . . But if he refuses to hear them, tell it to the believing community, and if he refuses to hear them, let him be to you as the pagan or the tax collector. . . . I tell you that if two of you agree on earth concerning what you ask, it shall be done for them by my Father who is in heaven. For where two or three are gathered in my name, there I am in their midst" (Matthew 18:15-20).

Here Jesus laid out a tolerant, wise and orderly plan

for disciplining a sinning brother. The wronged individual was first to seek direct remedy in private, then if necessary to go with two or three, and only as a last resort publicly to involve the local assembly of believers. The offender had three chances to repent before he could be cut off from the believing community. Believers should not fear to enforce such discipline, Jesus taught, because when accompanied by prayer it would be guided and ratified from heaven. God would be at work in the midst of his people, even when they number but two or three.

FOUR HUNDRED AND NINETY FORGIVENESSES!

This caused Peter to ask, "Lord, how often will my brother sin against me and I forgive him? As many as seven times?" (v. 21)

Peter was bothered because a guilty party could obtain forgiveness so easily by Jesus' method. He wondered if it had limits. The scribes taught that if a sinning Jew repented his friends should forgive him only three times. Peter generously increased it to seven.

Jesus answered:

"Therefore the kingdom of heaven resembles a king who wished to settle accounts with his servants, and as he began to settle them, a man was brought to him who owed over one billion dollars. And as he was unable to pay, the master ordered that he and his wife and his children and all that he had be sold for payment.

"The servant fell down before him, saying, 'Be patient with me, and I will repay you everything.' The master had compassion on that slave, released him and forgave him the debt. But the servant went out and found one of his fellow servants who owed him two thousand dollars and seized him and began to choke him, saying, 'Pay back what you owe.'

"His fellow servant fell down and entreated him, saying, 'Be patient and I will repay you.' But he was unwilling and went and threw him into prison until he repaid what he owed. . . .

"Then the master summoned him and said, 'You evil

servant, all that debt I forgave you since you entreated me. Shouldn't you also have pitied your fellow slave as I pitied you?' And since he was angry his master handed him over to the torturers until he should repay everything. So also will my heavenly Father do to you unless each of you forgives his brother from your heart" (vv. 22-35).

A ONE BILLION DOLLAR DEBT

Forgiveness limited to a certain number was no forgiveness, Jesus indicated. He reinforced the point with a striking parable. A servant owed the king "ten thousand talents," according to the original Greek. The talent was a unit of money equal to six thousand days' wages. If we translate this into our modern economy, with a days' wage of twenty dollars, ten thousand talents amounts to over one billion dollars!

What servant could have owed one billion dollars? Jesus exaggerated the amount to dramatize the immense moral debt each man owes God. The king's forgiveness of the huge debt symbolizes God forgiving us. The servant who refused to forgive his fellow servant a comparatively small amount pictures the bitter, hate-filled person who has not understood the immensity of God's forgiveness. Such a man does not genuinely believe and in the parable suffers punishment from the "torturers"—a picture of eternal destruction.

Yet God's forgiveness was still largely theoretical for the apostles. But shortly they would see their master hanging on a cross and then would begin to grasp the depths of the divine pardon.

INVALUABLE HOURS

Jesus' retreat into the outlying areas was over. His appointed destiny in Jerusalem was drawing close. But the hours he had spent with the twelve were not wasted. He had spectacularly displayed his deity. He had showed them their constant need for faith. He had taught them about the living community he would establish and the revolutionary principles of his kingdom. He had exalted humility, self-forgetfulness, love, and forgiveness by illustrating them in his life.

A new people was in the making—a worldwide family that would challenge the insolence, greed, and tyranny which have so dominated history.

THIRTEEN

◆ ◆

The Smartest People
can be Stupid

◆ ◆

The greatest Jewish festival of the year was the Feast of Tabernacles. This October celebration concluded the agricultural year, and the people gladly left the rocky fields where they had labored through the summer heat to travel to Jerusalem for the festival. The feast commemorated God's provision for Israel in the wilderness and his continuing provision of rain and crops in the preceeding year. One hundred and fifty thousand pilgrims packed into the city for the most joyous occasion on the religious calendar.

Jesus' brothers encouraged him to attend the Feast of Tabernacles and resume his public ministry in Jerusalem. "Leave here and go into Judea in order that your disciples may see the miracles you're doing. For no one who seeks to be known publicly keeps working in secret. Since you're doing these things, show yourself to the world!" (John 7:3,4).

Jesus had spent several weeks in Jerusalem at the beginning of his ministry and he went again during Passover and healed the man at the pool of Bethesda. But most of his time had been devoted to Galileen towns, and lately he had even avoided them. His brothers couldn't fathom this. A man of Jesus' signifi-

Once a Carpenter

146

cance should spend his time in the capital where the great rabbis were.

"My opportunity has not yet come," Jesus told them. "But any time is all right for you. The world cannot hate you. But it hates me because I testify that its works are evil. You go up now to the feast. I am not yet going up to this feast, because my opportunity has not yet come" (vv. 7, 8).

Jesus' brothers posed no threat to the religious leaders, but the carpenter-teacher was a marked man in Jerusalem. He must carefully choose the time to encounter his enemies.

NO WELCOME MATS HERE

After his brothers had left, Jesus and his disciples started toward Jerusalem privately through Samaria. He had planned all along to attend the feast, but quite differently from the public manner which his brothers suggested. He sent some of the disciples ahead to a Samaritan village to secure accommodations, but they found the Samaritans unwilling to show hospitality to a group of Jews going to the temple.

Reporting back to Jesus, James and John raged: "Lord, do you want us to call down fire from heaven to consume them?" (Luke 9:54).

The hot-tempered brothers arrogantly assumed they had power to bring down such judgment even though Jesus never used his power to retaliate. They got a stinging rebuke from Jesus (v. 55).

FAIRWEATHER FOLLOWERS

As Jesus continued the journey he encountered Jewish pilgrims along the route. Realizing he had little time left to offer the gospel, Jesus invited various ones to follow him. "I will follow you wherever you go," one said with great enthusiasm (v. 58).

But Jesus apparently detected that the man was looking for the rewards of the Messianic kingdom rather

147

than the persecution which was bearing down on him and the apostles. "The foxes have holes and the birds of the air have nests, but the Son of Man has nowhere to lay his head," Jesus answered (v. 58). The animals had homes, but Jesus, like a hunted criminal, had been rejected in Samaria, before that in Galilee, and soon would be executed in Jerusalem.

"Let me first go and bury my father," another man bargained (v. 60).

"Let the dead bury their own dead, and go and announce the kingdom of God," Jesus replied.

The man was not asking to bury a father who had just died, but to follow Jesus after his aged father finally passed away—perhaps years off. Jesus advised that other family members with no spiritual interest could handle that task.

Yet another responded, "I'll follow you, Lord, but first allow me to return and say goodbye to my family."

"No one who puts his hand to the plow and looks back is fit for God's kingdom," Jesus said, discerning his reluctance (vv. 61, 62). The man wanted a lengthy and grand farewell—evidence that his heart was more with his family than with Jesus. A man who plows, like a man who drives a car, can only look forward. This man wanted to cling to his past.

These encounters showed again how far apart Jesus and his nation were. The sacrifice, dedication, and urgency of his call were incomprehensible to many in Israel.

WHO WAS REALLY IGNORANT?

When Jesus arrived in Jerusalem he laid low for a few days while the crowds sought to locate the controversial prophet. Suddenly in the middle of the feast Jesus entered the temple area and began to teach the people. The listening Pharisees scoffed: "How does this man know Scripture without any education?" (John 7:15) Jesus had studied under none of the Jerusalem rabbis. The Pharisees considered him no more than a common peasant.

"My teaching is not mine, but from the one who sent me. If anyone wants to do his will, he will know concerning the teaching, whether it is of God or whether I speak only from myself," Jesus answered (vv. 16, 17).

Jesus lacked rabbinic education, but his statements proved repeatedly that he knew Scripture better than his challengers. He had gotten his doctrine straight from God, and any man who submitted to God would submit to Jesus' instruction.

"I did one miracle and you are all startled," he continued. "Because Moses has given you circumcision . . . you circumcise a man even on the Sabbath. If a man receives circumcision on a Sabbath in order that Moses' law may not be broken, why are you upset with me because I healed a whole man on a Sabbath? Stop judging according to surface appearances, but judge with righteous judgment" (vv. 21-24).

By healing the man at the Bethesda pool on a Sabbath Jesus incurred the Pharisees' wrath. But they circumcised the eighth day from birth, even when that day fell on Sabbaths, so restoring an entire body on the Sabbath should receive their approval.

A DRAMATIC EVENT

This stirred the controversy all the more, with the crowds lining up pro or con concerning Jesus. Deciding on drastic action, the Pharisees sent temple police to arrest him and end their problems. But as the guards were about to seize Jesus, one of the most dramatic events in his ministry occurred.

The final day of the Feast of Tabernacles was known as "the great day." It concluded a week of the most splendid, colorful, and moving pageantry in Israel's religious calendar. Each of the seven days the priests marched from the temple to the pool of Siloam, about a half mile away, where they filled a golden pitcher with water, and returned to pour it at the base of the great Jewish altar, along with another golden pitcher of wine. This was an acted out prayer, pleading for rain and prosperity for the coming year. The rabbis also taught that the pouring of the water symbolized the pouring out of the Spirit of God. The solemn pilgrimmage was attended by trumpet blasts, rousing music, and tens of thousands of people waving palm and myrtle branches and chanting, "Save now, we beg you O Jehovah: O Jehovah, we beg you, send now prosperity." On the seventh day the pageantry culminated in the priests' circling seven times around the altar, then pouring the wine and water. After this came a pause before the offering of sacrifices.

Probably during that pause, while the chanting crowds were hushed, Jesus stood before the masses and shouted, "If anyone thirsts, let him come to me and drink. The one believing in me, as the Scripture has said, rivers of running water will flow from his innermost being" (vv. 37, 38).

THE LOST OPPORTUNITY

Jesus' offer promised to the people the spiritual water they needed. Even more, he said torrents of this living water would flow from all who believed to the rest of the world. John explains that this water symbolizes the Holy Spirit, who came upon Jesus' followers after his resurrection and ascension. "He said this concerning the Spirit, whom the believers in him were about to receive. For the Spirit had not yet been given, because Jesus was not yet glorified" (v. 39). The book of Acts records that the Holy Spirit came so abundantly on the Day of Pentecost that within less than a generation spiritual water had indeed spread from Jerusalem over much of the Roman Empire.

Perhaps no more dramatic moment for receiving the Messiah ever visited Israel than on this feast day. Jesus was unequivocal: all they needed to do was to believe in him. Though some did, the majority raised old objections: "The Messiah certainly doesn't come from Galilee, does he? Hasn't the Scripture said that the Messiah will be David's offspring and from Bethlehem?" (vv. 41, 42)

The Judaeans so despised Galilee they could not

imagine Messiah coming from there. Had they investigated, they would have discovered that Jesus was in the direct line of David and born in Bethlehem of Judea!

"EVERYONE IS WRONG BUT US!"

At the end of the day the officers sent to arrest Jesus returned to the Pharisees and Sadducees empty-handed. handed.

"Why didn't you bring him?" they were asked.

"No one ever spoke as this man speaks," they answered.

"You haven't been fooled, too, have you?" the Pharisees retorted. "None of the rulers or the Pharisees have believed on him have they? But this crowd who doesn't know the law are accursed!"

The Pharisees threw up their hands in dismay. Jesus had outwitted them again. Their only recourse was to denounce everyone but themselves. These arrogant men not only despised Gentiles and Samaritans, they scorned the typical Israelite who came to worship at Jerusalem! The six thousand Pharisees alone, it seemed, were the only enlightened people on earth. Yet one of their number did not agree. Nicodemus, whom we have met before, suggested they be more open-minded.

"Does our law condemn a man without first hearing from him and knowing what he's doing?" (v. 51)

The Pharisees had never been objective about Jesus since the day he lined himself up with the razor-tongued John the Baptist. They now accused Nicodemus of being like the ignorant Galilean crowds, and went off to their homes trying to figure out a new way to catch their tormentor from Nazareth.

By morning they had fashioned a trap. As temple crowds again flocked to hear the Galilean, some Pharisees burst upon the scene dragging a disheveled, sobbing woman. Thrusting the woman before Jesus they inquired with a pretense of piety: "Teacher, this woman has been caught in the act of adultery. Now in the law Moses commanded us to stone such women. Therefore, what do you say?" (John 8:4, 5)

Jesus was on the horns of a dilemma. If he agreed to

stoning the woman, they could embroil him in a controversy with Roman authorities, who did not allow the death penalty for such crimes. Furthermore, Jesus would appear to be merciless toward the sinner and the outcast whom he had so often championed. But if Jesus took the woman's side, he would be denying the clear teaching of Moses, whose law he claimed to uphold in every detail.

Jesus' immediate response was to say nothing. Rather he simply stooped and began to write in the dust with his finger. We do not know what he wrote, but the effect was to heighten tension to the breaking point. The woman's life possibly hung on his answer, and his reputation would stand or fall with his next words.

THE UNWORTHY EXECUTIONERS

After what seemed an eternity, Jesus stood, looked at the Pharisees and uttered one short, unforgettable sentence: "The one without sin among you, let him be the first to throw a stone at her" (v. 7).

The crowd's eyes now turned to the Pharisees. Suddenly *they* were on the horns of the dilemma! Moses' law wisely insisted that the witnesses whose testimony convicted the guilty party must be the first to stone the condemned (Deuteronomy 17:6,7). The Pharisees claimed to be the witnesses of the woman's adultery, but if they stoned her *they* would get in trouble with Rome instead of Jesus!

Furthermore, the whole incident was so obviously trumped up that they were in every sense unworthy executioners. Their motive was not to banish adultery and uphold the holiness of Moses' law. They had probably been aware of the woman's adulterous relationship for some time. She was only a pawn in their effort to trap Jesus.

Under the searching scrutiny of the crowd, the Pharisees stared at each other to see if any dared step forward and proclaim himself a worthy executioner. Then, aware of another defeat, they filed out in frustration.

Jesus and the woman faced each other in the midst of

the crowd. "Woman, where are they? Did no one condemn you?" he said.

"No one, sir," she replied in hushed tones.

"Neither do I condemn you. Go: from now on stop living in sin."

A more compassionate scene hardly occurs in the Gospels. The judge of mankind forgave her. Yet he forgave her without approving her sin, for he told her to leave the illicit relationship and straighten out her life. We suspect that she did, and a few months later, after the day of Pentecost, she probably became an active and ardent member of the New Testament community. In fact, this may be the reason why her story is included in the Gospel record. Like the Samaritan woman, she had probably shared this incident in private with John, and after her death, he recorded it in his Gospel.[1]

TRUE LIGHT

Jesus resumed his teaching as the astonished audience hung on every word: "I am the light of the world. Whoever continues to follow me will not walk in darkness, but will have the light of life" (John 8:12).

John notes that Jesus spoke by the temple treasury (v. 20). This was located in the same area where giant candlelabras were erected and lit on the first evening of the feast. The flames were so bright that they lit up the entire city. Against this background, Jesus claimed to be the true spiritual light, just as he had claimed to be the true spiritual water. As the light of mankind he would banish the fearful darkness which causes men to stumble into destruction.

Pharisees again protested, but Jesus told them to stop judging according to their defective standards. He pointed out that he did not judge that way, but judged truly as God's representative in union with him (vv. 15, 16).

Then he continued, "I am going away, and you will seek me, and die in your sin. Where I go you can't come. You are from below, I am from above. You are of this

153

world, I am not of this world. If you don't believe I am
he, you will die in your sins."

"You! Who are you?" they taunted (v. 25).

To perceptive listeners Jesus began to expose the
great gap between himself and these proud religious
leaders. He would leave them and return to heaven, but
they could not follow him. Instead, they would die in
their sinful rebellion and go to destruction. They and
others could escape hell only if they believed his great
claim to deity, "I am he," which was uttered by Jehovah in the Old Testament.

HOW TO BE FREE

John mentions that part of Jesus' audience seemed to
believe and to agree he was the divine Messiah (v. 31).
Yet their faith, like that of many who responded earlier,
was fickle. Knowing this, Jesus began to expose the
flaws in these false followers.

"If you continue in my teaching, you are really my
disciples, and you will know the truth and the truth will
set you free," he told them (vv. 31, 32). His words
implied that they had taken the first step to freedom,
but were not yet there. They must move on to grasp the
whole realm of his teaching. But his suggestion that they
were enslaved insulted them.

"We are Abraham's descendants, and have never been
enslaved to anyone!" they replied indignantly (v. 33).
These were strange words coming from people who had
been under the Roman yoke for almost a century! But
Jesus went on to show he was not even thinking of
political servitude.

"Everyone practicing sin is a slave of sin. The slave
does not stay in the household always, but the son
remains forever. If the Son frees you then you will really
be free!" (vv. 34-36) Jesus specified that their bondage
was to sin. This was illustrated by a slave who has no
permanent security, and might be sold any time. But a
son in the family is born to freedom. Jesus was *the* Son
in God's household, and he offered slaves adoption into
the family if they would follow him.

FATHERS AND SONS

"I know you're Abraham's descendants," Jesus continued. "But you keep seeking to kill me because you have no room for my teaching. I am speaking what I have seen with the Father. You therefore are doing what you have heard from your father" (vv. 37, 38).

"Abraham is our father!" they shouted.

"If you're children of Abraham, you would do the works of Abraham," Jesus countered. "But now you seek to kill me, a man who has spoken the truth to you which I heard from God. Abraham didn't do this!" (vv. 39, 40).

"*We* were not born of immorality," they retorted. "We have only one Father—God!" These professed "disciples" were revealing their true colors. In attitude they were one with the leaders who sought to arrest and execute Jesus. Stung by Jesus' changes, their recourse was to accuse him of being illegitimate! (see Chapter One)

The controversy sharpened as Jesus continued: "If God were your Father, you would love me. You are of your father the devil, and you want to do the desires of your father. He was a murderer from the beginning and didn't stand in the truth, because there is no truth in him. When he speaks the lie, he is true to his nature, because he is a liar and the father of it. But because I say the truth, you don't believe me. Which one of you can point to sin in my life? If I speak truth, why don't you believe me?" (vv. 42-47)

The crowd was enraged at Jesus' bluntness. "Doesn't this show we're right when we say you're a Samaritan and demon possessed?" they shouted (v. 48).

"I'm not demon possessed, but I have the Father and you dishonor me. I tell you, if anyone holds to my teaching, he will never taste death" (vv. 48-51).

"Now we know you're demon possessed! Abraham died as well as the prophets. . . . You're certainly not greater than our Father Abraham. . . . Who do you claim to be?" (vv. 52, 53)

"Your father Abraham was glad to see my day, and

155

he saw it and was overjoyed," Jesus answered enigmatically (v. 56).

"You're not yet fifty years old, and you've seen Abraham?" they shot back (v. 57).

"I tell you, before Abraham was born, I am!" came the stupendous claim.

At that the fuming mob scrambled for stones to bombard Jesus, but he slipped away through the throngs and was gone. The crowd which had begun to imagine a sympathy with Jesus was now estranged. He had exposed their superficial affinity and unshakable self-righteousness. They assumed their birth assured them possession of Abraham's faith and rewards, and their life-long resistance to self-examination flared at Jesus' probing of their hearts. The truth was too excruciating to face—they were the devil's slaves.

A THEOLOGICAL QUESTION

As Jesus and some of his disciples left the temple area through one of the gates, they noticed a blind beggar waiting hopefully for money. One of the disciples evidently knew the beggar and asked Jesus, "Rabbi, who sinned, this man or his parents, that he should be born blind?" (John 9:2)

What a revealing question! For Jesus' disciple, the beggar stirred no compassion, only theological speculation. He held the popular viewpoint that tragedy struck individuals in retribution for their sin. Some scribes theorized that infants could sin in the womb and be penalized by deformity at birth, and Jesus' disciple even considered this possibility.

"Neither this man sinned, nor his parents; but this happened so that the works of God might be displayed in him," Jesus answered (v. 3). He exploded the view that personal sin lay behind every ill, but he hinted that God had a special purpose in the life of this blind beggar.

AN AMAZING HALF-MILE RUN

Jesus spit on the ground and kneaded some dust into a thick paste. He stood up and spread the wet dirt on the man's eyelids, then told him to wash it off in the pool of Siloam. The ancient pool, which still exists, is down a hill about a half mile, on the fringes of the city.

Groping his way through the crowded street the ragged beggar was a strange sight with his mud-caked eyes! But when this same beggar came running up the hill with twenty-twenty vision a few minutes later, the crowd was aghast.

The Gospels record that Jesus healed more blindness than any other malady. But this miracle was unique because an adult blind from birth who suddenly received sight would be unable to judge space and distance, and certainly could not run up a crowded street. The healing took care of all this in seconds.

The beggar immediately went home and his neighbors, burning with curiosity, asked how his sight was restored.

"The man called Jesus made clay, put it on my eyes and told me, 'Go and wash in Siloam,' and I went and washed and I saw," he replied simply (v. 11).

The healing, like so many others of Jesus', occured on a Sabbath, and some self-appointed guardians of holiness therefore took him to the Pharisees to retell his story.

LOOKING FOR A LOOPHOLE

This phenomenon split the Pharisees. Some insisted God could not have healed the man because it was done on the Sabbath! Others felt that only God could perform such a miracle. Turning to the object of attention, they asked his opinion.

"He is a prophet," the jubilant beggar replied (v. 17).

Before he had only referred to Jesus as "this man." Now, as he listened to the Pharisees argue, he realized that a man with such power must be a prophet of God.

The frustrated Pharisees summoned the man's parents. The leaders desperately wanted to discredit this extraordinary miracle. But the parents acknowledged the beggar was their son, that he was born blind, and that he had never been able to see (vv. 20, 21).

The Pharisees' manner was threatening as they returned to the beggar a second time to try to shake his story. "Give glory to God," they commanded. "We know that this man is sinful" (v. 25).

"I don't know if he's sinful," the man replied. "One thing I know: I was blind and now I see!" (v. 26)

The Pharisees would celebrate the miracle if they could detach Jesus from it, but the illiterate man was too smart for that. Then they asked him to repeat his story, hoping to uncover a flaw.

"Why do you want to hear it again?" asked the beggar impatiently. "You certainly don't wish to become his disciples also, do you?" (v. 27)

"DON'T CONFUSE US WITH THE FACTS!"

The Pharisees were furious. An ignorant beggar was reprimanding the learned leaders of the land! "*You* are this man's disciple, but *we* are Moses' disciples," they retorted. "We know God has spoken by Moses. But we don't even know where this man is from."

His reply shook them. "Now this is amazing. You don't know where he is from, and he opened my eyes. Since time began no one has ever heard of opening the eyes of a man born blind. If this man was not from God, he could do absolutely nothing!"

"You were born covered with sins, and *you* are teaching *us*?" (vv. 28-35)

And with that they threw him out the door.

In its own way this is one of the most humorous yet tragic scenes in the Bible. The unschooled beggar had outwitted the shrewd Pharisees in debate. With irrefutable logic, the beggar questioned how true religious experts could belittle a man who had performed such a miraculous and merciful feat. Such an accomplishment was evidence God was with Jesus. Their only recourse was to attack the beggar's "sinfulness," established in their opinion by his blindness. In saying this, they admitted he was blind, that he now saw, and that an unanswerable proof of Jesus' Messiahship was looking at them straight in the eyes!

LOVE AT FIRST SIGHT

Hearing of the beggar's banishment, Jesus found him and asked, "Do you believe in the Son of Man?"

"Who is he, sir?" the beggar answered.

"You have both seen him and he is the one talking to you," Jesus replied.

"I believe, Lord." Then he worshipped Jesus (vv. 35-38).

Though the man had heard and been touched by Jesus, he had never laid eyes on him until this moment. Now he saw what the antagonistic Pharisees were blind to: that Jesus was God's Messiah.

"For judgment I came into this world—that those who don't see may see, and those who see may become blind," Jesus said as he looked at the man.

Some Pharisees asked, "We're not blind also, are we?"

"If you were blind, you would have no sin. But now you say, 'We see,' and your sin remains," he answered (vv. 39-41).

The miracle pictured the great irony of Israel. The sinners and outcasts, who were spiritually blind, believed in Jesus and received spiritual sight. But Israel's leaders, who claimed to see, refused to believe and became spiritually blind. If they had humbled themselves and admitted they too were sinful, they could have responded to Jesus. But their insistence that they knew it all doomed them to blindness.

How often this irony has repeated itself! Those who should believe, don't; but those who shouldn't believe, do.

FOOTNOTE FOR CHAPTER 13

[1] This story is strangely missing from the best manuscripts of John's Gospel. Perhaps an early copyist removed the incident because he thought it would encourage immorality. Even if the incident does not belong in John's Gospel, it is obviously a genuine episode.

◆ ◆

FOURTEEN

The Most Beautiful Stories in the World

◆ ◆

Lonely, sturdy shepherds were familiar figures in Israel. The high rocky plateau which stretched down the backbone of Judea resisted farmers' tools, but welcomed shepherd's flocks. Though rigid Pharisees despised the shepherds who, because of their occupation, could not observe endless scribal traditions, the Bible honors the image of the shepherd and his sheep. David spoke of the Lord as his shepherd in the beautiful Twenty-Third Psalm, and other psalmists described Israel as the sheep of God's pasture. The Messiah was portrayed as a shepherd, as were Israel's leaders. Shepherds, of course, were the first witnesses of Jesus' birth.

So it was natural for Jesus to use the imagery of the shepherd and the sheep to teach profound truths to the Jerusalem crowds. He had just left the former blind beggar and once again a crowd of both friends and foes surrounded him.

"I tell you, the one who doesn't enter through the door into the sheepfold, but climbs up another way is a thief and a robber. The one who enters through the door is the shepherd of the sheep. . . . and his sheep hear his voice, and he calls his own sheep by name and leads them out. When he brings all his own sheep out, he goes before them and his sheep follow him because they know his voice. They certainly won't follow a stranger, but will run from him because they don't know a stranger's voice" (John 10:1-5).

A FAMILIAR PICTURE

The picture was familiar to his audience. Towns had public sheepfolds, with strong walls and solid doors or gates, where sheep could be left. Thieves might try to climb the walls to steal sheep, but the shepherd came through the door, which a doorkeeper would open for him.

When the shepherd led his sheep to pasture, he used a special call to which only they would respond. Palestinian shepherds, who spent many lonely hours with their sheep, became very attached to them, and even gave them names. Since sheep were used more for wool than food, the same sheep might remain for years in the same flock with the same devoted shepherd.

Jesus pictured himself as Israel's true shepherd who would call those in touch with God to himself. They would follow him and respond to him, but they would resist false teachers. Fresh on his mind was the blind beggar who, despite his ignorance, withstood all the attempts of the Pharisees to undercut his loyalty to Jesus.

But the audience didn't catch Jesus' spiritual analogy, so he spelled out his meaning:

"I tell you that I am the door for the sheep. All who came before me were thieves and robbers, but the sheep didn't listen to them. I am the door. Whoever enters through me will be saved and go in and out and find pasture. The thief comes only to steal, kill, and destroy. I have come that they may have life and have it abundantly" (vv. 7-10).

A LIVING DOOR

Jesus changed the illustration slightly. Outside the towns were sheepfolds that lacked doors or gatekeepers. The shepherd himself would lie down and sleep across the entrance and thus become the door. Jesus claimed to be the door to God and eternal life; he said those who claimed it before him were frauds—they were like thieves and robbers. He was not referring to the Old Testament prophets, of course, who never claimed to be Messiah or the way to eternal life. He was speaking of the many false Messiahs who misled Israel both before and after Jesus' time.

"I am the good shepherd," he continued. "The good shepherd lays down his life for the sheep. The hireling is not a shepherd to whom the sheep belong, and he runs and leaves the sheep when he sees the wolf coming. . . . I lay down my life for the sheep" (vv. 11-15).

Because shepherds owned and loved their sheep they risked their lives to protect them. Mere hirelings, working for wages, did not. Jesus proclaimed his absolute devotion to God's flock, in contrast to many of the Sadducees, who were religious leaders mainly for the money.

The crowd must have wondered what Jesus meant when he spoke of laying down his life, so he went on: "I have other sheep that are not of this fold. I must bring them in also . . . and these will be one flock and one shepherd. . . . I lay down my life in order to take it again. No one takes it from me but I lay it down voluntarily. I have authority to lay it down and authority to take it again. This commandment I received from the Father" (vv. 16-18).

With these illustrations Jesus was teaching all who would hear what he had proclaimed earlier to the twelve. He would found a new community which would reach beyond Israel. It would include Gentiles—"the other sheep"—and would unite under the one leader, Jesus himself, who would die for the flock and rise again as part of his voluntary submission to the Father.

When the events Jesus intimated came to pass, many in the audience would look back and understand, but others would insist he was demonic to their dying day. Though he contrasted himself to the long line of spiritual robbers and religious hirelings who had ravaged Israel, many in his audience would soon hail his crucifixion and gladly commit themselves to the hirelings and thieves who engineered his death.

A CHANGE OF SCENERY

Jesus left Jerusalem and apparently devoted himself to ministering in the nearby Judean countryside and across the Jordan in Perea. Galilee and Jerusalem had heard and largely rejected Jesus, but the heavily Jewish Judea and the mixed population of Perea were to see and hear the carpenter-Messiah during his last six months on earth. Most of our information about this period comes from Luke's Gospel. Since Jesus was reaching a new audience, some of his words repeat what he had already spoken in Galilee. The twelve disciples do not seem to accompany him the whole time, and he gathered additional unnamed disciples here who served him faithfully though they are anonymous.

In Perea Jesus selected a group of seventy disciples, instructed them as he had the twelve previously, and sent them two-by-two to spread the message of God's kingdom in towns he was going to visit (Luke 10:1-16). Jewish tradition taught there were seventy nations in the world; the recently completed Feast of Tabernacles sacrificed seventy bullocks for these nations. Jesus' commissioning of this number probably symbolized his concern to carry his message eventually to every nation on earth.

Their mission completed, the seventy returned with the excited report: "Lord, even the demons submit to us in your name!" (v. 17)

"I saw Satan tumble from heaven like lightning," Jesus replied. "I have given you authority to tread on serpents and scorpions, and on all the power of the enemy. . . . Nevertheless, stop rejoicing that the demons submit to you, but rejoice that your names have been recorded in heaven" (vv. 18-21).

Their success reminded Jesus that his life and death would soon seal the defeat of Satan himself, mankind's great enemy. He envisioned Satan as thrown out of his heavenly place of power and cast down to destruction.

163

Yet, like a long war, the spiritual campaign is won in stages and final victory only comes at the end. Then Jesus warned his followers against boasting over their success. Their own redemption was more important than the results of their ministry.

SEEKING HEAVENLY BROWNIE POINTS

Sometime after this, a Jewish legal expert approached Jesus with a profound question, "Teacher, what must I do to inherit eternal life?" (v. 25) The question revealed a Pharisaic mentality—eternal life must be *earned* by human merit.

"What stands written in the law? How do you read it?" Jesus answered (v. 26).

"You shall love the Lord your God with all your heart, with all your soul, with all your strength, and with all your mind, and love your neighbor as yourself," he replied (v. 27).

"You gave the right answer. Do this and you'll live," Jesus answered.

But the man faced a deep dilemma. If eternal life is earned through such good deeds, no one is worthy because no one is good enough! The only hope was to lower the commandment's requirements by redefining its terms. The Pharisees defined neighbor to mean only good Jews, and thus justified their hatred for outcasts, Samaritans and Gentiles. The legal expert had such a definition in mind as he insolently asked, "And who is my neighbor?"

In answer, Jesus told him this story:

"A man was going down from Jerusalem to Jericho when he fell among robbers who stripped off his clothes, beat him, and left him half dead. By chance a priest passed the same way, and seeing him, moved to the opposite side of the road. So also a Levite. . . . And a Samaritan as he journeyed came upon him, saw him, took pity, and went and bound up his wounds . . . put him on his own beast, brought him to an inn, and cared for him. The next day, he took out forty dollars and gave it to the innkeeper and said, 'Whatever you spend in addition, I will repay when I return' " (vv. 30-35).

RACISM REJECTED AGAIN

The tale of the "good Samaritan," justly enshrined among the world's greatest stories, was more than a match for the bigoted Pharisee. The twenty mile road which descended thirty-six hundred feet from Jerusalem to Jericho was often the scene of such robberies as Jesus described. But the real villains of the story were the priest and Levite, representatives of the religious aristocracy, who went out of their way to avoid helping even a fellow Jew. In them Jesus scathingly condemned non-involvement in the face of human need. The hero, on the other hand, was the Samaritan whom every Pharisee despised. For Jesus to tell this audience of the "good Samaritan" would be like telling the story of the "good Nazi" to Jewish people today!

Jesus now looked at his interrogator and challenged: "Which of these three do you think became a neighbor to the man who was robbed?" (v. 36)

The Pharisee probably gulped as he replied, "The one showing mercy on him." He chose not to use the word "Samaritan"!

Jesus commanded simply, "Go, and you do the same" (v. 37).

Jesus got the Pharisee's grudging admission that a foreign Samaritan had become a neighbor to a Jew, while a Jewish priest and levite had become "foreigners." Neighbor can not be defined by race and nationality. The elite Pharisee should seek, like the Samaritan, to become a neighbor to all humans and help whoever is in need. Once again Jesus attacks bigotry and racism wherever they rear their ugly heads.

THE OVERANXIOUS HOSTESS

Continuing his travels, Jesus turned toward Jerusalem and was invited to dine in the home of two women who, with their brother, become important characters in the Gospel history. The sisters Mary and Martha, along with their brother Lazarus, lived in Bethany just outside Jerusalem. They evidently had become acquainted with Jesus during his Jerusalem ministry.

Martha busily prepared the meal for their illustrious guest while Mary sat entranced in the living room listening to Jesus.

After a time Martha blew up. "Don't you care that my sister left me alone to do all the serving? Tell her then to help me!" (v. 40)

"Martha, Martha, you're anxious and troubled about many things," Jesus soothed her. "Only a few things are necessary—really only one. For Mary has chosen the good part which won't be taken from her" (vv. 41, 42).

Martha was anxious to make a big spread for Jesus and had undertaken far more than was necessary. Jesus was appreciative, but he tenderly pointed out that the really important thing was to hear the words of eternal life, which Mary had wisely chosen to do.

Again we see Jesus' concern to instruct the women, so neglected by scribes, as well as his patience with those like Martha who complicate their lives with unnecessary activities. Martha should have prepared a few simple dishes instead of making such a production out of the meal at the expense of her own spiritual welfare.

PERSISTANCE PAYS

As Jesus resumed his travels, he again instructed his followers about prayer.

"Suppose you have a friend, and you come to him at midnight and say, 'Friend, lend me three pieces of bread, since a friend of mine has arrived on a journey and I have nothing to set before him.'

"Then from inside he answers, 'Don't bother me, for the door is shut and my children are with me in bed. I can't get up to give it to you.' I tell you, though he won't get up and give because he is his friend, because of his persistence he will give him as much as he needs" (Luke 11:5-8).

Since hospitality was a sacred duty, the embarrassed host with no food for his late-arriving guest sought to borrow from his neighbor. He found the door bolted—a "do not disturb sign" in the ancient world. The whole family slept next to each other for warmth and put smaller livestock inside on the dirt floor, so for the neighbor to rise and get bread would rouse wife, children, and livestock! Yet the friend's persistence would rouse the family anyhow—and so the neighbor finally gave in. If persistence arouses an unwilling neighbor, Jesus suggested, how much more will persistence move God, our Father, who is always devoted to our welfare.

THE MAN WHO DIDN'T PLAN TO DIE

On another occasion as Jesus was teaching, one of his audience demanded that he help him in a financial controversy with his brother. Jesus rebuked the man for attempting to use him simply to gain money, then he told this story.

"The land of a certain rich man produced plentifully, and he thought to himself, 'What will I do because I have no place to store my crops?' Then he said, 'I'll do this—I'll tear down my barns and build larger ones, and I'll store all my crops and wealth there. Then I'll say to myself, 'You've stored up wealth for many years, now take it easy: eat, drink, and be happy.' But God said to him, 'You fool, this night I demand your life! Then who will get that wealth that you stored up?' This is what it will be like for the one who piles up wealth for himself, but is not rich toward God" (Luke 12:16-21).

This man saw wealth as ultimate security and he piled it up higher and higher instead of giving to the needy and using it to promote God's kingdom. He never realized that his life and the enjoyment of his wealth were in God's hands—until God separated him from his "security." Then it was too late. Jesus warned against trusting uncertain riches for security instead of the true God, and implied that God will hold us accountable for selfish use of money.

AN ANCIENT AND HORRIBLE PHILOSOPHY

Sometime after this an audience in Judea told Jesus about some Galileans who were slaughtered by Pontius Pilate, the Roman governor. The Judeans apparently interpreted this as a divine judgment on the slain people, for they followed the popular but horrible philosophy that tragedy was the divine visitation for personal sin. Jesus resoundingly rejected this—revolutionary for his day.

"Do you think that these Galileans were worse sinners than all other Galileans because they suffered this?" he asked. "No, I tell you, unless you repent you will all perish in the same way. Or those eighteen on whom the tower of Siloam fell, do you think they were worse than all the people living in Jerusalem? No, I tell you, unless you repent, you will all perish in the same way."

To this sobering warning he added a story.

"A man had a fig tree planted in his vineyard, and came seeking fruit on it and found none. And he told the gardener, 'I have been seeking fruit on this fig tree three years and found none. Cut it down. Why exhaust the soil?' But he answered, 'Sir, leave it also this year that I may dig around it and fertilize it. Then if it bears fruit in the future, good! Otherwise, cut it down' " (Luke 13:1-9).

Jesus knew that sin lay behind all tragedy and death, but this did not mean that those who suffered misfortune were more evil than those who didn't. The parable of the fig tree held terrible but veiled meaning for Jesus' listeners. Israel was like a fig tree that bore no fruit, but the patient gardener was willing to give it one more chance. His warning to these proud Judeans went unheeded. They continued to reject Jesus for the next forty years, then foolishly rebelled against Rome, and were slaughtered by the same nation, in the same manner, as these Galileans they despised. They literally did "perish in the same way"!

CRUELTY TO HUMANS, BUT NOT ANIMALS

Luke records the final mention of Jesus in a synagogue and the scene is familiar. He was teaching worshipers on the Sabbath and noticed a woman whose spine was so curved she was completely bent over. She had suffered the condition eighteen years, and Jesus called her over and said, "Woman, you've been freed from your malady" (v. 12). Then he put his hands on her, and she straightened up shouting praises to God.

As usual, the synagogue ruler was enraged because Jesus had healed her on the Sabbath.

Jesus answered: "Hypocrites, which of you on the Sabbath does not untie his ox or donkey from the manger and lead it away to drink? And shouldn't this woman, who is a daughter of Abraham, whom Satan has bound all these eighteen years, be untied from this bond on the Sabbath?" (vv. 15, 16) Since they freed animals from their stalls on the Sabbath, he felt justified in freeing this woman from a bent back on the Sabbath. The Pharisees showed mercy to beasts but denied it to people, and thus crushed human dignity.

AN UNHAPPY HANUKKAH

About three months had passed since the Feast of Tabernacles, and Jesus returned to Jerusalem for the Feast of Dedication, or Hanukkah, which celebrated the defeat of the Syrians and the reconsecration of the temple nearly two hundred years before. As Jesus taught in the temple area, some opponents crowded near and badgered: "How long will you keep us in suspense? If you are the Messiah, tell us openly" (John 10:24).

Jesus knew their real intentions, and his answer spotlighted the vast chasm between them.

"I told you and you don't believe . . . because you're not my sheep. My sheep hear my voice and I know them and they follow me, and I give them eternal life and they will absolutely never be lost and no one will seize them out of my hand. My Father, who has given them to me, is greater than I, and no one can seize them out of the Father's hand. I and the Father are one" (vv. 25-30).

Jesus had read their minds. They demonstrated that they were not his sheep, for his sheep would respond to his voice and never forsake him. God's hold on his followers, which was much stronger than his followers' hold on God, guaranteed the permanence of their faith. Then Jesus capped it off by declaring his unity with God—they are absolutely one, though he is subordinate to the Father's greater position.

The audience was so enraged at Jesus' claim that they picked up stones to kill him on the spot. Yet he stopped them with words.

"I showed you many good works from the Father. For which work do you stone me?" (v. 32).

Deflated, but unrelenting, they replied they were not stoning him for good works (which was their own admission he had done them), but for blasphemy—claiming a oneness with God which exalted him to the very level of deity (v. 33).

Jesus replied, "Doesn't it stand written in your law, 'I said you are gods'? If he called those people gods to whom God's Word came—and the Scripture cannot be broken—why do you say to the one whom the Father set apart and sent into the world, 'You blaspheme' because I say I am God's Son? If I don't do the works of the Father, don't believe me. . ." (vv. 34-38).

Jesus again outmaneuvered these skilled debaters. He quoted an obscure Old Testament passage where the Lord said the Israelites were like gods compared to the pagan nations surrounding them, because with Israel was deposited the very Word of God. If sinful, human Israelites were figuratively called gods, then Jesus, the sinless, divine Messiah, certainly could call himself God's Son.

Then Jesus again referred to his works—if his miraculous deeds were not of God, they were free to reject him. This put the Pharisees against the wall. If they could have faulted his works at the moment, they would have done so. But the listening crowd would not accept that. Once more he had vanquished his foes.

MORE THAN A MEAL

Nevertheless the opposition was so intense that Jesus temporarily left Judea for Perea (v. 40), where he would be safe for at least a while. As he traveled through Perea, he was invited to a Pharisees's house for a sabbath meal.

Once again, this was to find some flaw in Jesus rather than to express hospitality. But it was to be the most unforgettable meal this Pharisee and his friends ever had.

One of the dinner guests was swollen with edema (dropsy), and Jesus shot a question at his antagonists: "Is it lawful to heal on the Sabbath or not?" (Luke 14:3). As the Pharisees stared open-mouthed Jesus healed the man and reduced his bloated body to normal size.

Then Jesus zeroed in on the custom of assigning status positions at special banquets. There were various seats of honor—a seat for the "worthiest" guest, the "next most worthy" guest, down to the "least worthy" guest! It is easy to imagine what kind of competition arose for the best seats under such a system.

"When you are invited to a wedding banquet, don't sit in the place of honor," Jesus said, "for someone more important than you may have been invited, and the host may come to you and say, 'Give this man your seat,' and then you will take the lowest seat with much embarrassment. . . . For everyone exalting himself will be humbled and everyone humbling himself will be exalted" (vv. 8-11).

Then he challenged them to make their big meals truly purposeful:

"When you give a luncheon or dinner, don't always invite your friends, brothers, relatives, and rich neighbors, so they will invite you and in return repay you. But when you give a banquet, invite the poor, maimed, crippled, and blind and you will be blessed even though they can't repay you. You'll get repaid at the resurrection of the righteous" (vv. 12-14).

The Pharisaic mentality was: "I'll scratch your back if you scratch mine." Jesus encouraged them to reach out to those who could never repay, and to avoid selfish motives when inviting friends who could repay.

HE GAVE A BANQUET AND NO ONE CAME

One of the dinner guests then piously exclaimed, "Happy is the one who will eat bread in God's kingdom." Since the Pharisees believed that the Messianic reign would begin with a great banquet for all Israel, the comment implied that all good Pharisees would be at the auspicious event. Jesus answered him with another story.

"A man gave a great banquet and invited many, and sent his slave at the appointed hour to tell the invited guests, 'Come because it is now ready.' But they all began to make excuses.

"The first told him, 'I bought a farm and must go see it. . . .'

"Another said, 'I bought five pairs of oxen, and I am going to try them out. . . .'

"Another said, 'I have just married a wife, so I can't come. . . .'

"Then the slave came and reported to his master. Then the head of the house, who was angry, told his slave, 'Go out quickly into the streets and lanes of the city and bring in the poor and maimed and blind and crippled.'

"Then the slave said, 'Sir, what you have commanded has happened and there is still room.'

"Then the master said to the slave, 'Go out to the country roads and lanes and exhort them to come in to fill my house, for I tell you not one of those invited will taste my banquet' " (vv. 16-23).

The man who gave the banquet pictured God, and the originally invited guests with their lame excuses represented the Jewish leaders who refused to respond at the announced time—during the ministries of John and Jesus. Gathering in the poor and crippled pictured the Jewish sinners and outcasts who followed Jesus. Those from the countryside were the Gentiles beyond Israel who would believe. Jesus was warning the complacent Pharisees seated around him that they had no guarantee of making the great Messianic banquet. In fact, by their attitude toward him they were in extreme danger of missing it. And in their place, ironically, would be many of the Jews they despised, and worse than that, Gentiles.

As the meal ended, the Pharisee who invited Jesus to trap him discovered he and his friends had been trapped instead. Their distorted values, selfishness, and complacency had been unmasked by this renegade rabbi they planned to outwit. None of them probably dared to ask him to dinner again!

PAYING THE PRICE

As Jesus continued traveling and teaching in Perea, crowds gathered wherever he stopped.

"If any man comes to me and does not hate his father and mother and wife and children, and brothers and sisters and his own life also, he cannot be my disciple. Whoever does not carry his own cross and come after me cannot be my disciple. For which one of you wishing to build a tower, first doesn't sit down and count the cost to see if he can complete it. . . . Or what king going to war against another king doesn't sit down first to consider whether he is able with ten thousand men to meet the one opposing him with twenty thousand. . . . So then, any one of you who doesn't say farewell to all his possessions can't be my disciple" (vv. 26-33).

These Perean Israelites had not yet rejected Jesus, but their views were similar to those of the Galilean defectors. They imagined the Messiah would establish an empire in Jerusalem, so Jesus warned of the cost of following him.

They must be so devoted to him that their attachment to family was like hate in comparison. He illustrated his call from real-life situations. A man who built a tower in his vineyard to protect it from thieves, and the king who went to war both had to calculate the cost before embarking on a successful project. The enthusiastic Pereans should calculate whether they were willing to lose family, possessions, and even their lives before following him. They probably couldn't understand what he was talking about. But within less than a decade his followers were paying just such a price for their faith.

OPPOSITE POLES

As the Pharisees hardened into deeper alienation, the common Israelites, including tax collectors and religious outcasts, were drawn more and more to Jesus. Despite his warnings of the dedication and sacrifice involved, these unlikely followers sensed loyalty to Jesus would be worth such cost. The Pharisees, on the other hand, mocked him for even associating with such rabble. Jesus defended his actions in three of his most striking parables.

"Which of you, having a hundred sheep and losing one of them does not leave the ninety and nine in the wilderness and go after the lost one until he finds it? And when he finds it, he places it on his shoulders and joyfully returns home and calls together friends and neighbors. . . . I tell you that in the same way there will be more joy in heaven over one repenting sinner than over ninety-nine righteous men who need no repentance.

"Or what woman, having ten silver coins, if she loses one coin, does not light a lamp and sweep the house and search carefully until she finds it? And when she finds it, calls together her friends and neighbors saying, 'Rejoice with me because I have found the lost coin' " (Luke 15:3-9).

Since sheep were not fenced in, they easily wandered, and shepherds had to track down and rescue them. Sheep were often owned communally, so a whole village would rejoice when they saw the shepherd returning with their lost sheep. Married women in ancient Israel wore a headband with ten coins, which was nearly equivalent to a wedding ring and was a valuable part of their dowry. Losing one of these ten coins was a great financial and sentimental loss for people with little money and few possessions.

In both parables Jesus portrayed the main figures as aggressively searching for their lost objects and rejoicing when they were recovered. This contrasted God and himself to the Pharisees who steered clear of the lost and seemed to rejoice over their destruction!

THE MOST TOUCHING STORY OF ALL

Then in one of the most touching stories he ever told Jesus now drove home his point.

"A man had two sons. The younger said to the father, 'Father, give me my share of the property.' So he divided the estate between them. Soon after, the younger son got all his money together and went to a far country, and there squandered everything living a wild life. But when he had spent everything, a severe famine came on that whole country and he began to be in need. And he went and got a job with one of the citizens of that country, who sent him to the fields to feed pigs. He longed to fill his stomach even with carob pods the pigs ate, and no one gave him anything else."

Jesus then told how the son came to his senses and decided to return home and cast himself on his father's mercy. As he was coming up the road, "the father saw him, and was moved with pity, and ran to meet him, and embraced him and kissed him." Before the son could even blurt out the apology he had rehearsed, the father called his servants and ordered a great feast because his lost son was found.

But the older son would not participate in the merriment. He told the father, "Look, I have slaved for you all these years and never disobeyed your commands, and you never gave me even a young goat so I could celebrate with my friends. But when this son of yours came, who has consumed your money on prostitutes, you killed the fatted calf for him!

"And the father told him, 'Son, you're always with me and whatever I have is yours. But we must be happy and rejoice because this dead brother of yours has come back to life, and he was lost and now is found' " (vv. 11-32).

"I SLAVED ALL THOSE YEARS!"

In the story the wayward son represents rebellious sinners whom the Pharisees so despised. He departed for a foreign country, lived with prostitutes, and finally his chaotic lifestyle brought him as low as a Jew could sink—living in a Gentile land, feeding pigs, and even longing to eat their food! Jesus implied that a rebellious life brings its own penalties. Though he generously forgave repentant sinners. Jesus never taught that sin did anything but blight human welfare.

The father pictures God. Though his son had rebelled without reason and caused untold grief, the father gladly received him back when he returned sincerely repentant. God freely forgives the sinner who turns from his rebellion, and holds no grudges against him.

But perhaps the most important character is the elder brother, who represents the Pharisees. At first glance, he seemed justified. His faithfulness generated no celebrations, whereas a rebellious brother got a banquet! But according to Jewish inheritance laws, he had received twice the inheritance of his younger brother, and all the wealth of his father's great farm was his. But he never enjoyed what he had; he described his relationship to his father as "slaving all those years."

Like the Pharisees, he tried to earn his father's favor like a servant, instead of enjoying what was free to him as a son. His relationship was based on merit, not love. Since he had cut himself off from his father's love, he could hardly enjoy having it bestowed on someone else. Never was a more touching yet tragic picture painted of the Pharisee than this.

Jesus' ministry in Judea and Perea was drawing to a close. The days spent among unsympathetic Jerusalem Pharisees, hardened Judean crowds, and misguided Perean throngs have bequeathed to history's pages some of the world's greatest teaching. Not in the foggy language of philosophers, but in words of common men and with stories from daily life Jesus taught Israel and the world the greatest truths of the ages. His listeners resisted his message, but they could not deny that it was more profoundly and beautifully presented than any message they had ever heard.

◆   ◆

FIFTEEN

A Tomb and a Tear

◆   ◆

Israel as a nation was poor. She had limited national resources, few fertile fields, no army, no navy, no conquered countries under her heel—she herself chafed under the Roman yoke. But her people were proud, hardworking, and occasionally well-to-do. Every good Jewish son learned an honorable and sometimes profitable occupation from his father. Jesus was a carpenter, Peter a fisherman, Paul a tentmaker. The national philosophy was that hard work and a righteous life would earn God's material blessing.

Because they were energetic and sometimes successful, materialism was a direct spiritual snare to the Jewish people. Jesus directed two more parables to this problem before leaving Perea.

"A rich man had a manager who was accused of wasting his possessions," Jesus began. When the manager was called to account, he devised an ingenious scheme so that his employer's tenants might hire him when he got fired. He called each one of the tenants and asked the first, " 'How much do you owe my employer?' " " 'Eight hundred gallons of olive oil,' he answered.

" 'Take your bill, sit down quickly, and write four hundred,' he said.

"Then to another he said, 'How much do you owe?' "   177

" 'A thousand bushels of wheat,' he replied.

" 'Take your bill and write eight hundred,' he said.

"And the employer of that dishonest manager commended him because he acted shrewdly. For the children of this world are far more shrewd with their own kind than the children of light. And I tell you, make friends for yourself with worldly wealth, that when it fails, they may welcome you into eternal dwellings.

"Whoever is faithful with very little is also faithful with much, and whoever is unrighteous with very little is also unrighteous with much. If therefore you haven't been faithful with worldly wealth, who will entrust to you the true riches? And if you have been unfaithful with what belongs to someone else, who will give you what is your own?" (Luke 16:1-12)

A WHEELER-DEALER

The manager in the parable was responsible to collect rent in the form of crops from tenants on his employer's estate. Frequently such managers would extort amounts over and above what was due and pocket the difference. This manager called in the tenants and reduced drastically the debts piled up through this malicious practice. The owner still got his due, and the manager lost the amount he usually raked off, but he hoped his generosity would endear him to the tenants so they would hire him when he got fired.

Jesus didn't commend the manager's dishonesty, which got him into trouble in the first place, but he did applaud his shrewdness in wiggling out of the situation. He then told wise listeners to use their money shrewdly. Unlike this manger, who simply provided himself a temporary job and shelter, they were to lay up treasures in heaven by using their money to make eternal friends. This probably refers to using money for spreading the gospel and bringing people to God. Then when death comes to these wise believers, and their money is no longer useful, those who had come to God because of these well-spent dollars would welcome them into heaven, an eternal habitation.

Jesus taught several profound truths through this parable. First, those who don't know God are often more industrious in promoting bad ends than followers of God are in promoting good ends. In our own day the followers of Marx and Lenin have vigorously spread their atheistic gospel with lightning speed while the followers of Jesus have often lumbered along with out-dated methods and strategies.

Then Jesus taught that money is relatively unimportant. It is one of the "little" things God entrusts to believers before he entrusts greater things. The twentieth century has indoctrinated us with a philosophy that says lack of money means misery and abundance of money produces happiness. But America, the world's wealthiest nation, is today engulfed in more misery and uncertainty than ever before.

Jesus also revealed that our use of money reveals our character. If we fail with money, Jesus says, we are likely to fail in the most critical areas of life. Later on the Apostle Paul warned against giving authority in the New Testament congregation to a man who loves money (I Timothy 3:3). Love for money and for God simply cannot co-exist.

THE MILLIONAIRE AND THE BEGGAR

The Pharisees who heard this parable ridiculed it (Luke 16:14). Though they were frugal, they loved money, considering it God's reward for righteousness. Jesus exposed the weakness of their viewpoint in graphic terms:

"A rich man used to dress in purple robes and fine linen and enjoy luxury every day. A poor man named Lazarus, covered with sores, was put at his door, and longed to eat the crumbs from the rich man's table. Even the dogs came and licked his sores. And the poor man died and was carried away by the angels to Abraham's bosom. The rich man also died and was buried. And in hades, while in torment, he lifted up his eyes and saw Abraham from afar. And he called, 'Father Abraham, pity me and send Lazarus to dip the tip of his finger in water and cool my tongue, because I am suffering in this fire.' "

Abraham replied that a great gulf existed between the rich man and Lazarus, so that no one could cross over it. Then the suffering man pleaded that Lazarus be sent back to the rich man's household to warn his relatives of the fate awaiting them.

"Abraham answered, 'They have Moses and the prophets. Let them hear them. . . .

" 'No, Father Abraham, but if someone from the dead would go to them, they would repent.'

"But he said, 'If they don't hear Moses and the prophets, neither will they be persuaded if someone should rise from the dead' " (vv. 19-31).

The story is a series of contrasts. One man was stupendously wealthy and wore purple robes. Purple dye was obtained from a special fish which only yielded a few drops of dye. The dye alone was worth its weight in gold, and purple robes were worth a fortune. The linen was imported from Egypt. This man was a millionaire.

The other man was impoverished. He was lonely, hungry, and sick. His only friends were the mongrels in the streets.

THE GREAT REVERSAL

Yet when death struck the men all was reversed. The rich man went to torment in "hades," a word which describes the abode of the dead before their entrance into final judgment. The poor man went to "Abraham's bosom," a Jewish term describing the place of comfort for the believer before his entrance into heaven with Messiah. The beggar once cried for crumbs from the rich man's hand; now the rich man longed for a drop of water from the beggar's finger.

This story showed the bankruptcy of Pharisaic theology. By their reckoning the beggar had been condemned to poverty and sickness because he was a sinner, and the rich man was rewarded with abundance because he was good. But Jesus revealed that many positions on earth will be reversed in heaven. Death will be the ultimate "future shock" for many.

Yet the rich man did not go to hades because he had too much money, nor the beggar to heaven because of his poverty. Rather the rich man denied God in life, and the beggar trusted him. The rich man never used his worldly wealth to make friends for the eternal dwelling in heaven. He paid no attention to Moses and the prophets. He was godless. This is what sealed his doom.

The last portion of the story added an ironic twist which would soon find literal fulfillment. Abraham said rejection of Moses and the prophets causes such hardness of heart that not even a resurrected person can pierce through it. Jesus often accused the Pharisees of rejecting the teaching of Moses and the prophets, and the proof of Jesus' statements was demonstrated when Jesus rose from the dead. Those same Pharisees who rejected Moses rejected a resurrected Jesus. Such a resistance to their own Scriptures made them incapable of yielding to history's most stupendous miracle!

INTIMATE FRIENDS

About this time a message reached Jesus that Lazarus, the brother of Mary and Martha, was desperately ill (John 11:1-3). Though the Gospels mention Mary, Martha, and Lazarus only sparsely, they imply that an especially intimate friendship existed between this family and Jesus. In their message to Jesus they said "the one whom you love is sick." Probably Jesus had spent many hours in their home and appreciated their kindness and hospitality all the more after a day spent in savage argument with Jerusalem Pharisees.

When Jesus received the message, he was about a day's journey from their home in Bethany, but, incredibly, he delayed two additional days instead of heading there immediately. When he finally left for Bethany, his disciples protested, "Rabbi, the Pharisees were just trying to stone you, and you're going there again?" (v. 8)

"Aren't there twelve hours in a day?" Jesus answered. "Whoever walks in the day doesn't stumble because he sees the light of this world" (v. 9). He suggested that his ministry was of limited duration and he must take advantage of every opportunity, with assurance that death couldn't reach him until his work was finished.

Jesus then informed the disciples that Lazarus, the reason for going to Jerusalem, had already died. The announcement grieved and perplexed them. It now seemed that this trip might bring Jesus and all the apostles to an untimely death. But since Jesus was determined to go, Thomas morosely offered: "Let's go also that we may die with him" (v. 16). If Thomas lacked a joyful faith, at least he had a loyal despair!

LIFE HERE AND NOW

As Jesus approached Bethany, Martha came down the road to meet him. "If you'd been here, my brother wouldn't have died!" she said. "And I know that even now, whatever you ask of God, God will give you" (vv. 21, 22).

She wondered why he had delayed coming. Yet in her sorrow she at least weakly believed that Jesus could raise Lazarus.

"Your brother will rise again," Jesus said.

"I know he'll rise again in the resurrection the last day," she answered, afraid to hope for something sooner.

"I am the resurrection and the life," Jesus said. "Whoever believes in me will live even if he dies, and whoever lives and believes in me will never die. Do you believe this?"

"Yes, Lord, I believe you are the Messiah, the Son of God, the one coming into the world" (vv. 23-27).

Jesus had uttered another of his staggering claims. He claimed authority not only to raise the dead physically at the end of the age, but to raise the spiritually dead and give life *right now*. He did not say, "I will be the resurrection and the life," but "*I am. . . .*" He said this life is eternal, so that even if a believer dies physically he will keep living. In fact, because his real life is eternal he will never die in the ultimate sense.

THE TEARS OF JESUS

Martha could not grasp all this, but she did know that Jesus was no ordinary man. She believed he was the Messiah, the Son of God, and the promised deliverer of the Old Testament who would come into the world.

Martha hurried back to the house and got Mary, who left the mourners to meet Jesus. When she saw him she broke down and began to weep and wail, according to the meaning of the original Greek (v. 33). Between her sobs she spluttered, "Lord, if you'd been here, my brother would not have died" (v. 32). By this time many of the family friends were surrounding them and sobbing too.

The scene touched the deepest recesses of Jesus' soul. John says that Jesus was "moved with indignation in his spirit" (according to the original Greek), and "troubled" (v. 33). Jesus felt a deep anger—certainly not at the helpless Mary, Martha, or their friends; he was furious at death, this great enemy of man which brought such sorrow and suffering.

Jesus followed Mary and her friends to the tomb where Lazarus was buried. There he was overcome by his emotions, and one of the shortest and most moving verses of Scripture reports: "Jesus shed tears" (v. 35).

The word here describes a quiet shedding of tears, in contrast to the loud wailing of Mary and the others. Though John's Gospel emphasizes the deity and power of Jesus, here John reveals the tenderness of Jesus. Jesus was no block of stone. He was a sensitive man—capable of great anger, great pity, and great love.

Then Jesus authoritatively commanded the bystanders to roll away the stone that covered the tomb entrance.

"But, Lord!" Martha protested! "By now he will give off a putrid smell. He has been dead four days" (v. 39).

"Didn't I tell you that if you would believe, you would see God's glory?" Jesus answered (v. 40). After the stone was moved away, Jesus stood before the door and shouted, "Lazarus, come out!" (v. 43)

The bound figure of Lazarus emerged, shuffling slowly in the wrappings which enfolded the dead. Gasping onlookers probably approached to help Lazarus free himself as soon as they could believe their eyes. And the little family rejoiced in an unforgettable reunion!

At least two other times Jesus had raised the dead, and he had given the apostles the same power on their preaching mission. But so far as we know, never had he waited four days after death—when decomposition would ordinarily have set in, and, according to Jewish tradition, the spirit of the dead would have permanently departed. Furthermore, this sensational miracle was done in the shadows of the city which had threatened his life and eventually would take it.

THE UNHAPPY SANHEDRIN

Many of Mary and Martha's friends as well as others in Bethany came to believe in Jesus because of this miracle, but the members of the Jewish Sanhedrin, Israel's religious court, were impressed differently.

"What are we doing? For this man does many miracles. If we leave him alone, everyone will believe in him and the Romans will come and take away both the temple and the nation," they fumed (vv. 47, 48).

But the crafty high priest Caiaphas soothed them: "You don't know anything! Nor do you consider it expedient that one man should die for the people and not have the whole nation perish" (vv. 49, 50).

The Sanhedrin feared Jesus would draw such a following that the Romans would consider him a revolutionary and send in troops to destroy the whole nation. Caiaphas had a better plan: Put Jesus to death and spare the nation. From now on the Sanhedrin would stop at nothing to execute Jesus.

In the Old Testament high priests often uttered prophecies to the nation. The godless Caiaphas had unknowningly done just that in prophesying Jesus' death for the people.

Because of persecution Jesus now retreated to northern Judea (vv. 53, 54). He left behind a reunited family, hundreds of converts, and a perplexed Sanhedrin. He had shown he was the master of death in the future and the bearer of life right now. Yet, as Caiaphas prophesied, he would pay the price of death himself to bring his people that life.

THE LAST JOURNEY

After a short residence in northern Judea, Jesus now traveled to the borders between Galilee and Samaria to join the throngs coming to Jerusalem for Passover (Luke 17:11). Jesus' time of destiny had come. It was the spring of the year, the season of new life. He had alternately confronted and evaded the Jerusalem authorities all fall and winter, and now he would run no longer—for his ultimate challenge waited on a hill adjoining the city.

Yet even as he traveled with the crowds, Jesus took advantage of opportunities to perform uplifting miracles and to give incisive instruction. As they approached one village, ten men with leprosy stood at a distance but pleaded for healing from the famed rabbi. "Go, show yourselves to the priests," Jesus told them, careful to observe these commands of Moses. As the lepers began to go to priests nearest their homes, they discovered they were healed. Ecstatic with joy, they raced off, except for one, a Samaritan, who returned to offer thanks.

"Weren't ten cleansed? But where are the nine? Was only this foreigner found returning to give honor to God?" Jesus asked pointedly (vv. 17, 18).

Again Jesus' own people showed spiritual callousness while a heretic Samaritan showed grateful love. All had believed Jesus' reputation for miracle-working, but the Samaritan alone gave thanks to the God of Israel and healed his soul as well—which the others apparently missed.

As Jesus journeyed on, he met some Pharisees who questioned him, "When will God's kingdom come?" (v. 20).

"The Kingdom of god doesn't come with observation," he answered. "Nor will people say, 'It's here,' or

'It's there.' Actually, the kingdom of God is in your midst" (vv. 20, 21).[1]

Jesus meant that the kingdom of God would not reveal itself with the special signs for which the Pharisees looked, nor would it localize itself and start in Jerusalem, the desert, or some hidden community like that of Qumram. Later he would spell out that his kingdom in its final form would descend in power suddently and universally.

But in another sense, the kingdom was staring the Pharisees in the face—for Jesus was the present and future king.

THE CASE OF THE CORRUPT JUDGE

After talking further about his second coming (to be discussed in Chapter Seventeen), Jesus taught another parable about prayer. "A judge in a certain town neither feared God nor respected man. And a widow in that town kept coming to him, saying, 'See to it that I get justice against my adversary!' " (Luke 18:2, 3)

The judge refused for a while, but finally gave in to the widow, not because he wished to uphold the law but to keep her from pestering him. Then Jesus added the divine meaning.

"And won't God certainly grant justice for his chosen ones who cry to him day and night, and with whom he is so patient? I tell you, he will see they get justice swiftly. Nevertheless, when the Son of Man comes, will he find faith on the earth?" (vv. 7, 8)

Jesus knew his second coming was a long way off and he wanted to encourage his followers to patient prayer and unswerving loyalty. In the parable, the judge contrasts with God. The judge is heartless, yet grants justice when pestered to do so. God, fair and compassionate, grants justice because he cannot do otherwise. Nevertheless, God's justice seems slow in coming. But God has not forgotten his followers; when he brings final justice it will be sure and swift—evil will be abolished, unfairness rooted out, and his followers vindicated in a moment. At that time real faith will be scarce, so his people need to cling to their belief even more firmly.

TWO MEN IN THE TEMPLE

Jesus followed with another parable which has taken its place among his most memorable portrayals.

"Two men went up to the temple to pray—one a Pharisee, the other a tax collector. The Pharisee stood and prayed to himself, 'God, I thank you that I'm not like everyone else—robbers, unrighteous, adulterers, or even like this tax collector. I fast twice a week, I tithe of everything I get.'

"But the tax collector stood far off and wouldn't even lift up his eyes to heaven, but beat his chest and said, 'God be merciful to me, the sinner!' I tell you this man went down to his house justified, rather than the other" (vv. 10-14).

The Pharisee was unbelievably arrogant. When he thanked God that he was not like everyone else, he divided humanity into two categories with himself on one side and the rest of the world on the other. He based his righteousness on fasting and tithing and ignored the love, faith, patience, humility, and inner purity Jesus commended.

The tax collector saw himself worse than most—he was *the* sinner. His view may have been correct, for tax collectors had little righteousness to brag about. But he was repentant, so God accepted him while rejecting the self-sufficient Pharisee.

Here in miniature was the heart of the conflict between Jesus and the Pharisees, between his teaching and theirs. They both believed—or said they believed—in the God of Israel. They both taught morality. But Jesus declared mankind couldn't save itself and needed him as its savior. The Pharisees believed that they weren't that bad, and that with enough effort they could achieve salvation on their own. This is why he threatened them. This is why they had to crucify him. Yet when they finally nailed him to the cross, they unwittingly helped provide the world with the very salvation they said wasn't needed. And more than that, by crucifying him, they proved how much they needed salvation themselves.

FOOTNOTES FOR CHAPTER FIFTEEN:

[1] Sometimes this is translated, "The kingdom of God is within you." The context does not allow this interpretation, because in no sense was God's kingdom within these Pharisees.

◆ ◆

SIXTEEN

O Jerusalem, Jerusalem

◆ ◆

As Jesus and the Passover pilgrims caravaned toward the holy city, even the warm March air seemed heavy with tension. Judas was turning over in his mind a plan to defect. The Pharisees, now joined by the Sadducees and the high priest, were waiting for Jesus' arrival like soldiers ready to ambush. And Jesus, who had lived all his life under the shadow that he would die at this Passover, now had to face that his hour had come.

Yet as Jesus traveled, instead of seeking privacy and rest in the face of the looming crisis, he gave himself to the people without reserve, reaching out to anyone who would respond, sorrowing if they turned away, and never hesitating to match wits with the Pharisees who hounded him. These relentless opponents staged another confrontation as a group of them accosted Jesus with the question: "Is it lawful for a man to divorce his wife for any reason he wants to?" (Matthew 19:3).

Two views of divorce prevailed among the rabbis—one very liberal, the other very strict. The liberal view was the most popular, and Jesus had already rejected it in the Sermon on the Mount. The Pharisees were hoping he would denounce it again. It would arouse the anger of the masses, and perhaps even provoke the enmity of Herod and Herodias who had killed John the Baptist.

But Jesus replied: "Haven't you read that in the   189

beginning the one who created them male and female said, 'For this reason a man will leave his father and mother and come into union with his wife, and the two will become one flesh'? So they are no longer two, but one flesh. Therefore what God has joined together, let not man separate."

"Then why did Moses command a man to give her a certificate of divorce and send her away?" they retorted.

"Moses, because of the hardness of your heart, permitted you to divorce your wives. But it was not this way from the first. I tell you that anyone who divorces his wife, except for unfaithfulness, and marries another woman commits adultery," he answered (vv. 4-9).

BACK TO THE GARDEN OF EDEN

Jesus grandly swept aside the wearisome theological minutiae of the scribes and went back to the family's foundation in the Garden of Eden. From this he drew the truth that divorce in any form is really a violation of the divine purpose, for God intended one man and one woman to live together permanently. Then he showed that Moses' permission to divorce was only a concession to human sinfulness, not a command to divorce, as these Pharisees taught.[1] Finally, he revealed that divorce and remarriage constitute adultery unless adultery has already occurred.

Jesus' disciples were shocked. "If this is how it is for a man and his wife, it's better not to marry," they said (v. 10). Their apprehension reflected the male dominance of their culture. A woman could be stuck for life with a deplorable husband, but the husband could easily escape a disagreeable wife. When Jesus challenged his disciples to the same lifelong faithfulness which they expected of women, their response was that it's better not to marry at all!

SINGLE AND SATISFIED

Jesus took their words and made them the basis of further instruction: "Not everyone grasps this saying, but only those to whom it has been granted. For some are born eunuchs, others were made so by men, and some make themselves eunuchs because of the kingdom of heaven. Whoever can grasp this, let him grasp it" (vv. 11, 12).

Jesus agreed it is best for some people not to marry. Then he referred to "the eunuch" who was a castrated male placed by Gentile kings in charge of their harems. Some "eunuchs" are born this way—that is, incapable of marriage and sexual relations because of a congenital defect. Some were made this way by men, as a cruel punishment. But others voluntarily renounce marriage so as to serve God better. The prime example of this in the Bible is Paul. If he had been married, he would not have been so free to travel and risk his life in spreading the gospel.

It's better to be single—*if* God has called you to the single state. Yet no one should remain single from revulsion toward sex or to exhibit superior holiness. The valid reason was the possibility of working for God's kingdom in a way they couldn't otherwise.

SOME GOOD JEWISH MOTHERS

As the disgruntled Pharisees left the scene, another very different group approached. Some earnest Jewish mothers brought their infants and small children for Jesus to bless them (v. 13). Occasionally mothers brought their children to a rabbi for such blessing. The Pharisaic objections to Jesus had evidently gone over the heads of these simple Hebrews, who figured that anyone with Jesus' teaching and healing abilities must have a special hold on God, so they desired his prayers for their children.

But this was too much for the disciples. They thought it was important for Jesus to discourse with Pharisees or themselves, or to heal the sick, but he certainly was too busy for these ignorant women! But Jesus rebuked the disciples' rudeness and welcomed the mothers and children, once again reminding his followers that "of such is the kingdom of heaven" (v. 14).

These two scenes—the discussion over divorce and the

blessing of the children—give important insights into Jesus' view of the family. In Israel the liberal view of divorce especially penalized women. Among the Romans, to whom Jesus' message would soon be preached, divorce was so common that one satirist charged that Roman women kept track of the years by the number of their husbands. Jesus elevated marriage to the highest possible level: it was to be a lifetime commitment. If husbands and wives did not observe this because of callousness, they still must acknowledge the divine ideal. Jesus also elevated women to a new level, for they were the major victims of divorce.

Jewish people loved their children, but most would not expect a great rabbi or the Messiah to take time for infants as Jesus did here. The Romans were often brutal to their children, and sometimes even put their newborn infants to death simply because they were girls instead of boys! But Jesus reached down to the children and lifted them up to a special place, for they are highly regarded in God's kingdom.

Although Jesus never had a wife and children, he enshrined the family as a divine institution, not to be tampered with by man. Wherever his teachings have been adhered to, the family and society have achieved new happiness and stability.

WHO IS REALLY GOOD?

Shortly after this a wealthy young synagogue official, probably one of the finest specimens of Jewish manhood Jesus had ever seen, approached him and asked: "Good teacher, what should I do to inherit eternal life?" (Mark 10:17)

"Why do you call me good? Only God is good," Jesus answered (v. 18).

The Jewish people usually reserved the word "good" for God alone. In his answer Jesus did not deny he was good, but he challenged this man to think deeply about what he was saying. If he really considered Jesus "good," he must also consider Jesus' claim to be God! Jesus went on, "You know the commandments:

'Don't kill, don't commit adultery, don't steal . . . honor your father and mother.' "

"I've kept all these since I was young," the man answered (v. 20).

"Jesus looked at him, loved him, and said to him, 'One thing you lack. Go, sell your possessions, give to the poor, and you will have treasure in heaven, and come, follow me' " (v. 21).

A REPLACEMENT FOR JUDAS?

This personable young man not only had a defective view of Jesus' goodness, but of his own as well. He thought he was keeping the whole law of God by keeping his outward life free of gross sins. But when Jesus asked him to give away his material security and adopt the humble life of the disciples, the man's deficiency was exposed. He had broken the first commandment: "You shall have no other gods before me," making money his real god. He was violating this law every day.

What potential he had, and what a mistake he made as he rejected Jesus' invitation and went away! Perhaps he could have replaced Judas and become a fruitful apostle. Instead, he slipped back into his supposed material security. By the time he was old, he would see Roman armies march over the land, confiscate his wealth, and send his children and grandchildren into exile. Perhaps then he would realize his tragic mistake and surrender to the true God, but still he could never recapture this crucial moment or restore the wasted years.

As Jesus sadly watched him leave he said, "How hard it is for the rich to enter God's kingdom. . . . It is easier for a camel to go through the eye of a needle than for a rich man to enter God's kingdom!" (vv. 23, 24)

This shocked his followers, who, despite all his instruction, still believed wealth was a reward for goodness. If a man rewarded by God couldn't make heaven, then no one could, they thought, as they asked in consternation, "Who, then, can be saved?" (v. 26)

"With men it's impossible. But not with God. For with God all things are possible," Jesus answered.

Jesus attacked the self-sufficiency of the rich. A rich man only receives salvation when he gives up all trust in riches, and with the humility of a child trusts in God alone. This is so impossible for them that they cannot do it on their own. But when God works a miracle in their heart, *even they* can then enter heaven.

Unlike his disciples, Jesus looked upon the rich as perhaps the most unfortunate, easily-deceived people on earth. They seldom faced the basic questions of life because money appeared to provide all the answers. Yet their problem was not so much wealth—Jesus never asked his disciples to sell their possessions as he did this man—the problem was their attitude toward wealth, an attitude which imagined money would provide the security and happiness which only comes from God.

THE GREEDY DISCIPLES

As their journey continued, Jesus tried to correct other distorted views of the disciples. When they boasted of the great rewards they were anticipating in his kingdom, he told them a parable of workers in a vineyard (Matthew 20:1-16). Some of these workers toiled only one hour and got the same wages as those who labored all day.

Heavenly rewards would not be earned by simply piling up more good deeds than the next believer, Jesus taught. The believing thief on the cross, for example, had few good deeds to his name since he knew God only a few hours of his life, but his devotion doubtless gained a great reward. Paul, who perhaps was one of the Pharisees taunting Jesus in Jerusalem while the apostles watched, would also have a great reward though he believed later.

Yet immediately after this James and John had the audacity to request the two top positions in Jesus' kingdom, and he had to remind them that greatness was found in serving, not in aspiring to great positions (Mark 10:35, 45). He illustrated his desire to serve by healing two blind men on the outskirts of Jericho, as they left Perea for the last time (Matthew 20:29-34).

In Jericho Jesus encountered a man who proved to be a stark contrast to the wealthy synagogue ruler, the money-grubbing Pharisees, and the reward-seeking apostles. He was the unpromising Zacchaeus, chief tax collector at the important Jericho customs station, and a man of immense wealth. If anyone was a slave to his riches, it should have been Zaccaheus. But after Jesus visited in his home, much to the consternation of the local Pharisees, Zacchaeus' conversion caused him to donate half his fortune to the poor, plus restoring fourfold the amount of money he had extorted from the local populace (Luke 19:1-9). How this must have lifted Jesus' spirit after the frustrations with the Pharisees and his own followers on the journey!

Nevertheless, as Jesus climbed the twenty miles from Jericho to Jerusalem for his final week of life on earth, he must have been exhausted. The eighty mile journey from Galilee on foot tired him. The ever contentious Pharisees tired him. The spiritually dull disciples tired him, though he never gave up on them. On top of all this, after three and a half years of ceaseless teaching, healing, and praying for his people, in seven days Jesus would face the most horrible death a man would ever die.

THE DRAMATIC ENTRY

After resting on the Sabbath, the final week opened in a most dramatic manner. Jesus sent two of his disciples into the Jerusalem area to untie and bring a donkey and her colt to him. Apparently he had prearranged for their use. Mark notes that the colt had never been ridden (11:2). In Israel, animals designated for sacred purposes were never to have been put to ordinary use, and this colt was set aside this day for the most sacred purpose any animal would ever have.

Jesus rode into Jerusalem on the colt, with its mother walking alongside. Crowds from Jerusalem had been traveling to Bethany to gawk at Lazarus, the man who had returned from the dead. These crowds began to follow Jesus as he came over the Mount of Olives and descended into the Kidron Valley on his way into the city. When crowds of pilgrims in the city saw the procession, they went out to meet Jesus also. In their exuberance they began to lay their coats down on the road before him, and wave palm branches, as they shouted: "Hosanna to the Son of David. Blessed is he who comes in the name of the Lord. Hosanna in the highest!" (Matthew 21:9)

Their reception of Jesus—the clothes on the road and the waving of the branches—was the traditional way of welcoming a king. Their shout of Hosanna—taken from Psalm 118—meant they saw Jesus as Messiah. With some, a real faith no doubt was there. They had heard him teach and seen his miracles, including Lazarus coming out of a tomb. Others believed he was Messiah as the Galileans had—one who would give them a banquet and break Rome's power. Nevertheless, the scene was spectacular.

Still, one part of the scene seemed utterly incongruous for the trimuphal entry of the Messiah King. He was riding on a donkey colt. Horses were the animals of conquest and victory, donkeys symbolized humility and peace. No ancient king would have ridden victoriously into a city on a donkey! But over five hundred years earlier, the prophet Zechariah had said: "Rejoice greatly, O daughter of Zion! Shout in triumph, O daughter of Jerusalem! Behold your King is coming to you; he is just and endowed with salvation, humble, and mounted on a donkey, even on a colt, the foal of a donkey" (Zechariah 9:9 *NASB*).

Ironically, the Jewish rabbis had difficulty reconciling Zechariah's prophecy with other prophecies about the Messiah. They concluded that if Israel was worthy, the Messiah would come out of the clouds of heaven. If unworthy, on a donkey colt!

THE FRUITLESS FIG TREE

Jesus returned from the city to Bethany that night, no doubt to lodge at Mary and Martha's house. The next morning, Monday, he entered the city again. On the way, he observed a fig tree in full leaf, unusual so early in the spring. Jesus was hungry and thought that the tree might have some prematurely ripe figs since it had premature leaves. He discovered it did not and pronounced a curse on it (Mark 11:12-14). The next day, when they passed the tree again, it was withered clear to the roots (v. 20). The disciples were astounded, but Jesus used it as an occasion to teach that faith can work miracles (vv. 23-25).

Yet the strange incident seems to have a deeper, more symbolic significance, for Jesus would hardly curse a tree simply because it didn't have figs. The pretentious tree sprouting leaves but no figs seemed to symbolize Israel in Jesus' time, as the ensuing week demonstrated. Israel made great religious pretensions and was filled with religious activity, but she bore no spiritual fruit, and thus incurred the judgment of God which fell on Jerusalem in A.D. 70.

Of all Jesus' miracles this alone was a judgment. Many times Jesus could have brought supernatural catastrophe on his opponents, as Moses did on Egypt or Elijah did on Israel. Yet the only destruction he ever wrought was on a tree. His miracles saved rather than destroyed, because he came to save, not to destroy his people.

SAME SONG, SECOND VERSE

When Jesus entered Jerusalem after cursing the tree, he went straight to the temple. There he beheld the same scene which had so repelled him three Passovers earlier. The corrupt money changers and merchants were selling their wares and cheating the people the same as before, and Jesus' response was the same as before—he threw them out (Mark 11:15-18).

Despite his three years of ministry and the preaching of John the Baptist, the religious leaders of Israel showed not one ounce of repentance. They were as bound in corruption as when he came.

In contrast to these corrupt men, some Gentiles who, like the Roman centurion, had come to worship the God of Israel, now sought an interview with Jesus (John

12:20-22). They had no doubt heard of his amazing healings and revolutionary teachings—perhaps they were from the heavily Gentile Perea where he had just been.

What Jesus said to them is unrecorded, but their request reminded him afresh that he would soon die, not only for Israel, but for the world beyond. With deep emotion he compared himself to the grain of wheat which can bear fruit only when thrown into the cold ground and buried. Only when the seed thus suffers and "dies," is it fruitful, and only by suffering and dying could Jesus save others from spiritual death.

He then revealed his inner conflict: "Now is my soul troubled, and what should I say? 'Father, rescue me out of this hour?' But because of this I came to this hour" (vv. 25, 26). Jesus was deeply disturbed by the thought of the approaching cross. He naturally shrank from a death which, as will be seen, went far beyond physical suffering. But overriding his apprehension was a firm resolution to die for the world and to save it. Despite Jesus' supernatural power and sinless perfection, the prospect of that death on the cross was becoming harder to bear. It would take every ounce of his strength to go through with it. The reward for his submission to such a death was great, but that could not make the terrible task any easier or the hideous pain any less.

THE DEBATING SOCIETY AT IT AGAIN

The next day, Tuesday, Jesus returned to the temple area to teach. There the Sadducees and Pharisees, for what seemed the millionth time, lured him into debate. They hoped to discredit him before the crowds and establish grounds for his arrest. They felt that only his popularity lay between them and success.

"By what authority are you doing these things?" they demanded (Matthew 21:23). Fresh on their minds was the expulsion of money changers from the temple the day before. Beyond this was his lack of accreditation by any rabbinic school or great rabbi. If he said no one gave him authority, they could arrest him for unauthorized actions. If he claimed God was his authority, they would charge him with blasphemy—for God commissioned no one, they maintained, to disturb temple operations!

But Jesus answered their question with a better one: "Was John's baptism from heaven, or only of human origin?" (v. 24)

Once more, it took only one pregnant sentence to confound them. If they said John was from God, then John's baptism of Jesus served to accredit him. If they said John was not from God, the crowd would turn on them.

THREE DEADLY TALES

But as they retreated in humiliation, Jesus drove even one more nail into their coffin, as he directed three telling parables at them. First, he told of a man with two sons. One son refused to obey his father but later gave in. The other son promised to obey his father but later refused (vv. 28-31). Jesus accused them of being like the second son who agreed to obey but never did, whereas the tax collectors and prostitutes had first disobeyed God, then repented under the teaching of John and Jesus. "I tell you the tax collectors and prostitutes are going before you into God's kingdom!" he said as the shocked crowd looked on (v. 31).

Next he told of a farmer who planted a vineyard, rented it to tenants and went abroad. When he sent his servants to collect the rent, the tenants beat some and even killed others. Finally, he sent his own son in hopes they would respect him, but the murderous tenants also killed him! Then the owner came himself and killed the tenants and rented the farm out to others who would obey the law (vv. 33-41).

The parable was true to life, for great landed estates owned by absentee landlords dotted Palestine. Occasionally the tenants would revolt against the landlords, and if the tenants could secretly kill the owner of the estate and his heirs they could gain legal possession of it. But when such rebellions occurred owners could bring government troops and execute the rebels.

The vineyard pictured Israel, the owner was God, and the tenants were Israel's religious leaders. The servants were prophets, such as John, whom they rejected. The Son, of course, was Jesus. The massacre of the tenants was fulfilled in the Roman destruction of the Jewish state. Handing the vineyard over to another group of tenants pictured the inauguration of the new community of God and, at the end of the age, a generation of Jewish people who would respond and believe.

Jesus concluded the story with a quotation from Psalm 118:22: "A stone which the builders rejected, this became the cornerstone." Ancient builders were superstitious about which stone would be the cornerstone of a building. They would reject many before choosing the exact one which suited them. Jesus said the Old Testament prophesied these leaders would reject their own Messiah, but he would become the cornerstone of a new people of God.

Jesus' third parable was similar to one he had told earlier about the great feast which the invited guests refused to attend because of feeble excuses. But in this parable a king was holding a wedding for his son. When the invited guests, who were probably the nobility of his country, refused to come and even killed the servants who invited them, it was an act of political rebellion. The king soon sent an army to destroy "their city." Then he invited the common citizens to the wedding instead. All of the guests who came, according to ancient custom, were provided with a wardrobe for the occasion by the king himself. But one guest rejected the proffered wardrobe and wore his own. When he was discovered, he was thrown out (Matthew 22:1-13).

This parable also condemned the leaders who refused God's invitation and were replaced by common Israelites, Samaritans, and Gentiles. As a judgment "their city," Jerusalem, was destroyed. But of those who responded to the wedding invitation, the one with his own clothing pictured the false believer such as Jesus described in the parable of the wheat and the tares. Thougn outwardly professing faith in Jesus, he was trusting in his own good deeds—his own suit of clothes—rather than allowing God to clothe him with divine righteousness.

Jesus added this turn to the parable to warn the crowds that even though they might profess to follow him, they had to abandon hope in their own merit and humbly accept God's provision for salvation.

GIVE TO EACH HIS DUE

Another groups of religious leaders, a combination of Pharisees and Herodians, baited Jesus. "Is it lawful to pay taxes to Caesar or not?" they asked (v. 17).

This was another loaded question. If he said "Yes," his popularity would vanish with the people, who hated Roman taxation, and the Pharisees could arrest him without opposition from the crowds. If he said "No," the crowds would love him but the Romans would jail him.

"Show me the tax money," he replied (v. 19). Then they brought him the Roman denarius. "Whose image and inscription is this?" he asked.

"Caesar's," they replied.

"Give then what is Caesar's to Caesar and what is God's to God" he answered (v. 21).

The Roman denarius had Caesar's image and inscription, which showed it belonged to Caesar. When Judeans paid taxes to Rome, they were only returning Rome's money to Rome for services rendered, and Jesus said this was only fair. On the other hand, the inscription on the coin stated Caesar was a god. Jesus said coins belonged to Caesar, but not worship—that went to God alone.

In a dozen words Jesus summed up for the whole age the relationship of the believer to the state. What philosophers, social activists, and theologians have devoted volumes to, he summed up magnificiently in a sentence! Even the Pharisees and Herodians were amazed that such wisdom could pour forth on a moment's notice.

THE WOMAN WITH SEVEN HUSBANDS

As the chargrined Pharisees and Herodians left, the Sadducees entered. This religious group denied a future resurrection of the dead and were confident Jesus could not escape their snare. They proceeded to tell the fantastic story of a woman married in succession to seven brothers who died one after the other. When God raised the dead, they asked, which of the seven would justly be her husband? (vv. 23-28)

Jesus answered, "You are in error, because you don't know either the Scriptures or God's power" (v. 29). He went on to explain that at the resurrection believers would be like angels because they would not marry or have families. The intimacy of family life, so necessary on this lonely planet, would be unnecessary in heaven where sin cannot block human relationships. Heaven would be populated with people who never age and never die, so reproducing children would be needless.

Then Jesus had a statement for them to answer about resurrection: "Haven't you read what God said to you, 'I am the God of Abraham, and the God of Isaac, and the God of Jacob'? He is not the God of the dead, but of the living" (vv. 31, 32).

The Sadducees believed only in the first five books of the Old Testament and thought Moses, their author, denied resurrection. They believed death was extinction and future life was non-existent. Jesus quoted from the scene in the book of Exodus where God appeared to Moses. God implied he was the God of Abraham, Isaac, and Jacob at that moment, though they had been dead hundreds of years. That meant they were still alive—and the Sadducees' theory was dead! Another presumptuous balloon had been punctured.

A WISE PHARISEE

The Pharisees now regrouped to come up with another question. One of their number decided to test Jesus' wisdom honestly rather than attempting to trap him. "Teacher, what's the greatest commandment in the law?" he queried (v. 36).

Behind the question was the Pharisaic theology which divided the law into 613 commandments—248 of them positive and 365 of them negative—and then debated which ones must be observed to gain salvation.

Jesus replied: " 'You shall love the Lord your God with all your heart and with all your soul and with all your mind.' This is the first and greatest commandment. The second is like it: 'You shall love your neighbor as yourself.' On these two commandments hang all the law and the prophets" (vv. 37-40).

Jesus swept aside Pharisaic technicalities once again, and in only three sentences went to the heart of the Old Testament. Obedience to these basic commands would cause all the others to be kept. The inquiring Pharisee recognized Jesus' wisdom and commended his answer (Mark 12:32, 33).

Jesus' response was revealing: "You are not far from God's kingdom" (v. 34). Perhaps as this man returned home to meditate on Jesus' words, faith was born in his heart and he moved from the outskirts to residence in God's kingdom.

THREE IN ONE

With his foes silenced, Jesus now put them to the test. "What do you think about the Messiah? Whose son is he?" he asked.

"David's," they answered.

"How come, then, David speaking by the Spirit, calls him 'Lord'? He says, 'The Lord said to my Lord: sit at my right hand until I put your enemies under your feet.' If David calls him 'Lord,' how come he is his son?" (Matthew 22:42-45).

The couldn't answer a single word! Of course Messiah was David's descendant, but much more—he was David's Lord from heaven. In fact, Jesus referred here to the trinity: the Spirit of God inspired David, who spoke of

two divine personalities: "the Lord" and "my Lord."
Hence the Father, the Son (Messiah), and the Holy
Spirit—three persons, though one God—are drawn by
Jesus from the Old Testament.

Perhaps this set the Pharisees thinking. Was this only
a man who raised Lazarus and performed miracles? Was
this only a man who read their thoughts and constantly
outwitted them? Or was this God incarnate?

THE SEVEN WOES

As the Pharisees pondered this puzzle, Jesus launched
his most scathing criticism on these men who had im-
placably resisted and bitterly maligned him. He said the
Pharisees should be honored as Israel's teachers, and as
they expounded her law they should be followed (Matthew 23:1-3). But he declared that their lives contra-
dicted their words, and they made serving God a heavy
burden through their mass of traditions (v. 4).

Their great problem, Jesus went on to say, was that
their piety was only to impress men. They made boxes,
called phylacteries, which contained Scripture passages,
and strapped them around their heads and left arms
during prayer, all for display. Then they made the straps
especially wide to draw more attention to their supposed piety. Similarly the four tassels attached by every
devout Israelite to his coat were enlarged to a supersize
to attract special notice (vv. 5-7). They loved the public
seats of honor and special titles, like "Rabbi," "Spiritual
Father," "Great Leader." But it was all for show, and
militated against the humility and brotherhood Jesus
taught.

Jesus sternly pronounced seven great woes on these
men. He condemned them for blocking the entrance of
God's kingdom for themselves and others through their
opposition to Jesus; for going to fanatical lengths to
convert recruits to their corrupt system; for clever use
of oaths to promote deception; for elevating such trivia
as tithing plants from their garden while neglecting the
crucial issues of life; for making ritual their religion; for
measuring life by outward appearances; and for boasting

of their allegiance to dead prohpets while defaming the greatest prophet of all (vv. 13-32).

A SAD FAREWELL

In righteous anger, Jesus called them a bunch of snakes and reptiles and warned: "Upon you will come all the righteous blood that has been shed on earth, from the blood of righteous Abel to the blood of Zechariah . . . whom you murdered between the temple and the altar. I tell you, all this will come on this generation" (vv. 35, 36).

The first book of the Bible recorded Cain's murder of Abel, and Chronicles, the last book in the Jewish arrangement of Scriptures, recorded the death of Zechariah at the hands of the evil king Joash. Between these two godly men flowed a river of martyrs' blood. Instead of learning from the past, these Pharisees were about to kill the greatest prophet of all—and seal their dreadful fate.

Jesus could not think of Jerusalem's judgment without sorrow, and as he prepared to leave the temple for the last time, he looked over the city and uttered those memorable and tear-stained words: "O Jerusalem, Jerusalem, the one killing the prophets and stoning those sent to her! How often I wished to gather your children as a bird gathers her young under her wings, and you refused. Your house is left to you desolate. I tell you, you won't see me again until you say, 'Blessed is he who comes in the name of the Lord' " (vv. 37-39).

Jesus looked at this great city—the spiritual capital of the world and the home of the temple—and prophesied its desolation. Its citizens, who longed for their Messiah but were deaf to his call when he came, would not see him again—not until the end of the age.

TRUE DEVOTION

Then the sorrowing Messiah noticed a poor widow putting her meager offering into the temple coffers, and his heart rejoiced as he noted: "This poor widow has put more than anyone else into the treasury, for they put in from their abundance, but this woman out of her poverty put in all the money she had" (Mark 12:43, 44).

The Gospel writers probably never forgot this obscure incident because it contrasted so sharply with most of the temple activity. This ragged widow was a picture of true devotion and piety, while the arrogant Pharisees and Sadducees were pictures of the ultimate in hypocrisy.

When Jesus first came to the temple as a baby in his mother's arms, a poor widow named Anna honored him. When he left the temple for the last time, he honored another poor widow. Though at the bottom of the social ladder, such widows ranked among God's heroes to Jesus.

Jesus now sorrowfully left the temple, his public ministry to Israel ended. She would not see his face, listen to his voice, or feel his healing touch again for centuries. Multitudes of common Israelis loved and responded to Jesus, but the leadership could not endure him. Despite their impressive credentials, the leaders tried to mix spiritual devotion with pride. They were proud they were Abraham's descendants, proud they were rabbis, Pharisees, and Sadducees. They were proud of all their piety. They dreamed they were in a class by themselves, instead of sinners in need of redemption like the rest of mankind.

It is easy, of course, to condemn them. But if Jesus reappeared today, the human race gives no evidence it would be any more humble.

FOOTNOTE FOR CHAPTER SIXTEEN:

[1] See Chapter Six.

SEVENTEEN

◆ ◆

"I Shall Return"

◆ ◆

Adjacent to the Holyland Hotel in modern Jerusalem is a fascinating model of the ancient temple and the holy city as they stood in A.D. 66—four years before Titus' Roman legions leveled them. The reproduction, constructed by the painstaking labors of Jewish scholars and craftsmen, captures on a small scale what must have been the staggering beauty and grandeur of the Jerusalem temple, which covered one sixth of the city. "He who never saw Herod's edifice has never in his life seen a beautiful building," the rabbis used to say.

This temple of Jesus' time resembled the original temple built by King Solomon some thousand years earlier. The Babylonians destroyed that structure in 587 B.C., and a smaller temple was built by Ezra seventy years later. Nearly five hundred years after that, when King Herod came to power, he decided to re-create the ancient glory of Solomon's temple and more, in a vain attempt to win loyalty from his hostile Jewish subjects. He and his successors spent over eighty years constructing one of the architectural wonders of the ancient world, only to have the Roman armies destroy it all in a few months.

As Jesus and his disciples walked through those magnificent temple grounds on their way out of the city at the close of his public ministry, some of his followers stopped to remind him of the magnificence of the buildings, and perhaps to show him a newly completed addition. Jesus had just announced that Israel's house would be left desolate (Matthew 23:38), and they couldn't fathom why God would forsake such a beautiful structure as this!

"You see all this?" Jesus said. "I tell you one stone won't be left on another which won't be thrown down" (Matthew 24:2).

Some of the temple stones were over forty feet long, twelve feet high, and twenty feet wide, according to the historian Josephus, and must have weighed over a hundred tons! For Jesus to speak of that mass of limestone being leveled stunned the disciples.

Walking up the slope of the Mount of Olives east of the city, Jesus decided to sit down to rest, and his followers, dying of curiosity, begged him: "Tell us, when will this be, and what is the sign of your coming, and the end of the age?" (v. 4)

By this time the disciples had grasped that Jesus was going away and would return as a conquering king, but they apparently thought his absence would be brief, and they still could not conceive that his departure would be by death. As they listened eagerly for Jesus' answers that afternoon, the beautiful city with its beautiful temple glistened across the valley in the glow of the setting sun. Jesus began to reveal the future of that city and temple, and ultimately their effect on the whole world, in his famous "Olivet discourse"—a discourse in the process of literal fulfillment today.

NOT A PRETTY PICTURE

"Watch out that no one misleads you. For many will come in my name saying, 'I am the Messiah, and will mislead many, and you'll hear of wars and rumors of wars, but see that you're not terrified. For this must happen, but the end is not yet. For nation will rise against nation, and kingdom against kingdom, and there will be famines and earthquakes in different places, but all this is the beginning of labor pains.

"Then they will hand you over to affliction and will kill you, and you will be hated continually by all the nations because of me. And then many will be offended, and will betray each other and hate each other and many false prophets will arise and lead many astray, and because anarchy increases, many peoples' love will grow cold. But the one who endures to the end, he will be saved. And this gospel of the kingdom will be proclaimed in the whole world as a testimony to all the nations, and then the end will come" (vv. 4-14).

Silence must have gripped the disciples at these sobering words. Distress and destruction were to characterize history between his first and second coming. False messiahs would delude the Jewish people. The world in general would be plagued by ceaseless warfare and natural disasters such as famines and earthquakes. Terrible persecutions would pursue Jesus' followers, false prophets would mislead the masses, and increasing anarchy would smother human compassion. Finally, a world-wide proclamation of Jesus' message—the only positive sign—would signal the end of the age.

Jesus was no dreamer. He knew that sinful man on a cursed earth could never usher in a golden age, and that science, education, economic theories, or international organizations could never create utopia. Twenty centuries of world turmoil, culminated by the universal crises of our time, have verified beyond dispute Jesus' view of history.

During the ebb and flow of the years, of course, these signs have ebbed and flowed. Natural disasters have been sporadic, persecution of believers has flared and subsided, the gospel has penetrated new areas and periodically retreated, and wars have given way to brief periods of peace. Jesus revealed that such upheavals are not the end of the age—they are the labor pains brining to birth God's new era. His followers should endure these trials knowing that they do not necessarily mean his second coming is just around the corner.

THE DOOM OF A GREAT CITY

At this juncture, an important prophecy omitted in Matthew's and Mark's accounts appears in Luke's Gospel.

"But when you see Jerusalem being surrounded by armies, then know that her desolation has drawn near. Then let those in Judea run to the mountains, and let those in the city get out, and let those in the area not enter in to it. For these are the days of punishment in fulfillment of what stands written. . . . For there will be great distress upon the land and wrath on this people, and they will fall by the edge of the sword and will be led prisoners to all the nations, and Jerusalem will be trampled down continually by the Gentiles until the times of the Gentiles are fulfilled" (21:20-24).

The disciples had asked when the temple would be destroyed. Jesus said its doom and the city's was sealed when armies surrounded it. Between A.D. 66-70 the events Jesus described were literally fulfilled. Ironically, the Jewish revolt against Rome which issued in Jerusalem's destruction was sparked partially by the belief that Messiah would deliver the nation at this time. As the doom of Jerusalem drew near, tens of thousands of men, women, and children flocked into the city destined for seige by Roman armies because they wanted to witness Messiah's victory! But Jesus had instructed his followers to abandon the city because her plight was hopeless. Thousands of Israelis were slaughtered, but those who believed Jesus' words escaped.

Jesus also taught that Jerusalem would be under the Gentile heel from then on until his second coming. Since her destruction in A.D. 70 Jerusalem has languished under the oppression of Gentiles—until 1967. But even the Six-Day War did not really free Jerusalem from Gentile domination. On Israel's sacred temple site stands a Moslem mosque today which Israelis dare not disturb. Only a minority of ancient Jerusalem's residents are Jewish, and both the city and nation lie under the continual threat of war from surrounding Gentile states.

EVEN MORE SPECTACULAR REVELATION

As Jesus' disciples listened in numb amazement, he continued his vivid sketch of the future with prophecies which made even what they had already heard seem tame.

"So when you see the abomination which desolates, spoken by Daniel the prophet, standing in the holy place—let the reader understand—then let those in Judea run to the mountains. . . . And pray that your flight won't be in winter or on a Sabbath, for then there will be great tribulation, such as has not happened from the creation of the world until now, nor ever will happen again. And except those days had been cut short, no human would have been saved, but because of the chosen ones those days will be cut short" (Matthew 24:15-22).

A search of the Old Testament book of Daniel turns up three references to the "abomination" cited by Jesus—Daniel 9:27; 11:31; and 12:11. The first and last descriptions are not found in history, but many scholars agree that Daniel 11:31 was fulfilled in 168 B.C.

At that time a Syrian ruler named Antiochus Epiphanes conquered Jerusalem, took possession of the temple, and set up an altar to Zeus in the sacred santuary where he offered a pig! This revolting desecration of the temple so infuriated Israel that it fomented a revolt which eventually expelled Antiochus. His "abomination which desolates" pictured the event predicted by Jesus for the future—a prediction unfulfilled for more than nineteen hundred years.

Some scholars insist that the abomination Jesus prophesied was the destruction of the temple by the Romans. But Jesus warned his followers to flee when they saw the abomination. Such a warning would prove useless after the city was conquered, its inhabitants taken captive, and the temple in the process of destruction. Jesus described an act of terrible idolatry while the temple was still standing. History records no incident which parallels Antiochus' desecration of the sanctuary.

Furthermore, Jesus explicitly timed the future abomination during a period of such "great tribulation" that nothing before or since would equal it. All of life would be exterminated if the time was not shortened. This was not true of the destruction of Jerusalem. Jesus was obviously predicting an event which has not yet occurred.

THE GREAT DICTATOR

What is this ominous event? The rest of the New Testament sheds further light. Paul wrote to the Thessalonians of a future world leader described as a "man of lawlessness" who "opposes and exalts himself above everything that is called God and receives worship, so as to seat himself in God's temple, proclaiming himself to be God" (2 Thessalonians 2:3, 4).

Paul says the most evil, satanically-inspired genius of all history will enthrone himself in the Jerusalem temple and demand the worship of Israel and the world! When this event occurs, said Jesus, any believer who lives in Israel should flee immediately from Jerusalem, for terrible persecution and tribulation will soon follow.

How could such a seemingly far-fetched state of affairs come about? The last quarter-century has set the stage for this prophecy to be fulfilled. The Jerusalem temple would have to be reconstructed, which necessitates a state of Israel and a population with Jewish laws, for Jesus noted that Jewish sabbath restrictions would hamper travel (Matthew 24:20).

In 1948, despite the combined forces of surrounding Arab states and the opposition of many leading nations, a small number of Jewish statesmen and soldiers brought to birth the modern state of Israel. In 1967, Israel captured Old Jerusalem and the temple area from Jordan. In 1973, the Arab oil embargo guaranteed that Israel increasingly would become the focus of international tension. In 19?? the temple may be reconstructed and an evil leader may establish himself as dictaor over the earth, demanding the ultimate worship that unleashes world-wide persecutions, eventual atomic holocausts, and the greatest tribulation period of history. What seemed like an apocalyptic fairy tale fifty years ago is now conceivable reality!

THE FINAL WRAP UP

For believers on earth during this holocaust, Jesus gave further advice.

"Then if anyone says to you, 'Here is the Messiah,' or 'There he is,' don't believe it. For false messiahs and false prophets will rise up and perform great miracles. . . . If someone says to you, 'He's in the desert,' don't go out. . . . For as the lightning starts in the east and flashes to the west, so will the coming of the Son of Man be. Wherever the carcass is, there will the vultures gather. . . . And then the sign of the Son of Man will appear in the sky, and then will all the people of the earth mourn, and they will see the Son of Man coming on the coulds of the sky with power and great glory" (vv. 23-30).

The coming of the true Messiah cannot be mistaken, for like the lightning it will be a public event filling the sky; and as vultures gather over a carcass so will he and angelic hosts gather to judge and cleanse the world.

This was the spectacular coming which Israel and Jesus' disciples longed for. He would not enter the human scene secretly and live in obscurity, as at his first appearance. He would suddenly take over with the most fantastic display of supernatural power in all history. He would dazzle and stun like the cosmic Messiah the disciples saw transfigured. Both lines of Old Testament prophecy—that of a humble, suffering Messiah, and that of a ruling, glorious Messiah would find their fulfillment in the one Messiah who would appear two distinct times.

THE LAST GENERATION

But when would Jesus consummate his kingdom? The disciples must have yearned to know. Jesus used an illustration of a fig tree whose new leaves indicate that summer is near. Then he added: "When you see all these things, know that it is near, right at the door. I tell you this generation won't pass away until all this takes place" (vv. 34, 35).

The generation of people that sees the abomination which desolates, the era of great tribulation, and the other horrors he described would be the same generation which sees his return. These terrible events would not unfold over the centuries—they would all transpire in less than a generation. With Israel now in possession of Jerusalem and world crises mounting, the present generation seems a candidate to be the final one. But Jesus left the time indefinite so every generation would watch and pray expectantly. Paul felt his generation might be the last, and other believers have named their own.

Jesus emphasized that only God the Father knew the day and hour of Messiah's return (v. 36). Even Jesus did not know, for while on earth he was bound by the limitations of human flesh. In light of this, his followers certainly need not demand to know.

Then he added some startling new information. "For as it was in the days of Noah, so will the coming of the Son of Man be. For as in the days before the flood, they were eating and drinking, marrying and being given in marriage, until the day Noah entered the ark; and they understood nothing until the flood came and swept them all away. So also will be the coming of the Son of Man. Then two men will be in the field—one will be taken, one will be left. Two women will be grinding at the mill—one will be taken, one left" (vv. 37-41).

MILLIONS SUDDENLY VANISH

Jesus said that some people would suddenly vanish from the earth to be with him at his coming—one would be taken, one left. This event would occur unexpectedly when people were pursuing life as usual, indifferent to warnings of judgment, as in the days of Noah. Paul later described this dramatic event in I Thessalonians 4:16,

17, speaking of believers being "caught up" to meet the Lord in the air at his second coming.

This event, called "the rapture" by many biblical scholars, is one of the most spectacular prophecies in the Bible, but its timing is a matter of great debate. The comparison of Noah's days gives some clue. It is difficult to imagine life proceeding as usual during the great tribulation upheavals. Cosmic disturbances, worldwide conflicts, and persecution of believers would hardly permit the marrying, eating, drinking, and working in the field which Jesus pictured.

Jesus seemed to imply that his second coming would comprise a series of events covering several years, just as his first coming was a series of events which covered at least thirty-three years. The first event would be the sudden "catching up" of his followers at any unexpected moment, for which they are to watch keenly. This would be followed by the abomination which desolates, the terrible crescendo of tribulations, and finally his appearance in the clouds as conquering king. Yet during the period of tribulation many would become believers, even though believers alive at the time of the great "catching up" would be gone.

The disciples had looked and longed for the spectacular. The Pharisees had charged that Jesus' miracles were not spectacular enough. But this almost unimaginable course of events pictured by Jesus to the apostles was overwhelming. And this same Jesus, whose words had proved so trustworthy in all else, then said, "Heaven and earth will pass away, but my words will never pass away" (Matthew 24:35).

PRACTICAL PICTURES

Jesus devoted the rest of the discourse to a series of parables about his second coming. These were like practical pictures which made what he had said applicable to life. He refused to teach prophetic truth simply to satisfy curiosity about the future. He wanted it to change lives.

First, he told of the owner of a house who failed to protect it against thieves, then of a slave put in charge of other slaves while his master was on a journey (vv. 42-50). The owner never knew when a thief might come, and the slave never knew when his master would return. Both parables illustrated that believers must be ready for their "catching up" at any time. Unbelievers, in contrast, would suddenly find themselves swept into tribulation judgments, and beyond that, in many cases, to hell itself.

Then Jesus told of ten female wedding attendants who waited for the procession of the bride and groom to come down the street late at night, according to ancient custom. Some had oil to light their lamps for the procession, and others did not. When the bride and groom came unexpectedly, the negligent girls could not light their lamps and enter the wedding banquet. Again, this contrasted the believer who prepared for the return of Jesus and the unbeliever who was unprepared and missed the rapture (Matthew 25:1-13).

Jesus followed this with a parable of slaves who were each entrusted by their master with several thousand dollars and given instructions to invest the money while he was gone. Two of the slaves invested and reaped handsome dividends, as well as additional rewards from their master on his return. But the third buried his money and was condemned by his master (vv. 14-30). This parable encouraged the disciples to invest all of their abilities in serving Jesus. The slave who refused such an investment pictures the unbeliever who passes by the opportunity to follow Jesus, to his ultimate ruin.

UNCONSCIOUS ACTS OF FAITH

Jesus concluded his discourse by picturing the final judgment of the nations at his second coming. The individuals in the nations are divided into two classes: "sheep" and "goats." The sheep enter his kingdom and the goats are cast into hell. The basis of judgment is whether they performed merciful acts toward believers or ignored them (vv. 31-46).

Jesus had often taught that anyone who gives a cup of cold water to even the least of his followers because they are his followers, will not lose his reward (Matthew 10:42). He viewed such acts of mercy as ultimately springing from a faith in him and his cause, though the person might be unaware of it at the time. During great persecutions of believers, many who have risked their lives to help them have through such acts come into faith themselves. Jesus re-emphasized for his followers the importance of seemingly insignificant acts of mercy because the incredible revelations of this discourse could easily inflate their egos and promote a thirst for the spectacular. Feeding the needy and visiting the sick seem very unexciting, but Jesus taught they are deeds which make headlines in heaven.

ONE DAY . . .

As Jesus ended his discourse, and the sun set over the city and the temple, he looked at them with sorrow—sorrow over the Jewish rejection of him, sorrow over what would happen to his people. But he also knew that victory would finally be his. One day he would gloriously return. One day he would eliminate injustice in his city, his nation, and the world. One day that city would worship him. One day he would return, and it would all be different.

EIGHTEEN

◆ ◆

A Night to Remember

◆ ◆

As Jesus and his band of followers left the Mount of Olives that afternoon, on opposite sides of the hill opposite dramas were being enacted. To the west of the Mount of Olives, in Jerusalem, some of Jesus' worst enemies were searching for a secret way of arresting and eventually executing him (Matthew 26:3-5). At the same moment, on the eastern slope of the Mount, in Bethany, some of Jesus' dearest friends were busily preparing a festive meal to honor him.

The host for the meal was "Simon the leper" (v. 6), and assisting him were Mary, Martha, and Lazarus. As Jesus and his disciples reclined for dinner that evening, he looked into the eyes of one grateful man he had raised from the dead, and into the eyes of another he had healed of leprosy. Few of his friends appreciated him more than these two men and their families that night.

As the meal proceeded, Mary entered and made one of the most lavish gestures of appreciation toward Jesus he had ever known. She began to anoint him with oil, as was the custom, but she used an oil that was very special. It was contained in a special alabaster vessel, broken open just for the occasion, and its worth was actually a whole year's salary—equivalent to thousands of dollars today. It was probably a valuable heirloom, the most precious possession Mary had. Furthermore, she rubbed the fragrant substance on Jesus' feet as well as on his head, then let down her hair and wiped his feet (John 12:3).

Attending to the feet was reserved for servants, and for a woman to take down her hair in public was considered shameful. But Mary was so consumed with honoring the man who had resurrected her brother physically and herself spiritually that she humiliated herself before the wide-eyed audience.

A BEAUTIFUL GESTURE CRITICIZED

Judas Iscariot, however, objected to the extravagant display. "Why wasn't this ointment sold for thousands of dollars and given to the poor?" he complained (v. 5).

His objection seemed sensible, but John tells us he was dishonest, and, as the treasurer of the group, he habitually stole from their common funds (v. 6). He would have loved to get his sticky fingers on a whole year's wages!

"Let her alone," Jesus said, "for it is intended for her to preserve this for the day of my burial. You will always have the poor among you, but you won't always have me" (vv. 7, 8). Mark adds that Jesus declared, "Wherever this gospel is proclaimed in the whole world, what this woman did will also be told in memory of her" (Mark 14:9).

Mary's devotion received generous praise from Jesus because he recognized the gift as an emblem of deep love. In addition, Mary alone evidently understood that Jesus' death was imminent. Bodies were ordinarily anointed before burial, and she had provided a preliminary anointing while he was still alive.

The incident shows that Jesus appreciated acts of love and generosity even when they had little apparent practical value. Mary had not fed the poor or clothed the naked with her treasure, but she had done something on which no price tag could be placed, and the beauty of her act, like the beauty of an artistic masterpiece, belongs to the ages.

THE TRAITOR

When dinner ended, however, Judas sneaked away and made a bargain with Jesus' enemies. Incensed by Mary's lavish sacrifice and the rebuke he felt he had received, he agreed to hand Jesus to them secretly for thirty pieces of silver—the price of a common slave and less than half the value of Mary's oil (Matthew 26:14-16).

What a contrast Mary and Judas were! He was so greedy that he stole from his impoverished fellow workers. She was so generous that she gladly surrendered her most valued treasure. To her, Jesus was priceless—she couldn't do enough for him. To him, Jesus wasn't worth half as much as the oil, and he gladly handed him over to crucifixion. Few acts have been more tender than hers that night, and none more heartless than his.

THE MOST SIGNIFICANT PASSOVER OF ALL TIME

The next day, Wednesday, was apparently a day of rest for Jesus and the disciples. Then on Thursday, Nisan 14, on the Jewish calendar, they prepared for the Passover meal. Jesus sent Peter and John this fateful day to sacrifice a Passover lamb in the temple at mid-afternoon and then prepare the meal which would be eaten that evening (Luke 22:7-13). Since the Jewish day began at 6 P.M., Thursday evening became Friday, Nisan 15, and the actual Passover day.

Jesus instructed them to look for a man in the city carrying a pitcher of water and to follow him to his house. That man would provide them a room already prepared for their Passover celebration. As men rarely carried pitchers of water, this was evidently part of a pre-arranged plan, with secret signals already worked out by Jesus. He had to keep Judas ignorant of the feast's location or the authorities might have arrested him in the midst of his final meal with the apostles.

As the sun set that Thursday, Jesus and the other ten apostles joined the throngs converging on Jerusalem and came to the secret room where they met Peter and John. There the apostles prepared to eat what was to become, unknown to them, the most significant Passover of all time.

ANOTHER ARGUMENT

As they sat down to eat, a dispute arose among some as to which was the greatest, probably provoked by the seating arrangement (vv. 24-30). According to Jewish custom, since Jesus was the host, the most worthy guest should be on his left and the next most worthy on his right. Jesus himself disdained the system, but to the apostles, who should sit where was crucial.

As the meal began, Jesus rose from his reclining position and laid aside his clothing, so that like a slave, he wore only a loin cloth. With a pan of water and a towel, he began to wash the disciples' dusty feet. Such duties belonged only to slaves, but there were none present, so the most famous and illustrious member of the group took the servant's place and ministered to his quarreling guests.

How this must have shamed the twelve who had just been disputing over their greatness! When Jesus came to Peter, he felt the Messiah was performing such an incongruous act that he refused to allow it. But Jesus sternly reprimanded him: "Unless I wash you, you have no part with me."

"Then not my feet only, but also my hands and head!" Peter answered.

"Whoever has been bathed needs only to wash his feet. He is entirely clean; and you are clean, but not all of you," Jesus replied (John 13:8-10).

John discloses that Jesus refered to the member of the twelve whose soul was unwashed—Judas.

Peter's impulsive blunders often gave Jesus opportunities to teach profound lessons. As a man who went

221

out to dinner would bathe at home and only need his feet washed when he arrived, the eleven apostles were bathed spiritually through true faith in the Messiah. They might fail and need correction and subsequent cleansing, but this did not mean they needed another bath or re-entrance into his kingdom. Their spiritual bath was once and for all.

WASHING EACH OTHER'S FEET

There was further meaning in Jesus' service:

"You call me the teacher and the Lord, and you speak correctly, for so I am. If I, therefore, your Lord and teacher, have washed your feet, you also ought to wash one another's feet" (vv. 12-14).

Washing the feet of fellow believers symbolized a willingness to do menial tasks to help one another. If Jesus humbled himself to the task of a common slave, his true followers could do no less. The washing also symbolized the cleansing of sins which take place as believers exhort, correct, counsel, and restore each other. In Jesus' new community the brotherhood would humbly love and serve each other instead of competing for privileges and power.

THE BETRAYER ANNOUNCED

The Passover celebration continued until Jesus shattered its joyous mood with the announcement that one of the twelve would betray him (v. 21). The apostles still did not realize Jesus meant he would die soon, or that the betrayal he mentioned was connected with his death. They probably thought that one of them would prove disloyal in the future in some trying circumstance.

But Peter beckoned another apostle, who was next to Jesus, to ask who the traitor was. This apostle is anonymously described as the disciple "whom Jesus loved," who "leaned back" against Jesus to ask him the traitor's identity (vv. 23-25). Early tradition is unanimous that this apostle "whom Jesus loved" was John, the author of the Gospel, who describes himself this way several times. Since they did not sit in chairs, as pointed out earlier, but reclined with their feet stretched away from the table, leaning on their left elbows, John must have been on Jesus' right. When he leaned back, his head would be touching Jesus' breast, and he could quietly whisper the question to Jesus.

Jesus replied, "The one to whom I will give this piece of food when I have dipped it" (v. 26).

Probably John alone heard the answer. Jesus then dipped a morsel of food in the Passover sauce and handed it to Judas. Judas, suspicious that Jesus knew his plan, whispered back to Jesus, "Certainly, I'm not the one, am I?" (Matthew 26:25) Jesus confirmed that he was (v. 27).

THE GUEST OF HONOR GOES INTO THE NIGHT

For Jesus and Judas to have this private conversation, Judas must have been next to Jesus. Since John was on Jesus' right, Judas must have been on his left. The seat to the left of the host was reserved for the guest of honor, and Jesus' offer of food to Judas was an act of friendship. Perhaps as the disciples argued about seating arrangements at the beginning, Jesus settled the matter by inviting Judas to be the guest of honor. This would not be unusual, since Judas was the treasurer of the group. Yet at the precise moment when Jesus showed his love for Judas by offering the morsel, Satan entered into Judas (John 13:27).

Judas had a choice—either surrender to Jesus' love, or surrender to the devil's hatred. He chose the latter. Within a few minutes he quietly left the feast and was on his way to inform the Sanhedrin where Jesus was, so they could arrest him. John says "he went out immediately, and it was night" (v. 30). It was night in more ways than one, for Judas was never to bask in the light of God again.

THE NEW COMMAND

After Judas departed, Jesus began to prepare the

eleven for his crucifixion. "I'll be with you only a little while longer. . . . Where I go, you can't come," he said. "I give you a new command—that you love one another as I have loved you. By this everyone will know you are my followers, if you love one another" (vv. 33-35).

The command to love was not new, but the command to love as Jesus did was new. No Old Testament hero had given his life for the world. Never before had there been such an example to imitate! Yet Jesus' followers were not to love to earn Jesus' love; they were to love *because* he loved them.

But Peter was disturbed by Jesus' words that he was going away and none could follow. Peter insisted he could follow and was even willing to lay down his life for Jesus. But Jesus predicted Peter would deny him before morning came (vv. 36-38).

Peter and the others were proud of their loyalty to Jesus. They dreamed they would do anything for him—even die. But the shoe was on the other foot; Jesus would die for them. If they had boasted less of their loyalty, they might have had more of it when the need was so great, a few hours later. They had to learn humility the hard way.

LAST PASSOVER—FIRST SUPPER

As the conversation and eating continued, the little group in the upper room came to the high points of the Passover meal. Before the roasted lamb was served, the host would take a loaf of unleavened bread, break it in pieces, then distribute it to the guests. After the lamb was eaten, he would then ask God's blessing on a cup of wine which, after sipping, he would pass to each guest to sip in turn.

As Jesus broke and passed the bread, he said words which no Jewish host had ever pronounced before. "This is my body which is given for you. Do this in remembrance of me."

After they ate the sacrificed lamb, Jesus distributed the wine and said, "This cup is the new covenant in my blood, which is poured out for you" (Luke 22:19-20).

The Passover feast commemorated the deliverance of ancient Israel from Egypt, and, in particular, the deliverance from the death angel who "passed over" their houses, but brought death on all the first born sons of Egypt. This night Jesus closed down one memorial service and opened up another. The new Passover would no longer remember Israel's deliverance, but that of all believers everywhere. It would no longer mark salvation from Egypt, but salvation from sin. The basis of deliverance would no longer be the blood of a lamb, but the blood of Jesus, "the lamb of God."

On this historic and fateful night the old covenant with Israel ceased, and a new covenant with Israel and the world beyond began; the religion of Moses evolved into the religion of Jesus, the sacrifice in the temple gave way to the sacrifice on the cross, and the Passover Feast become "The Lord's Supper."

WAITING FOR THE COBWEBS TO CLEAR

Of course, Jesus didn't expect the befuddled little group of former merchants and tradesmen to grasp all this that night. Yet he knew that shortly the cobwebs would clear—after his death and resurrection they would begin to understand. So as supper ended, he continued to plant great truths in their hearts which would later bloom and flourish.

"Stop letting your hearts be troubled. You trust God, trust in me also. In my Father's house are many rooms. Otherwise, I would have told you. For I am going to prepare a place for you. And if I go and prepare a place for you, I will return and take you with me that where I am, you may be also" (John 14:1-3).

The apostles were still distressed because Jesus had announced he would depart. They had burned every bridge and built all hopes upon him—and now he was leaving! Jesus tried to allay their fears by saying they could trust him as completely as they trusted God. He was going to the Father's house—heaven—and prepare a place for each of them, then he would return and take them to that place.

The word "take," which Jesus used here was the same word he used when he spoke of believers being caught up at his second coming (Matthew 24:40, 41). At that time dead believers also would be caught up to receive a resurrection body, Paul said (I Thessalonians 4:16, 17). Jesus here gave his personal promise of returning to take his followers to their indescribable reward of a new physical body and a new, divine home.

THE WAY, TRUTH, AND LIFE

Anxious and bewildered, the apostles protested they still didn't know where he was going or how to get there.

"I am the way, and the truth, and the life; no one comes to the Father except through me," he answered (John 14:6). Many great leaders have demanded devotion to their causes but not to themselves. They have claimed their teachings would save men, not they themselves.

Jesus built everything about ultimate faith in himself. He said he was the road to God, and God's truth and life incarnate as well. He even told them that "he who has seen me has seen the Father" (v. 9). He claimed a union with God so unique that he was saying, in effect, he is God incarnate.

ANOTHER HELPER

Jesus then unveiled one of the greatest truths of all. "I will ask the Father," he said, "and he will give you another helper, who will be with you forever. The world cannot accept this helper, because it neither sees him nor knows him. But you know him, for he lives with you and will be in you" (vv. 16, 17).

The Greek word for "other" implies he is the same kind as the original helper, Jesus. So his followers are promised a helper distinct from Jesus but just like him—who will be in them forever! Moments later Jesus revealed more about him: "But the helper, the Holy Spirit, whom the Father will send in my name, will teach you everything and will remind you of everything I told you" (v. 26).

The scribes referred to the Spirit of God, or the Holy Spirit, because he was mentioned in the Old Testament. But they did not see him as a divine person distinct from the heavenly Father. Jesus had already implied that, though God is one in essence, the Messiah is a divine person distinct from God the Father. Now he explained that the same is true of the Holy Spirit. Though God is one, he consists of three persons: Father, Son (Messiah), and Holy Spirit.

Since the Holy Spirit is a spiritual being, he can live inside those who receive him and be present everywhere at once. The limitations of space and time, to which Jesus had subjected himself as a human, would not hinder the Holy Spirit. It was as if every believer, everywhere in the world, would have one just like Jesus living in him. The impact of this on the world would far transcend the impact that Jesus could make in his human limitations.

When the day of Pentecost came two months later, this is exactly what happened. On that day more believers were won than Jesus apparently gained in three years. Within a few years his followers, empowered by the Holy Spirit, would reach multitudes all over the ancient world.

THE VINE AND ITS BRANCHES

Jesus and his followers left the upper room—perhaps just ahead of Judas and the soldiers—and began to walk to the Garden of Gethsemane on the lower slope of the Mount of Olives. Along the way they stopped, perhaps near a vineyard, and Jesus further illustrated profound principles for the eleven's spiritual progress.

He told them he was the true vine and they were his branches, with the Father being the vinedresser (John 15:1). Over the temple gate hung a beautiful golden vine, an emblem of Israel. But Israel had never born fully the fruit expected of her, because she was not really the true vine—Jesus was.

As unfruitful branches were pruned from a vine, fruitless branches would be severed from him, Jesus said (v. 2). On his mind, perhaps, was Judas—the branch with so much potential who, like the cursed fig tree, had leaves only. Judas was now severed forever from Jesus. In the same way, many professing to believe in Jesus resemble good branches, but lack genuine faith and fruit, and eventually become severed from the true body of believers or any profession of faith.

But other branches bear fruit, and God cleanses them to bear more fruit, as a vinedresser might wash off insect deposits. Jesus told the eleven that his words had already cleansed them (v. 3), and they could expect further cleansing through God's purifying work in their lives. As a branch cannot bear fruit alone, so they could not bear fruit unless they kept relying on Jesus—apart from him they could accomplish nothing for God (vv. 4, 5).

Then, perhaps thinking of Judas again, Jesus warned that those who depart from him will wither and face judgment (v. 6). Those who follow him all their lives, whatever the cost, will find they bear fruit and more fruit; but the superficial followers who attach themselves only for a while will find they have turned their backs on the only life and hope this world has. As they wither, die, and head to destruction, like Judas, they will awaken too late.

A FINAL WORD

Jesus also spoke of his love for the apostles, of the Holy Spirit's stupendous future ministry in them, and of persecution they would face. Then, as they listened in silent awe, he concluded with a moving prayer.

First Jesus asked God to honor him so he might honor God. He spoke confidently of finishing all that God had given him to do (John 17:1-8). Then he prayed for the eleven, that God would keep them from evil in an evil world (vv. 9-19). He prayed last for all who would believe through them, that they would be united in spirit, and that all who believed would join him in heaven (vv. 20-26).

For a man facing death, this prayer and all that Jesus had said that night seemed incredible. Only a year ago he had been at the height of his popularity, and now he was facing certain death and seeming defeat. Yet he spoke as if victory had been won and all was well! He had done all God wanted, he had made no mistakes, he had no regrets. He spoke as if on the verge of history's greatest conquest rather than in the shadow of a crucifixion.

For a man so to speak was not normal. For a man to have no sense of guilt whatever was astounding. Shining through the words and works of Jesus, now nearly finished, was again the inescapable fact that he was more than man—he was God in the flesh.

NINETEEN

♦ ♦

"Tetelestai!"

♦ ♦

It was one o'clock in the morning as Jesus and his disciples threaded their way down the slope from the city walls and crossed the Kidron Valley to a peaceful clump of olive trees. The small orchard, known as Gethsemane, was probably owned by friends, and it became Jesus' frequent retreat during his tempestuous Jerusalem ministry. It was to be his last shelter on an inhospitable earth.

Jesus told eight of the disciples to sit down while he took Peter, James, and John with him a little further to pray. But this was utterly different from his usual times of prayer—Jesus was obviously in a state of overwhelming agony greater than they had ever seen.

"I am terribly distressed, even to the point of death," he told them. "Stay here and watch with me" (Matthew 26:38). Then Jesus fell on the ground and prayed, "My Father, if it is possible, let this cup pass from me; yet not what I will, but as you will" (v. 39). After a short interval, he prayed again, "If this cup cannot pass away unless I drink it, let your will be done" (v. 42). Then he prayed a third time and got up.

Luke tells us this struggle was so great that an angel came and strenthened him, and that Jesus' suffering was evidenced by his sweat becoming "like clots of blood falling to the ground" (22:44).

What was happening? In this hour Jesus was enduring overwhelming torment over the prospect of dying for the sins of the world. It was his main mission on earth, for he had said: "The Son of Man came not to be served, but to serve and to give his life a ransom for many" (Mark 10:45). His death was destined to pay for the sins of mankind and to ransom those who believed on him from eternal death. But Jesus shrank from the horrible task. The terrors of his death would far exceed the physical torment of crucifixion. No one else would ever know what that death involved, but in Gethsemane at that hour, he knew, and he could hardly stand it.

A RARE MEDICAL CONDITION

Luke perceived some measure of the struggle in describing Jesus' perspiration as great "clots" of blood. It is possible that Luke, himself a physician, was noting a rare medical condition now known as haematidrosis. Under extreme emotional stress blood vessels expand so much that they break where they come into contact with the sweat glands. The suffering individual then actually sweats blood. As Jesus prayed in agony, Luke's Gospel accurately observes that he was covered with a bloody sweat.

The Garden of Gethsemane reveals, as perhaps no other place, that Jesus was a true man. Though he never sinned, he was not a robot programmed automatically and painlessly to obey God. He faced real choices of obedience or disobedience, and on this occasion chose obedience only through a frightful ordeal. The letter to the Hebrews, contemplating such incidents as this in Jesus' life, states: "For we do not have a high priest who is unable to sympathize with our weaknesses, but one who was tempted in all points like as we are, yet without sin" (Hebrews 4:15).

The Garden of Gethsemane probably witnessed the most difficult test of Jesus' life. In the wilderness temptation, Luke records that the devil left off his severe testings of Jesus "until an opportune time" (4:13). Though he tempted Jesus all through his ministry, Satan's fiercest ests were probably reserved for the beginning and end of Jesus' ministry, in the wilderness and in the garden. The garden was "the opportune time," when Jesus, worn by three years of selfless giving and the heightening stresses of his final week, was more vulnerable than at any other time.

While the first man failed in the Garden of Eden, this man triumphed in the Garden of Gethsemane. The devil's dreams crashed in a heap under the weight of those hated words: "Not my will, but yours be done."

A KISS OF DEATH

While this great drama was unfolding, James, Peter, and John, who swore they would go to death with Jesus, were peacefully sleeping. But their slumber was disturbed by the approach of Judas and a band of soldiers who, unable to get to the upper room in time, had now descended on Gethsemane, guided by the traitor's knowledge that Jesus often came here.

The final irony now took place as Judas greeted Jesus with a conventional kiss of friendship and said, "Hello, rabbi!" (Matthew 26:49) The kiss indicated Jesus' identity to the soldiers so they could capture him in the dim light. The guest of honor at the Passover now repaid Jesus' kindness with a fatal kiss of death.

But Jesus was more than the master of the situation. "Who are you looking for?" he said.

"Jesus of Nazareth!" they answered.

"I am he," Jesus' voice boomed back (John 18:4, 5).

The words "I am he" again suggested the Messianic claim. Judas and the soldiers, knowing that Jesus was a miracle worker, were probably afraid of a judgment miracle being called down on them. When Jesus uttered his great Messianic claim they fell back in terror (v. 6).

THE MASTER SUBMITS

Nevertheless, Jesus submitted to arrest. But the aroused Peter continued to descend into the blackest night of his life by grabbing a sword and slashing off part of the ear of Caiaphas' servant, who had accompanied the soldiers. Jesus, in his final miracle, restored the ear and rebuked his impulsive disciple:

"Don't you think I could ask my Father and he would send right now more than twelve legions of angels? But how then would the Scriptures be fulfilled that this must happen?" (Matthew 26:53, 54)

Twelve legions of angels would be seventy-two thousand. The Old Testament records that one angel slew 185,000 Assyrians and another killed all the first-born sons of Egypt! Jesus was making clear that his coming trial and death were not forced on him by circumstances over which he had no control. He chose to submit to them; he had said earlier, "no one takes my life from me, but I lay it down voluntarily" (John 10:18).

THE DESPERATE PROSECUTORS

Jesus began an exhausting trial that stretched through six stages lasting past dawn. Justice was swift then, so trial and execution could immediately follow arrest. Furthermore, the Jewish authorities would have to bring the case before Pontius Pilate, the Roman official, soon after dawn if they wished a decision that day; and they dared not prolong the issue that could arouse a fickle populace.

Jesus was taken first before Annas, a former high priest and the father-in-law of Caiaphas, the current high priest. As Annas shared the profits of the temple businesses which Jesus had disrupted, he was especially interested in examining the renegade rabbi. Annas, clever and corrupt, was probably the most powerful Jewish leader in Israel.

Annas asked Jesus about his disciples and his teaching, perhaps hoping to indict some of his followeres as well (John 18:19). Jesus said nothing of his disciples and requested Annas to bring forward witnesses against his teaching, according to the Sanhedrin's legal procedure. Jesus' request provoked a blow on his face from a temple officer (vv. 21-23), and Annas gave up on getting further answers. He ordered Jesus to be bound and taken to Caiaphas for formal Sanhedrin trial.

233

For the Sanhedrin to convict Jesus, it had to produce two witnesses against him whose testimony agreed. A number of witnesses testified, but they could not agree on any single charge. The best they could do was to charge him with profaning the temple, but even here the witnesses could not unite (Mark 14:55-59).

With the whole case threatening to dissolve, Caiaphas approached Jesus and asked if he was the Messiah.

Jesus answered, "I am, and you shall see the Son of Man sitting at the right hand of power and coming with the clouds of heaven" (v. 61).

The Sanhedrin had the charge it needed. This Jewish revolutionary, forsaken by his followers and standing before them in chains, could not possibly be the triumphant Messiah, they thought. They paid little attention to his ominous words that he would return on the clouds of heaven and one day judge them.

With Jesus convicted as a fraudulent Messiah, the court waited until dawn to pass a legal sentence of death. They quickly declared Jesus guilty of blasphemy, and sent him off to Pontius Pilate to secure Roman agreement to his death.

COURAGE TURNED INTO COWARDICE

While Jesus' trial was proceeding, two other lives were being radically affected by the night's events. Peter and the other disciples had fled from the garden, but Peter stealthily followed Jesus to the fringe of the courtroom scene. A slave girl in charge of the courtyard door noticed Peter entering, and she began to converse with other servant girls about him. When he drifted to a fire grate to warm himself, she and some of the others came over and said, "You were also with Jesus the Nazarene."

"I don't know or understand anything you're talking about!" he answered (vv. 67, 68).

But the slave girl was tenacious. She stirred up the questioning bystanders again, and Peter denied knowing Jesus the second time. Later, another servant, who was a relative of the man wounded by Peter's slash in the garden, began to accuse him.

Peter, fearful for his life, had had enough. He began

to curse and to swear that he did not know Jesus. He was not using profanity, but inviting curses from God should he be lying, and solemnly swearing in God's name that he had never known Jesus. This was as strong a denial as one could make. But as Peter uttered his oath, he heard the cock crow and he remembered that Jesus had said he would deny his Master three times before the cock crowed twice (v. 72). Crushed, the shamed apostle went out and wept bitterly (Luke 22:62).

A TRAGIC END

As Peter was going through his agony, Judas was also going through his. When the Sanhedrin pronounced Jesus guilty and sealed his death, Judas felt remorse, perhaps surprised that Jesus had not freed himself through a miracle. Judas brought back the thirty pieces of silver to the Sanhedrin and declared, "I have sinned by betraying innocent blood."

"What do we care. Take care of it yourself," they told him (Matthew 27:4, 5).

Judas threw down the silver and rushed out. In no time he had hanged himself, and his body fell to a field where it lay broken and drenched in blood—a tragic and gruesome end for the treasurer of the twelve apostles and the Passover guest of honor.

The hypocritical Sanhedrin felt it was illegal to keep the tainted money, so they used the thirty pices of silver to buy the land upon which Judas had died. The land, known as the potter's field, was converted into a burial plot for Jewish pilgrims (vv. 6-8, cf Acts 1:18, 19). The Jewish leaders, who felt no twinges of conscience over Jesus' brutal crucifixion or Judas' tragic suicide, now scrupulously insisted that the money which helped finance both tragedies be spent legally and charitably. Such were their distorted values!

THE POTTER'S FIELD

Yet in all their callousness, they were so remarkably fulfilling divine prophecies that their actions would actually draw others to faith in Jesus. Over six hundred years earlier the prophet Jeremiah had stood in a field outside the city walls and announced the field would become a burial ground for Israel as a symbol of judgment upon her (Jeremiah 19). Reliable tradition says that very field, which became known as the "potter's field," became the place of Judas' death and the Sanhedrin's cemetery for Jewish pilgrims.

Over one hundred years after Jeremiah, the prophet Zechariah acted out a parable against the Jewish nation—he portrayed himself as a faithful shepherd, rejected by his own flock, and considered of no more value than the cheapest slave:

"And I said to them, 'If it is good in your sight, give me my wages, but if not, never mind.' So they weighed out thirty shekels of silver as my wages.

"Then the Lord said to me, 'Throw it to the potter, that maginificent price at which I was valued by them' So I took the thirty shekels of silver and threw them to the potter in the house of the Lord" (Zechariah 11:12, 13, *NASB*).

Perhaps unkowingly Zechariah was prophesying that Messiah would be valued at the insulting price of thirty pieces of silver. Judas threw the thirty shekels in the temple, and they were used to buy a potter's field, exactly as pictured by Zechariah five hundred years earlier.

Both Judas and Peter betrayed Jesus, and both repented. Yet Judas went on to destruction and Peter to eventual restoration. Why? Judas apparently hoped to force Jesus into political messiahship through betrayal. When he realized that Jesus would not take over as Messiah, but would die instead, he knew that all hopes of reward in the Messianic kingdom were gone. Judas loved rewards, money, and position. He repented that his plans had failed and that no place in Jesus' kingdom awaited him. But of his basic unbelief he never repented, and to his death he felt *Jesus had failed him.*

Peter, in contrast, repented that he had been such an arrogant braggart. He grieved, not that his plans had gone awry, but that *he had failed Jesus.* This crucial difference distinguished Judas and Peter. To one, Jesus was Messiah to be manipulated for his own ends; to the other, Jesus was Messiah who saved sinners.

It was the difference between heaven and hell.

AN OBSCURE MAN AND HIS DAY OF INFAMY

As dawn broke, Jesus was brought before Pontius Pilate, the Roman governor in charge of Judea from A.D. 26 to 36. Since Rome reserved the right to inflict the death penalty, the Sanhedrin had to convince Pilate that Jesus deserved death. Little could this obscure Roman official imagine that his verdict would bring him universal infamy for centuries to come.

The Sanhedrin charged that Jesus claimed to be a political ruler. The Romans cared nothing about a religious figure, but a claim to kingship might spark revolution. As the fastidious Sanhedrin pressed charges against their unrecognized Messiah, they refused to do so in Pilate's palace, because entering a Gentile's house would make them ceremonially unclean for observing the week-long Passover festivities (John 18:28). They did not hesitate to execute Jesus on the Passover, but meticulously observed their religious tradtions in the process. They strained out gnats and swallowed camels!

As Pilate questioned Jesus, he could find no evidence that Jesus claimed to be a political Messiah. In fact, Jesus told him: "My kingdom is not of this world. If it were of this world, my servants would be fighting to keep me from being delivered to the Jews. But now my kingdom is not from here" (v. 36).

It seemed to Pilate that the issue revolved around another of the endless theological debates of Judaism, and that somehow Jesus had humiliated the Jewish leaders and incurred their wrath. Yet if Pilate denied the Sanhedrin and set Jesus free, he would add to the problems he already had with this volatile people.

THE PLAYBOY KING AGAIN

At this point Pilate thought he saw a way out. He heard that the infamous king of Galilee, Herod Antipas, was in town. Since Jesus was a Galilean, Pilate sent him to Herod in hopes the king would take the matter off his hands. Unfortunately for Pilate, the playboy king only desired to be entertained by a miracle from Jesus, and when Jesus refused to oblige him, Herod sent him back. Yet the depraved monarch could not close out his history in the Gospel records without one more inhumane act. He joined his guards in ridiculing and mocking the Messiah (Luke 23:8-12).

Pilate now thought of another way out: it was customary to release a prisoner of popular choice at Passover, and Pilate had a notorious revolutionary named Barabbas in custody. If he offered the crowd a choice between Jesus and Barabbas, Jesus' followers would surely outshout Barabbas' supporters.

Pilate was sorely disappointed when he discovered the crowd went for Barabbas instead (Mark 15:11). The crowd had collected for political reasons, to see which prisoner Rome would release. Jesus' terrified followers and the truly devout of Israel were not among them. Faced with the choice of Barabbas, who was not a common criminal but a popular revolutionary, and the controversial spiritual leader who was opposed by their own Sanhedrin, the crowd chose Barabbas without hesitation.

ROMAN BRUTALITY UNLEASHED

But Pilate still was not ready to give in. He thought if he brutally scourged Jesus, out of pity the crowd would call for his release. The Roman scourge was a leather whip with several thongs, each containing pieces of bone or metal. A severe thrashing with this torture instrument could be fatal. Sometimes victims were beaten so that their bones were exposed or their intestines spilled out.

After beating Jesus with the scourge, Roman soldiers draped him in a bright garment and clamped a crown of dead thorns on his head. As Jesus stood before them, ready to collapse and in deep pain, they spit on him, beat him over the head with a stick, and bowed down before him in mock reverence! (vv. 16-19; John 19:1-3)

Pilate then led the pitiful figure, robed and crowned,

out to the crowd. But instead of sympathy he heard: "Crucify! Crucify!" (John 19:6) Pilate continued to insist that he found no reason to crucify Jesus, but the leaders answered that Jesus was guilty of blasphemy—a capital crime under Jewish law—because he claimed to be God's Son (v. 7).

Pilate was superstitious and this struck fear into him. He took Jesus back into his palace and questioned him further (vv. 8-11). His wife had dreamed that Jesus was an innocent man and urged Pilate to free him (Matthew 27:19). But the chief priests told Pilate he would be Caesar's enemy if he did not crucify this threat to the empire, and Pilate weakly gave in (John 19:12). The Roman emperor was the paranoid Tiberius, with whom Pilate's status was never secure. Faced with crucifying an innocent but inconsequential Jew, or having the Sanhedrin lodge a protest that he favored revolutionaries, the governor surrendered. The battered prisoner was led off to crucifixion.

The soldiers escorted the stumbling man to a skull-like hill outside the city wall and nailed him on a cross between two other victims, probably revolutionaries like Barabbas (Mark 15:27).[1] On the way, Jesus was required to carry part of the cross until his strength gave out, and a man named Simon of Cyrene was forced by the soldiers to help. Mark mentions that Simon was the father of Alexander and Rufus, who were evidently well-known believers (v. 32). Simon's heart-wrenching involvement may have caused him and later his two sons to become believers!

SADISM AT ITS WORST

The crucifixion Jesus underwent was not different from what thousands of criminals endured, but this didn't make it any less cruel. Jewish capital punishment, by stoning, brought almost instant death; but Roman crucifixion was a slow, excruciating torture. When the victim was nailed to the cross, the spikes were driven through the wrists just below the palms of the hands, which caused maddening pain. The feet were then nailed one on top of another with one large spike, and the body's weight pulled on these ragged wounds.

If the victim hung limply, his chest muscles cramped and breathing became impossible. To keep alive he had to lift himself up by his lacerated hands and feet. So he alternately sagged and straightened up until exhaustion and pain killed him. Even strong men could not long endure such a procedure, so the ·sadistic Romans invented various props to extend the victim's agony. Crucifixion was reserved for none but the lowest criminals, and forbidden if one was a Roman citizen.

A THOUSAND-YEAR-OLD DETAIL

As Jesus hung on the cross, some of his faithful Jewish followers mingled with the mocking crowd which witnessed the horrible scene. His friends wept at the terrible injustice and Jesus' awful pain (John 19:27-31). The pitiless Roman soldiers divided Jesus' clothing among themselves, as he possibly hung naked on the cross. One got his sandals, another the undershirt, another his belt, and another his head covering. Since there were five articles of clothing for the four of them, for his outer robe they drew straws.

Little did these pagan Gentiles realize that they were fulfilling what King David had written a thousand years earlier: "They divide my garments among them, and for my clothing they cast lots" (Psalm 22:18, *NASB*). How could David forsee—except by divine revelation—such a little detail ten centuries earlier: most of the garmets divided, but for one piece they cast lots!

It was customary at crucifixion for the victim's crimes to be posted on the cross. Ironically, over the protest of the Sanhedrin, Pilate wrote: "Jesus the Nazarene, King of the Jews" in three languages (John 19:19, 20). He got grim vengeance on the leaders for their badgering him into the crucifixion, and also announced to the world Jesus' true identity!.

As Jesus slowly weakened, he noticed his mother in the crowd and he asked "the beloved disciple," John, to care for her in this time of need (vv. 26, 27). A careful comparison of Matthew 27:56, Mark 15:40, and John 19:25, shows that Mary was John's aunt, since she was the sister of his mother, Salome. In her hour of desperation, Jesus placed his mother, whose soul had now been pierced with the sword of Simeon's prophecy, in the care of her nephew.

SEVEN FINAL WORDS

Often the crucified would cry out profanities and insults—their final act of rebellion against the authorities they despised. But the cries of Jesus were different. He cried for God to forgive his enemies (Luke 23:34); he promised eternal life to one of the revolutionaries hanging next to him who had believed on him (v. 43); he asked John to care for his mother; he screamed, "My God, my God, why have you forsaken me?" (Mark 15:34); he called, "I thirst" (John 19:28); he announced, "It is finished" (John 19:30); and he prayed, "Father, into your hands I commit my spirit" (Luke 23:46).

When he cried, "My God, my God, why have you forsaken me?" the crowd thought he was calling for Elijah since the words "Elijah" and "My God" sound similar in Aramaic (Mark 15:34-36). According to popular folklore, Elijah was supposed to come in the hour of need to save the innocent. Actually, Jesus was uttering the cry of the Twenty-Second Psalm, the same psalm prophesied not only the dividing of the garments but this entire crucifixion scene.

Jesus shrieked in despair because at that moment he was truly being forsaken by God for the sins of the world which he bore in his body. He was at last draining the cup of God's wrath that he had begun to sip in Gethsemane. The experience was indescribable agony, infinitely worse than the pains of crucifixion.

"TETELESTAI!"

The cry "It is finished" translates the one Greek word *tetelestai.* John chose this word to translate Jesus' cry of triumph. By it Jesus meant that all was complete—the biblical prophecies of his earthly life and atoning death were fulfilled. He also meant that all he was sent to do was finished—nothing left undone. He also meant that the redemption of his people everywhere was accomplished; their sins were paid for. When stamped on receipts the word meant "paid in full." Probably many of John's readers were struck by the wonder that all sins were now paid in full.

By three o'clock Jesus was dead. To make sure of his death, a Roman soldier drove a spear into his side, probably into his heart, and blood and pericardial fluid, which would accumulate in the heart of the dead, flowed out (John 19:31-34). Jesus' legs were not broken, though this was usually done to hasten death. Broken legs forced the victim to hang limp, which prevented him from breathing.

The Passover lamb must be a perfect lamb, sacrificed, prepared, and eaten without breaking a bone, according to the Old Testament (Exodus 12:46). On this Passover day, God's true Passover lamb was sacrificed without a bone broken, to redeem a people from bondage. But this was not the end of the story. It was only the beginning, as the events of the next few days would reveal.

WHO CRUCIFIED JESUS?

Controversy has flared recently over who was responsible for Jesus' crucifixion. Prestigious scholars have suggested that Jewish leaders of Jesus' time were not the real culprits. Underlying these scholarly views is a laudable desire to oppose every form of anti-semitism.

But removing blame from the Pharisees and Sadducees in the interests of anti-semitism is unnecessary. Jewish people today are not accountable for mistakes of their ancestors twenty centuries ago any more than a Southerner today is accountable because his distant forefather may have imported slaves in 1750.

The New Testament places primary blame for the crucifixion on a few thousand Pharisees and Sadducees.

Beyond them, it points an accusing finger at a cowardly Gentile, Pontius Pilate, and a fickle Jerusalem mob who chose Barabbas over Jesus. In contrast, thousands of Jesus' Jewish contemporaries embraced him as Messiah. During its first two decades, most of the early church was Jewish and every New Testament author except Luke was a Jew. Though the majority of Israel eventually rejected Jesus, the majority of every Gentile nation has since done the same, despite their pretentious claims to be "Christian" countries.

God doesn't hold anyone now living accountable for Jesus' crucifixion. But he does hold us accountable for rejecting Jesus as Messiah. For this sin no one can blame his ancestors—he can only blame himself.

FOOTNOTE FOR CHAPTER NINTEEN:

[1] The Greek word which describes them could mean either thief or revolutionary, but thievery was not punished by crucifixion, whereas revolution was.

"Tetelestai!"

◆ ◆

TWENTY

"O Death, Where is Your Victory?"

◆ ◆

In his book, *Who Moved The Stone?*, Frank Morison begins with a startling chapter entitled, "The Book That Refused To Be Written." In it he describes how he intended to refute Jesus' resurrection, but instead after careful research he became convinced of its reality. The resulting book turned into a brilliant defense of the resurrection, much to the author's surprise.

Jesus' followers were destined for a similar surprise on Sunday, Nisan 17. The crucifixion had blasted every hope. Yet as events began to unfold, they slowly realized that the most spectacular miracle of all time was staring them in the face—Jesus had physically risen from the dead.

Jesus died about 3 P.M. on Friday. His followers hastened to provide him with a decent burial before the Sabbath began at 6 P.M. But who would dare associate himself now with this executed revolutionary? Annas had sought to discover his followers; those who buried him might be subject to arrest and execution.

Ironically, the two who stepped forward to bury him were the least likely. Joseph of Arimathea and Nicodemus, both prominent Sanhedrin members who had secretly favored Jesus, now openly declared themselves his followers by requesting the body from Pilate (John

19:38-39). While the supposedly courageous apostles hid, these two former cowards declared their faith for all the world to see.

ANOTHER AMAZING PROPHECY

Yet behind their courage was the fulfillment of a final detail of one of the most amazing prophecies of the Old Testament. Seven centuries before Jesus' birth, Isaiah had written:

"He was despised and forsaken of men, a man of sorrows and acquainted with grief. . . . Surely our griefs He himself bore, and our sorrows He carried. . . . He was pierced through for our transgressions, He was crushed for our iniquities. . . . All of us like sheep have gone astray, each of us has turned to his own way; but the Lord has caused the iniquity of us all to fall on Him.

"He was oppressed and He was afflicted, yet He did not open His mouth; like a lamb that is led to slaughter, and like a sheep that is silent before its shearers. . . . He was cut off out of the land of the living, for the transgression of my people to whom the stroke was due. His grave was assigned to be with wicked men, yet with a rich man in his death; although He had done no violence, nor was there any deceit in His mouth" (Isaiah 53:3-9, *NASB*).

The prophecy pictured an innocent victim who would die silently and without complaint for the sins of his people. The ancient scribes often puzzled over this. If this passage spoke of the Messiah, how could he suffer such rejection and death, yet come from the clouds of heaven to rule and reign? The solution that one Messiah would appear two times was hidden from them until Jesus came. Jesus' trial and crucifixion fulfilled Isaiah's prophecy of Messiah's first appearance to the letter.

Isaiah's final statement about his death was puzzling because it predicted his persecutors intended a criminal's grave for him, but he was rewarded with a rich man's burial instead. A penniless and condemned criminal could hardly expect his body to be wrapped in fine linen, generously covered with sweet-smelling spices, and placed in a new tomb. This was the burial awarded to heroes or nobles, yet this is what Jesus received. Joseph and Nicodemus had put the final pieces in the puzzle of this amazing prediction.

THE EMPTY TOMB

On Saturday, Nisan 16, Jerusalem and Jesus' followers rested. But one group who hated Jesus for his supposed Sabbath violations were violating the Sabbath themselves. The Pharisees and chief priests sought Pontius Pilate's permission for a guard around the tomb and a wax seal on the stone rolled over its entrance (Matthew 27:62-66). They wanted to guarantee that his body stayed in the tomb, but their efforts were to be in vain.

On Sunday morning at the crack of dawn several women made their way toward the tomb to finish anointing Jesus' body. They were in a quandry over how to get inside because of the great wheel-shaped rock rolled into a groove at the entrance. They were probably unaware that the soldiers had been assigned to guard it.

When they arrived, they found no soldiers, no stone over the door, and no body of Jesus! Instead two angelic visitors informed them he had risen from the dead (Luke 24:1-8). The women, with Mary Magdalene leading the way, now ran to tell the apostles the unbelievable story (vv. 9-12, John 20:1, 2). Peter and John immediately ran to the tomb to see for themselves (John 20:3).

As the sun's first rays shone in the doorway, "Simon Peter . . . went into the tomb. and stared at the grave clothes. The cloth which had been around Jesus' head wasn't lying with the other wrappings, but was wrapped in a place by itself" (vv. 6, 7).

Slowly the truth began to dawn on Peter and John. If Jesus' body had been stolen, the linen wrappings would be gone or left in disarray. Apparently they were undisturbed from the time Nicodemus and Joseph had left the tomb, except Jesus' body had vanished from underneath them! The cloth around his head, in a place by itself and covered with ointment, probably was etched with the very outline of his face. Peter and John "saw and believed" (v. 8). Their weak and wavering faith was beginning to admit what the wrappings told them—Jesus had risen from the dead.

THE FIRST TO SEE

In their excitement they bolted out the entrance and headed off a few seconds before Mary Magdalene arrived. She came, looked in the tomb again, and saw the two angels who had now reappeared. But still she could not fathom the mystery. She thought Jesus' body was stolen, and broke down in tears—not only was he dead, but now someone had taken him off! (vv. 11, 12)

Suddenly, she sensed someone behind her. She turned around and a familiar voice said, "Why are you crying?"

"If you have taken him away, tell me where you've laid him, and I'll take him away," she answered, not recognizing who it was (vv. 13, 14).

"Mary," came the one-word reply. Only one person had ever said her name that way. She began to clutch Jesus' arm and hold tight as the mystery finally began to unravel for her.

"Stop clinging to me," Jesus said, "for I have not yet ascended to the Father, but go to my brothers and tell them I ascend to my Father and your Father and my God and your God" (v. 17).

Mary was so overwhelmed by Jesus' presence that she wanted to hold on to him, afraid he would soon leave and never return. Jesus wanted to reassure her that he would remain for some time—his ascension was still many weeks off. Yet that ascension would surely come. When it did Jesus would be closer to Mary than human touch—through the Holy Spirit he would live in her heart.

Jesus' appearance to Mary Magdalene, from whom he had driven out seven demons (Luke 8:2), was his bountiful reward for her unusual devotion. Since the ancients gave little credence to a woman's word, this story of Mary would never have been invented by Jesus' followers. Both this and Jesus' next appearance were to women, because he wished the world to know that the portion of the human race which has suffered so much indignity at the hands of men has attained a new dignity in his kingdom.

As the rest of the women returned to the tomb, Jesus met them also. He allowed them to touch his feet to assure them he was real, because unlike Mary Magdalene, they were not trying to cling to his physical presence (Matthew 28:9, 10).

A LAME EXCUSE

In the meantime, the guards, who had left the tomb earlier in a panic when an angel appeared and an earthquake rolled away the stone, reached the Sanhedrin (vv. 2-4, 11). The superstitious soldiers, squeamish about guarding the tomb of a miracle worker who had said he would rise from the dead, were now in a state of terror.

The Sanhedrin bribed them to say that while they were asleep the disciples came and stole the body. Then the Sanhedrin guaranteed Pilate would not punish them for sleeping on duty (vv. 12-15). Yet, who could believe that a whole Roman guard would fall asleep when such dereliction could cost their lives? Who could believe that they all would sleep through the disciples' frantic efforts to roll back the stone? Finally, who could believe that such sound sleepers would know what had happened while they slept? However, the hardened Sanhedrin would rather perpetrate such a lame alibi than admit Jesus had arisen.

AN UNFORGETTABLE JOURNEY

As this memorable Sunday wore on, two formerly obscure followers of Jesus became the next resurrection witnesses. As they returned to Emmaus, a few miles outside Jerusalem, Jesus joined them for their journey. Apparently his appearance was altered, so they did not immediately recognize him. The alteration had the value of preventing outsiders from recognizing him; perhaps it was caused by his body entering a new dimension, for he was no longer subject to space and time.

As Jesus began to engage the two in conversation, they told him of the crucifixion, the empty tomb and the women who claimed he was risen. They were more bewildered by all this than prepared to believe the truth.

Finally Jesus said, "Foolish men and slow of heart to believe all that the prophets have spoken! Wasn't it necessary for the Messiah to suffer these things and then to enter into his glory?" (Luke 24:25) Jesus then unravelled for them that Messiah's death, as Isaiah had said, was a prerequisite to his coming reign.

By this time the two were so astonished by the teachings of their strange companion that they invited him to eat with them in their home at Emmaus. When they sat down to dinner, he prayed over the food and gave it to them, probably in a similar fashion as they had seen him so doing during his life on earth. They suddenly realized it was Jesus, and became the first men among his followers to see him risen.

THE SURPRISE GUEST

The two were so excited they hurried back to Jerusalem before sunset to tell the apostles. When they arrived, they found that Jesus had also appeared to Peter, and that the apostles and other disciples were beginning at last to grasp the great truth before them. As the two disciples, the apostles, and the others present were marvelling over this, Jesus suddenly appeared in their midst.

They were terrified at first, but Jesus reassured them, showing them his hands and feet, still scarred by the nail prints. Then he ate a piece of broiled fish in their presence (vv. 42, 43), and, in a symbolic gesture, breathed on each of them and said, "As the Father has sent me, so I also send you. . . . Receive the Holy Spirit. Whoever's sins you forgive, they are forgiven. Whoever's sins you retain, they are retained" (John 20:21, 22).

Jesus taught them that his resurrection was not an end in itself, for he would send them into the world, as

he had been sent. Through this symbolic breathing he
deeply impressed on each one that he would receive the
Holy Spirit. Apparently this promise of the Holy Spirit
was fulfilled only in symbol that night. The literal
fulfillment came at Pentecost.

Jesus also told them again that they would be door-
ways of divine forgiveness. Of course, they had no
power to dispense such forgiveness of their own. Guided
by the Spirit, they later dispensed it as they spread
Jesus' message of forgiveness through the empire. He
again declared that they were entrusted with the most
important task on earth as his channels of the salvation
message.

THE MAN WHO MISSED THE EXCITEMENT

The resurrection Sunday passed. Jerusalem and the
followers of Jesus were astir. But one man had missed
the excitement. Thomas had not been present when
Jesus appeared to the others. As an eternal pessimist
who had previously predicted they all would perish with
Lazarus, Thomas found the good news of resurrection
hard to accept. For the entire next week he protested
that the resurrection was impossible—only if he could
touch Jesus' nail prints and wounded side would he
believe (vv. 24, 25).

Eight days after resurrection Sunday, as the apostles
met together again, Jesus miraculously appeared once
more, singled out Thomas and said, "Reach your finger
here and see my hands, and put it into my side. Stop
doubting and start believing" (v. 27).

"My Lord and My God!" Thomas exclaimed.

"Because you have seen me, you have believed.
Happy are those who have not seen, and yet have
believed," Jesus answered (v. 29).

Thomas was so startled that he swtiched from stubborn unbelief to the greatest exclamation of faith any
follower of Jesus had yet uttered! Jesus was more than
Messiah, he was Lord and God. Jesus accepted this
enthusiastic confession, but cautioned that faith should

be built on more than sight. Those followers of Jesus who couldn't behold him physically but believed because of the reports of his claims, his life, and his teaching, would be as well off as Thomas.

ANOTHER FISHING EXPEDITION

The disciples, obeying Jesus' command, left Jerusalem for Galilee. After several days there, bewilderment seemed to creep over them. Where was Jesus? What would happen? What plans did he have?

Finally, impatient Peter could stand it no longer. He decided to take up fishing again, and several of the others joined him. As on that night nearly three years earlier when he had caught no fish, so on this night he caught nothing. At dawn they came in toward shore, and in the first light of the new day someone on the beach called, "Have you anything to eat?" (John 21:6)

When they answered no, whoever it was told them to put their nets down on the right side of the boat. Suddenly their nets were filled. By this time the sun had arisen and they realized that the stranger on the beach was Jesus. He had started a charcoal fire, and as the disciples came to shore he put some fish on the coals and prepared for them a memorable breakfast.

After they had eaten, Jesus looked at the remaining fish and asked Peter, "Do you love me more than these?" (v. 15) Peter, of course, affirmed he did.

Jesus asked a second time, "Do you love me?" Again Peter protested he did. Jesus asked a third time. This angered Peter, so he vehemently protested. Jesus then uttered a mysterious prophecy over Peter: "When you were younger, you fastened your belt and walked where you wanted. But when you are old you will stretch out your hands and someone else will fasten your belt and carry you where you don't want to go" (v. 18).

John notes that this was a prophecy of Peter's martyrdom (v. 19). An early tradition records that Peter was crucified. Jesus' description of his death would describe a victim with stretched-out hands, tied to a cross, going to crucifixion. Peter would finally have his boast fulfilled—he would die for Jesus, and even die like Jesus.

Though he probably couldn't grasp it then, Peter was getting recommissioned as an apostle. As at Peter's original call, when Jesus filled empty nets and commanded him to fish for men, so Jesus filled the nets again and commanded Peter to tend God's flock. As Peter had warmed himself by one fire and denied Jesus three times, so now Peter warmed himself by another fire and asserted that he loved Jesus three times.

The apostle who blew so hot and cold at last had achieved stability. After bitter lessons, he was ready to inaugurate the great movement which would soon begin in Jerusalem.

THE FINAL APPEARANCE

Shortly after this, Jesus made his seventh appearance. He appeared to the eleven and apparently several hundred others and gave them one of his greatest commands: "All authority in heaven and earth has been given to me. Go therefore and make disciples of all nations, baptizing them in the name of the Father and of the Son and of the Holy Spirit, teaching them to observe everything I have commanded you, and surely I will be with you always, to the end of the age" (Matthew 28:18-20).

He claimed to hold ultimate authority in the universe. He ordered his followers to evangelize the entire world. They were to baptize in the one name of the Father, the Son, and the Holy Spirit. The one name implied the oneness of God. The three persons implied a plurality of personalities, of whom Jesus was one.

He said that they should teach everything he commanded and that he would be with them forever. He had made astounding claims like this before, but the disciples had not comprehended them. The concept of Jesus as the final authority, of spreading one faith over the whole world, of the oneness and plurality of God, of Jesus' eternal presence—all of this seemed incredible.

But the man who uttered the words had now risen from the dead. That was also incredible.

Jesus made three more recorded appearances before he ascended. One to his half-brother James (I Corinthians 15:7), another to the apostles (Luke 24:44-49, Acts 1:3-8), and a final one when he ascended back to heaven from the Mount of Olives (Acts 1:9-12).

As the apostles and disciples now waited for the Day of Pentecost, they could only marvel over the events of the previous weeks. When all seemed lost, he had risen. At first, they were skeptical. But the proofs became so overwhelming that this little group of disillusioned followers changed into men and women with supreme confidence in their crucified, risen leader and his message.

ATTEMPTED EXPLANATIONS

Of course, many in their nation and the world since have not shared that confidence. Some have charged that the resurrection is a product of the superstitious and overactive imaginations of his followers. The distraught disciples only thought they saw Jesus. But this cannot explain either the empty tomb or the nature of his ten appearances. Can we really believe that Peter, John, Mary Magdalene and the others only imagined that the tomb was empty? Can we believe that the Roman soldiers and the Sanhedrin imagined the same thing? Can we believe that his followers imagined touching him, eating with him, talking with him, listening to his instructions, and even having him fix their breakfast?

Others have suggested that his body was stolen. But his enemies would not have stolen the body—they put the guard around the tomb. His followers probably could not have stolen the body from the sealed and protected tomb; and even if they had, can we believe that they would endure hardship, persecution, and death for what they knew was a fraud? Furthermore, this leaves totally unexplained Jesus' many and varied resurrection appearances.

253

Still others have suggested that Jesus did not really die. He was hastily removed from the cross before his death, and recovered in the tomb. But what we know of crucifixion shows that he must have died because his body hung limp. The wound in his side, from which blood and pericardial fluid flowed, is evidence of death. If he didn't die, he would have required months of constant nursing to recover from the ordeal. We can hardly imagine such an emaciated, bed-ridden Jesus becoming the basis of the resurrection accounts. Was this stroke of luck what caused Peter to preach with unheard of boldness that Jesus had risen from the dead, when all the while he knew better?

Perhaps the most popular theory is that the resurrection is a myth manufactured by the followers of Jesus. But myths grow up over time and distance. The first New Testament books were written only twenty years after his death, and these reflect a belief in the resurrection which goes back to the event itself. Belief in Jesus' resurrection began where and when it happened, not hundreds of years and thousands of miles away. And if the resurrection is a myth, what dramatic event transformed his forlorn followers? How did they enlist thousands of fellow Jewish converts through proclaiming the resurrection of a man obviously lying in a Jerusalem tomb?

THE REAL TRUTH

No, a miracle happened that Sunday morning. The Sanhedrin hoped it would go away. But it has not gone away. The Sanhedrin, Pontius Pilate, and the Roman Empire have gone away. That miracle is still with us today. Jesus, the Messiah, rose from the dead, and today he lives in the hearts of his followers. He will enter the lives of all who wish to believe in him. Perhaps very shortly, he will return physically to rule this earth.

Once he was a carpenter, now he is savior, soon he will be king.

"O Death, Where is Your Victory?"